THE GARDENING WHICH? GUIDE TO

PATIO AND CONTAINER
PLANTS

THE GARDENING WHICH? GUIDE TO
PATIO AND CONTAINER
PLANTS

SUE FISHER

CONSUMERS' ASSOCIATION

Which? Books are commissioned and researched by
Consumers' Association and published by
Which? Ltd, 2 Marylebone Road, London NW1 4DF

Distributed by The Penguin Group:
Penguin Books Ltd, 27 Wrights Lane, London W8 5TZ

First edition 1996

British Library Cataloguing-in-Publication Data
A catalogue record for this book is available from the British Library

ISBN 0 85202 609 9

Credits
Designed and typeset by Keith Watson Art Direction
Edited by Alistair Ayres, Editor, *Gardening Which?* with assistance from
Jonathan Edwards, Kate Hawkins and Martyn Hocking.

Gardening Which? Themed Gardens

Gardening Which? has a series of ten themed gardens. These small
gardens simulate real-life situations and are designed to inspire visitors, demonstrate
much of the advice given in the magazine and provide a valuable resource when
trying out new techniques and design ideas. You can visit the *Gardening Which?*
Demonstration Gardens at Capel Manor, Bullmoor Lane, Enfield, Middlesex EN1 4RQ.
Phone 0181-366 4442 for details of opening times.

Gardening Which? magazine

You can find up-to-date information on all the latest plants, gardening products
and techniques in *Gardening Which?* magazine. It regularly carries out tests and
trials of plant varieties and suppliers, as well as gardening equipment and sundries
such as composts and fertilisers. Each issue is packed with ideas, practical advice
and results of the magazine's independent evaluations.

Gardening Which? magazine is available by subscription only. To try it free for 3 months
write to *Gardening Which?*, Consumers' Association, Freepost
Hertford X, SG14 1YB or Freephone 0800 252100.

Colour reproduction by Kestrel Digital Colour Ltd

Printed and bound in Great Britain by Butler & Tanner, Frome, Somerset

Contents

How to use this book

Finding the right plant

The plants in this book are categorised by type. If you are looking for summer colour, the A-Z of annuals and tender perennials contains details of both common and unusual plants grown for their stunning flower displays. For permanent plants, the shrubs section contains a good selection that perform well in containers. Bulbs, perennials and alpines provide seasonal highlights, while many of the ferns and grasses provide year-round interest. If you want a productive patio display, consult the herb, vegetables and fruit sections for recommended types.

Annuals & tender perennials

Bulbs

Climbers

Roses

Shrubs

Herbaceous perennials & alpines

Grasses

Ferns

Herbs, vegetables & fruit

Shape and size

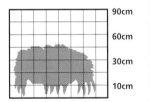

90cm
60cm
30cm
10cm

The icons in the major plant sections indicate the habit and the likely height of the plant when grown in a suitable container. Plant size will be restricted, however, if the plants are in too small a container or do not receive adequate nutrients.

Position

The icons show whether plants are suited to growing in a hot, sunny position or whether they need a situation in light or full shade.

Full sun or sun for more than half the day

Light shade or some sun e.g. for less than half of the day

Full shade

Overwintering and hardiness

The icons indicate how hardy the plants are and the best method for keeping them through the winter. For more information on overwintering, see pages 20-21.

 7°C
 5°C
 5°C
 5°C

Plants under cover at 7°C (45°F)

Plants under cover at 5°C (43°F)

Store bulbs under cover at 5°C (43°F)

Cuttings under cover at 5°C (43°F)

 7°C

 0°C
Treat as Annual

Cuttings under cover at 7°C (45°F)

Plants frost-free

Hardy plant but insulate the pot to prevent compost freezing

Annual or best grown from seed each year

Compost

The compost icons tell you the best type of growing medium. Plants requiring acidic conditions can be grown in peat-based, multipurpose composts and do not require a specialist ericaceous compost. For more advice on composts, see pages 16-17.

Multipurpose

Well-drained - use an equal mixture of multipurpose compost and sharp sand or grit.

John Innes No2

Containers

The icons offer guidelines as to the types of container to which the plants are most suited.

Window-box *Hanging basket* *Single specimen* *Dot plant in tub* *Filler for a tub*

Watering

How little watering can you get away with? The icons give you a guide to the drought tolerance of various plants.

Will tolerate drying out for short periods *Will tolerate occasional drying out. Should not need watering more than once a day in summer* *Need to be kept constantly moist. May need watering several times a day in summer*

Feeding

Once a month during the growing season *Once a fortnight during the growing season* *Once a week during the growing season*

Features calendar

Use the features calendar to help plan your displays for seasonal interest.

Flowers		Scented flowers		Berries or attractive fruit	
Jan	Feb	Mar	Apr	May	June
July	Aug	Sept	Oct	Nov	Dec

Seasonal foliage tints *Seed pod*

Growing guide

The growing guide gives you tips on getting the best from each plant as well as details of propagation and dealing with the problems you are most likely to face when growing the plants.

Which variety?

This is a guide to the varieties most commonly sold by seed suppliers, garden centres and nurseries. It will help you decide whether it is worth seeking out a particular variety or settling for an alternative. Be wary of plants that are not labelled with the variety name as these could turn out to be inferior types.

Buying tips   *Plant quality can be very variable and availability of some plants is very seasonal. Use these tips to avoid the pitfalls.*

The icons also give guidance on the types of containers to use

Other books in the series:

The Gardening Which? Guide to Successful Propagation

The Gardening Which? Guide to Successful Pruning

The Gardening Which? Guide to Successful Shrubs

The Gardening Which? Guide to Small Gardens

To order, p&p free, freephone 0800 252100 (credit cards) or write to Which? Books at Castlemead, Gascoyne Way, Hertford SG14 1LH.

Planting up your patio

A standard pelargonium can look imposing on your patio

A patio is an extension of the house that is halfway between a room and a garden. If you are starting with a bare block of paving, think of arranging your patio very much as you might when furnishing a room. The chances are that you will want space for a table and chairs for al fresco dining, somewhere to put out a sun lounger and maybe even a barbeque or, if you have young children, a sandpit. Having established the position of your basic furniture and the thoroughfares, you can then decide on containers and plants. The important viewing points for a patio are generally from inside the house, sitting on the patio and from further down the garden. Before spending a lot of money, it is often a good idea to take some snaps from these viewing points. Using tracing paper or acetate overlays, you can then do a few rough sketches to try out ideas for different types of containers and plants. The following guidelines should also help you establish your priorities and shortlist ideas.

Framing the garden

Consider which are the most attractive parts of your garden as well as any eyesores. Tubs containing evergreen shrubs are ideal for framing an attractive flowerbed say, or blocking an eyesore such as a rotary clothes line or oil tank from immediate view. Another possibility for screening would be to construct a wooden trough with trellis attached to the back as a support for climbers. Similarly, a tripod or obelisk on top of a large tub for training climbers creates height for framing a view.

The most attractive parts of the garden tend to change through the year. In summer, it may be an herbaceous border, while in winter it could be a combination of golden evergreens and red-stemmed dogwoods. By mounting your containers on castors, you can change the way you frame the garden according to the season.

Creating privacy and shelter

Strong prevailing winds and prying eyes can ruin your enjoyment of your patio. Containers can provide the solution. Several pots of taller bamboos are ideal for creating both privacy and shade. Large-leaved evergreens will serve the same purpose. Pergolas are also a good way of creating privacy on your patio but ideally they should only cover between the third and half of the patio or they can become rather oppressive.

A chimney pot makes an excellent focal point

Vigorous large-leaved climbers produce a high degree of privacy but create a lot of shade and you may find the dripping after a rain shower annoying. Less vigorous climbers such as a late-flowering clematis combined with a thornless rose such as 'Zephrine Drouhine' would be an attractive solution and you could attach sections of trellis to the pergola for added shelter and privacy. The climber can be grown either in large pots or you could lift a paving slab to create a planting hole.

Focal points

Attractive containers make excellent focal points and you can use them in a number of ways. When viewing the patio from indoors, position a container to attract your eyes towards a good-looking part of the garden. If there is a shady area on the patio, with an ivy-covered wall and couple of evergreens say, an ornamental urn can bring such a dull area to life. From the patio, positioning a container within the garden so that it is half hidden from view will help create an air of mystery and interest. With ornate containers,

Use a range of different sized pots for an eye-catching display

keep the planting very simple using specimens such as hostas which have bold outlines. Plain containers, such as earthenware jars, are suited to plants such as Japanese maples which have very intricate foliage.

Sun and shade

The aspect of your patio will largely determine when it gets the sun. While it is pleasant enough soaking up the rays on a sunny afternoon, it is equally enjoyable to laze back in the dappled shade and enjoy your garden without overheating. The ideal patio will provide both scenarios. You could accentuate the sun and shade theme with a group of terracotta pots full of Mediterranean drought-resistant plants such marguerites and pelargoniums in the sun, and a cool, shady corner adorned with lush hostas, ferns and large-leaved ivies. On a similar theme, you could create a haven of flowers in the shade and semi-arid feel to sun-scorched paving. Fuchsias and impatiens do best in light shade as they will scorch and wilt in full sun unless copiously watered. Plants such as agapanthus, agaves, cordylines and phormiums will keep hot areas looking hot, even when the sun goes behind the clouds.

Grouping containers

A collection of similar-sized pots each containing different plants will make your patio look more like a sales area than a place to relax. Try and create some linking theme amongst groups of containers.

Some ideas that you might like to try are:
- *Next to a doorway or at the start of a path matching containers with the same planting can look very effective.*
- *At the side of steps, an ascending line of identical plants in identical pots become like beacons showing you the way.*
- *A group of containers of contrasting shape in complimentary colours nearly always look good together. For example, a Victorian chimney pot with an Ali Baba-style urn and burnt-glazed flower pot.*
- *Where you have a mixed group of containers that do not look very different, try linking them with a number of varieties or colours of the same plant.*
- *Select plants to suit the shape of the containers - long trailers for tall pots, round bushy ones for urns.*
- *Plant a large container with a mixture of flowers and surround it with smaller pots, each filled with one of the flowers from the mixed planting.*
- *A shallow terracotta pot planted with thyme, two medium-sized terracotta pots, each planted with rosemary and a larger pot crammed with scented-leaved pelargoniums.*
- *If your pots are all the same size, create a stepped staging for them using a few bricks and pieces of wood. But make sure you arrange it against a wall so they cannot fall or get knocked over.*

Well-trained shrubs add a touch of class to a doorway

Colour all year

Even in the depths of winter, the patio is one of the most visible parts of the garden. So before you pack it out with pots of annuals and tender plants, plan for a few features that will keep it looking attractive and interesting right through the year.

Permanent plants

Though summer flowers are the most tempting, the best way to start planning for year-round display on the patio is to select a few evergreens that will look good during the winter and act as an anchor for summer groupings. *Nandina domestica* 'Firepower', the sacred bamboo, for example, has finely featured foliage which makes an excellent backdrop to bold flowers such as petunias and pelargoniums. In winter, it steals the show when its leaves turn bright red. Camellias put on a showy display in spring, while in summer their dark glossy leaves really highlight white and pastel flowers in neighbouring pots.

On a smaller scale, evergreen grasses such as *Carex hachijoensis* 'Evergold' and evergreen ferns such as *Asplenium scolopendrium* are well worth considering for any patio display. The golden variegated grass looks at home with bright summer bedding, while ferns can make an eye-catching combination with pots of *Lilium regale*, creating a cool, sophisticated effect. In winter, grasses and ferns help provide welcome colour and greenery, adding to the larger permanent plants.

Spring colour

Bulbs are the mainstay of spring colour and these can be planted in containers on their own or used to edge the tubs of permanent plants. Plant up some cheap plastic pots with bulbs in the autumn and keep them on hand to be plunged into large tubs or more decorative pots when they come into bud. Once they have finished flowering, the pots can then be removed and replaced with other spring flowers such as polyanthus or double daisies. Pansies and violas can be relied on to fill any gaps where you want extra colour and will carry on until you want to replace them with summer flowers.

Summer colour

The peak time for enjoying the patio is during the summer, when there are literally thousands of plants to choose from to provide colour and scent. Plants such as pelargoniums which bloom right through to the frosts are good value, but spectacular plants such as lilies which provide only a fleeting display can add greatly to the interest. These summer spectaculars can be moved to less prominent positions, once they have finished their display. In a hot summer, you can expect some plants to stop flowering prematurely. Lobelias are a notable example. This generally happens in August when garden centres tend to be low on cheap replacements. You can plan for this by sowing a few pots of annuals in late May to act as fillers.

Autumn and winter colour

In milder areas, plants such as impatiens and pelargoniums should carry the colour well into autumn. Japanese maples will be at their peak of glory and evergreen shrubs will start to take on a

Pansies will flower all summer in hanging baskets

Scaevola aemula 'Blue Fan' hanging underneath a half basket planted with Impatiens and Nicotiana

Skimmia and heather provide winter interest on the patio

new light. But what do you do with all the empty-looking pots that were a blaze of colour in summer? Winter-flowering heathers make a convenient stop gap as they are cheap to buy and exceptionally easy to grow from cuttings. Variegated ivies and periwinkles are ideal for trailing over the edges of urns and chimney pots. And then there are the ubiquitous Universal pansies. The problem with winter schemes is that the plants will hardly grow at all, so if you leave it until the last minute, you will have to spend a lot of money on large specimens or lots of plants to create an effective display. It is worth planning ahead and potting up some young plants or cuttings in the spring with winter in mind. Even with pansies, a few plants bought in August could yield dozens for your winter displays.

Another ploy is to choose containers that will look attractive in key positions even unplanted. An urn planted with bedding in the summer could be lined with polythene and become a bird bath during the winter, for example.

Heathers and ivies work well in winter containers

Which container?

The choice of pots is vast

If you visit any garden centre or DIY store, you will be confronted with an enormous variety of plant containers made of many different materials and at widely ranging prices. Pot sizes are generally quoted by diameter and the most useful sizes are 30cm (12in), 45cm (18in) and 60cm (24in). Small pots will dry out more quickly and very large ones can be a problem if you need to move them around.

When choosing containers, decide on a common theme for your patio rather than getting a mixed bag of different pots. A collection of Mediterranean plants, for example, would look stunning in a group of matching terracotta pots of different sizes.

Clay and terracotta pots

Clay and terracotta pots come in a wide range of sizes and designs. Simple machine-made pots are the cheapest and these are a good buy where the main focus of attention will be the plants and the container will be at least partly concealed. Ornate designs of machine-made pots are more expensive but still competitively priced. These are best suited to planting schemes where the pot is not hidden but viewed from a distance. However, none of the machine-made pots can compete with hand-thrown terracotta for richness of colour and overall appearance. Where budget is a major consideration, reserve these pots for specimen plantings in prime spots. Brand-new terracotta is generally a bright orange colour that will soon weather and take on a more mellow appearance. It only takes a few weeks for this to happen or, at the most, several months, though it is possible to speed up the process by giving the pot a wash of lime or spraying it regularly with liquid fertiliser.

Pros Can look stunning and harmonise with most planting schemes.

Cons Porous, so the compost inside them can dry out very quickly unless you line the insides with polythene. They can also be cracked in winter if the compost inside freezes and expands or if moisture trapped within the clay turns to ice. Pots guaranteed as frost-resistant should prove more durable but it is prudent to line the inside of the pot with bubble polythene to minimise risks. Alternatively, insulate the pot from outside (see pages 20-21).

Planting a tub

Crocks are not essential if you use good-quality compost, though they do add weight and stability. Cover large drainage holes to prevent the compost being washed out. If you are planting a large specimen, position the plant in its original pot on a layer of compost so that the surface is at the correct level. Fill the container with compost while the pot is still in place, firming the compost down well around the edges.

Finally, remove the pot and insert the plant into the ready-made hole in its new container. Leave at least 2.5cm (1in) clear at the rim to allow for watering.

With annual displays, start in the middle and work outwards, cramming in as many plants as will fit. Water all plants thoroughly before and after planting. Soak plants in a bucket of water if they look dry before you plant them.

Glazed earthenware pots

These come in all manner of colours and designs and have the advantage over terracotta in that the glazing prevents water loss through the sides of the container. Before spending a lot of money, look for a guarantee that the pot is frost-resistant and check that it has adequate drainage holes and that the glaze is not damaged.

Pros Glazing prevents the pots drying out so quickly.

Cons Pots may crack if the compost freezes. The glaze may also crack. Not all pots have drainage holes.

Plastic pots and tubs

Plastic pots range from cheap polythene pots to ornate mock-terracotta moulded from polypropylene. Most plastic pots are stabilised against the effects of ultra-violet rays, though they will all inevitably fade and become more brittle with time. The cheap pots are ideal for annual displays where the plants will hide most of the container. They are also useful liners for more expensive pots, allowing you to change the display very easily. Some of the more expensive pots are convincing imitations of terracotta. Besides being lightweight and frost-resistant, the thicker polypropylene pots also provide insulation for the compost. In addition, brightly coloured pots can look very effective in contemporary designs. Plastic tubs often have their drainage holes sealed over and you should drill these out before planting up.

Pros Light, frost-resistant. Thicker pots are good insulators.

Cons May not have enough stability for tall plants. Highly decorated pots tend to look cheap and do not combine well with the plants.

Line terracotta pots with green polythene to retain moisture

Spot the difference: plastic or terracotta?

Concrete

Concrete pots are available in many designs and mouldings. They are ideal for permanent hardy plants that are unlikely to be moved around. They can take many years to develop aged appearance. For growing acid-loving plants, it is best to treat the concrete with a sealant as it can leach lime into the compost.
Pros Robust, very stable and frost-resistant.
Cons Heavy to move around. Can look stark.

Reconstituted stone pots

These are made from stone which is ground up and then moulded into a shape in the same way as concrete. The appearance is a cross between concrete and real stone. Like concrete containers, they are very slow to take on a weathered appearance. Otherwise, their properties are very similar.
Pros Robust, very stable, and frost-resistant.
Cons Heavy to move around. Can look stark.

Fibreglass

Fibreglass is used for simple modern planters, particularly self-watering designs. Its main attraction is the high gloss finish and range of colours available. Fibreglass pots offer most of the benefits of high-quality plastic containers, though they are more stable but slightly less durable.
Pros Stylish in the right setting. Stable but not to heavy to move around. Frost-resistant.
Cons Can crack or shatter on impact. Expensive.

Wooden barrels

Wooden half-barrels make popular plant containers and are available as recycled barrels or replicas. Look for solid construction and check that the metal bands around the barrel are in good order.

Some of the replicas have plywood bases and packing-case-quality metal bands and so are unlikely to last very long. Barrels are commonly sold without drainage holes so you may need to drill your own. Once you have planted up the barrel, make sure you keep the compost moist at all times. If you do not the barrel is likely to dry out and fall apart.
Pros Attractive in the right setting. Stable and frost-resistant. Easy to attach handles for moving about.
Cons Needs regular maintenance to prevent the metal bands from rusting. Will fall apart if the wood dries out. Whiskey barrels may have residues that are toxic to plants.

Ornamental containers

Urns

Make sure that urns are stable and cannot fall over. They should be attached securely to a plinth or a pedestal.

Bowls

These tend to dry out very quickly and are too shallow for most plants. However, they can look attractive when planted with drought-resistant succulents such as sempervivums (houseleeks).

Troughs

Tufa or stone troughs are the traditional containers for alpines but they are expensive. See page 195 for instructions on how to make one.

Window-boxes

Many of the window-boxes on sale are too small. For best results, choose one that is at least 23cm (9in) deep and a suitable length for your window.

Security

Stunning containers and hanging baskets can, unfortunately, attract the attention of thieves. A precaution worth taking for permanent containers, particularly in front gardens, is to drill a hole in the paving or concrete and cement a long bolt beneath the tub. This can then be passed through a drainage hole and secured to a piece of wood or metal within the container.

Window-boxes should be secured with brackets or chains attached to the brickwork or window frame. On sloping window sills, also use wedges to prevent the box leaning. These precautions prevent boxes falling off and act as a deterrent to thieves.

Hanging baskets need to be supported by strong brackets held firmly in place with wall plugs. Using a stronger chain and a padlock to attach the rim of the basket to the bracket will deter the opportunist, though will not stop a determined thief.

If you have a lot of expensive plants and containers, consider installing security lighting triggered by an infra-red detector.

How to plant hanging baskets

A cheat 'standard' with begonias and ivy, using a hanging basket on a pole

Before buying baskets and liners, take some time to look at the various options available. Some are a lot less work or are more attractive than others.

Types of basket

Wire baskets Traditional baskets made of plastic-coated wire have large holes making planting through the sides straightforward. The disadvantage is that they can dry out very quickly but this can be overcome by lining them with polythene. Black is the best colour if you want the basket to be inconspicuous while the plants get established.

Self-watering baskets These are more like plastic bowls with a water reservoir built into the bottom. A piece of matting draws water up to compost as it dries out. The plants should thrive through the hottest weather when watered only every other day. The drawbacks are that they are much heavier than conventional baskets when the water reservoir is full and that you cannot plant up the sides. They are also around three times the price of wire baskets.

Plastic baskets You can buy plastic replicas of wire baskets but these often tend to have narrow gaps in the sides, which makes them difficult to plant in the same way. Most, however, are like self-watering baskets but with drainage holes and a drip tray instead of a water reservoir. In wet weather the drip tray can fill up and cause the compost to become waterlogged. On the plus side, they tend not to dry out as quickly as wire baskets. You cannot plant up the sides, so will need trailing plants to cover up the sides. The smaller sizes are the most widely available; you can find them in a range of colours.

Half-baskets and mangers These are designed to be screwed directly to the wall and are available in wrought iron or plastic. As they

STEP-BY-STEP

1. Stand the basket in a bucket to keep it steady and insert your chosen liner. Before adding the compost, place a circle of polythene at the base to act as a water reservoir.

2. Fill the basket one-third full of compost and then start planting up the sides. Slit the liner if need be and feed the plants through from the inside to prevent root damage. You can protect the foliage by wrapping it in a roll of newspaper.

3. Add slow-release fertiliser granules (eg Osmocote) to reduce the need for liquid feeding during the summer.

4. Fill the basket with compost and then plant up the top. Start at the centre with an upright, bushy plant and fill in with smaller plants and trailers around the sides.

contain only half the volume of a round basket, they need more frequent watering. However, they look attractive with older-style properties.

Liners

Sphagnum moss This is the traditional liner for baskets but its collection can pose an ecological threat to peat bogs. Moss collected from the lawn is a good substitute.

Conifer clippings Clippings from conifers such as Leyland cypress are alternatives to moss as they remain green until the basket becomes covered with plants. For best results, line the inside of the clippings with polythene to reduce water loss.

Recycled wool and cotton These preformed liners are generally dyed green to look like moss. It is easy to cut planting slits in them and some come with precut slits. Some have a polythene inner lining to aid moisture retention.

Coconut fibre These are similar to wool liner but made of a much coarser material through which water will run freely.

Foam liners These fit in the baskets easily but making planting slits is more difficult than with the recycled wool and cotton liners. They tend to look unsightly until the plants cover them.

Polythene Black or green polythene makes a cheap and effective liner though it looks slightly unsightly until the plants start to hide it.

Preformed wood fibre These rigid liners sit inside the basket and are generally dark brown in colour. However, it is more difficult to cut holes for planting up the sides, though they are useful where you want to have a succession of plantings as they can be lifted out and replaced with another preplanted liner.

A truly gorgeous cascade of petunias and pelargoniums

Which size basket?

As you can see from the table below, the larger the basket the easier it is to keep watered. Larger baskets also produce better displays. The drawback is that the cost increases with basket size. A 16-in basket is also very heavy and requires a heavy-duty bracket to support it.

	10in	12in	14in	16in
Compost	3 litres	5litres	7 litres	10 litres
Fertiliser	10g	15g	20g	30g
Min no. of plants	6	8	10	15
Weight	2.5kg	3.6kg	4.8kg	7.6kg
Daily waterings	3	2	1	1
Maintenance	high	high	moderate	low

5. Level off the compost leaving a gap of around 2.5cm (1in) below the top of the liner to allow for watering. Give the basket a thorough soaking before hanging it on a bracket.

Composts, watering and feeding

Types of compost

Choosing the right compost can make an enormous difference to your container displays. In the worst composts, plant roots can be killed by waterlogging or the foliage can be starved and stunted. In the best they will grow vigorously and produce an abundance of flowers, need less frequent watering and be less reliant on feeding for the first six weeks.

Three varieties of John Innes composts

Multipurpose composts are suitable for raising seeds, rooting cuttings and growing on plants. Their light weight and versatility makes them popular with gardeners. Most of the multipurpose composts are based on peat and these tend to be the most reliable. Peat substitutes are continually being developed but have yet to be perfected. Some of the peat-free composts tested by *Gardening Which?* are capable of producing reasonable results but they do require extra care. Composts containing coir dry out rapidly on the surface but remain moist underneath so it is very easy to overwater your plants. Composted bark tends to be very free-draining and plants grown in it need more frequent watering and feeding than in other compost. Those based on organic waste have a tendency to rot down even while they are in the bag, leading to a loss of structure and an unpredictable nutrient content. While you may prefer not to use peat for environmental reasons, we recommend that you try peat substitutes alongside tried and trusted brands as some peat-free products that have been sold as composts simply are not fit for the purpose of growing plants.

Hanging basket composts are similar to multipurpose composts except that they contain a wetting agent to make them easier to water if the compost dries out. Multipurpose composts can be difficult to rewet if they become too dry,

The use of different composts is clearly shown here with these pelargoniums

though you can add a tiny drop of washing-up liquid to a watering can full of water to remedy this. There is a slight advantage in using specialist composts for hanging baskets though they are generally more expensive.

John Innes composts are composts that are made to the John Innes formulae and they contain a mixture of loam, peat and sand, together with lime and a base fertiliser. There are four different formulae but in practice you may find it difficult to obtain them all. Seed and Cutting contains very little fertiliser and is used for sowing seeds and rooting cuttings. No 2 and No 3 contain the most fertiliser and are the ones to choose for growing established plants in containers. No 1 is used mainly for growing on nutrient-sensitive seedlings until they are large enough to be potted on into a No 2 compost. John Innes composts can vary a lot, depending on the quality of the loam used - the worst are like heavy clay or builders' rubble; the best have a fine, crumbly texture. A good-quality John Innes No 2 is generally the best choice for permanent plants in containers as they hold their structure well for many years. Peat and peat substitutes tend to break down after a few years. The other advantage of John Innes compost is that it is a lot heavier than multipurpose compost and provides stability for tall plants.

Saving money on compost

If you have a lot of containers to plant, your compost bill can soon mount up. For annual displays, consider using the compost from growing bags. This is generally around half the price of multipurpose compost and will produce

---

Acid-loving plants

It is often recommended that plants that require acid conditions, such as azaleas and camellias, should be grown in an ericaceous compost. However, in Gardening Which? *trials, ericaceous composts were not found to be significantly more acidic than multipurpose composts after growing plants for two years. Multipurpose composts are generally cheaper.*

Problems can occur with both types of compost if you live in a hard-water area. To combat the build-up of lime in containers, use rain water or add a used tea bag to the watering can every couple of weeks. Once or twice a year, flush the pots through with rain water.
Should you see signs of iron and magnesium deficiencies, noticeable as pale or yellowing leaves, apply a tonic such as Miracid or Sequestrene.

reasonable results over one season. Even growing bags used for tomatoes can support a crop of flowers if you flush the compost through with fresh water and replenish the fertiliser.

For large tubs, you could consider mixing the compost with garden soil to save money. As long as your soil is not sticky clay or solid chalk, this should produce acceptable results. Expect to find weeds growing in your containers though and do not use soil for raising seeds and cuttings as they should be grown in a sterile medium.

Watering devices

If you have a large selection of pots and containers, using a watering can to keep them watered can be strenuous and time-consuming. A hosepipe can save time but you can waste water and compact the compost unless you use it carefully. A hose lance gives you control over the flow rate and allows you to direct water right into the pots. It also gives you extra reach for hanging baskets.

The easiest way to keep your containers watered is to plumb them in. You can buy micro-tubing and drip nozzles which allow you to connect all your containers to a single hose. The water can then be controlled by a timing or volume control device fitted to the tap. If you don't already have an anti-siphon device, you will need to fit one.

Watering systems and some hose lances can be used to deliver fertiliser separately too, but it is better to apply a liquid fertiliser to using a watering can or use slow-release fertilisers when planting up.

Feeding

Plants potted into fresh compost can generally go for four to six weeks without feeding. After that, it is recommended that you apply a liquid feed at least once a week throughout the growing season. Annual displays can be fed right through the summer. With permanent plants, gradually reduce feeding during August and stop by the end of the month. This will prevent them producing a lot of soft growth during the autumn which will then be vulnerable to frost damage.

To produce the best flower displays, use a general-purpose liquid fertiliser until they are in full bloom then switch to a high potash fertiliser, such as a tomato feed, for the rest of the season. As you will see from this book, not all plants respond well to regular feeding, so use the icons as a guide.

It's easy to forget to use a liquid fertiliser

Watering

Plants in containers need regular watering throughout the summer. The following tips should help prevent your from plants drying out and reduce the need for watering.

1. Use a good-quality, moisture-retentive compost.

2. Consider mixing a water-absorbing gel with the compost before potting up plants. This will certainly improve the performance of poorer composts.

3. Grow plants in the largest container practicable.

4. Line porous containers, such as terracotta pots and wire hanging baskets, with polythene to reduce water loss.

5. Group containers together so the plants create a moist microclimate around their leaves and shade the compost.

6. Water containers in early morning and evening rather than in the heat of the day.

7. Water the compost, not the foliage.

regularly. The alternative is to apply slow-release (sometimes called controlled-release) fertiliser granules such as Osmocote. There are different formulations which last from three to nine months. Slow-release granules produce reasonable results with most plants, but fast-growing plants will perform best with supplementary liquid feeding.

Whatever fertiliser you use, remember that plants can only take up nutrients as long as the compost remains moist.

Watering a hanging basket can be made easier by using a hose lance

Buying plants

Don't buy bedding strips until you are ready to plant them out

There are a number of different options for buying annuals and tender perennials. Which you choose depends on your budget, how much time you have got and what facilities you have for raising seeds and growing on plants.

Seeds

Many of the plants in the A-Z of annuals and tender perennials can be grown from seed. Some, such as alyssum and nasturtiums, are very easy to grow without any special facilities. To grow a wide range of plants from seed you really need a heated propagator with an adjustable thermostat for germination, a greenhouse for growing plants on, and a cold frame for hardening off plants ready for their life outdoors.

Growing plants from seed is generally the most economical way if you want a lot of plants. However, where you only want a few specimens, or where the seed is expensive as in the case of F1 pelargoniums, buying seedlings or plantlets can be a lot more cost-effective.

At garden centres and shops, you'll find the best choice of seeds between January and April. Mail-order seed varieties offer the latest varieties and a wider range. Their new catalogues come out around mid- to late October each year.

Seedlings

Some tender perennials and bedding plants are sold as seedlings. These are sold in pots or small trays at garden centres in February and March and can also be ordered from the mail-order seed catalogues for early spring delivery.

Seedlings overcome any problems that you might have with germinating the seed but you still need to prick off the plants into trays or individual pots and grow them on somewhere warm and light.

Plantlets

These are sold under a variety of names including tots, plugs and Jiffy sevens but they are all seedlings or rooted cuttings, generally with two or three pairs of leaves. The peak season for plantlets at garden centres is February to early May. Mail-order seed suppliers also stock them though it is prudent to place orders by around the end of February.

The big advantage of plantlets is the enormous range of varieties sold this way, including many of the more unusual tender perennials. They do work out considerably more expensive than bedding strips, so don't buy common bedding plants this way.

As with seedlings, plantlets need to be potted up individually and grown on under glass until the risk of frosts has passed. Alternatively, you can use them to plant up the sides of hanging baskets, providing you keep the basket under cover for frost protection.

Bedding strips

Bedding strips usually contain between six and twelve small plants which are ready to plant out. Bedding strips become available from early April and are on sale to early June. There is often a great temptation to buy plants early, plant up your containers and put them outside too soon while frosts still threaten. In most parts of the UK, it's best to wait until late May or early June before putting out summer containers. If you do plant up containers and frosts are forecast, keep a double layer of horticultural fleece handy to cover the plants at night.

Individual pots

Large plants in individual pots will give a near instant effect but are by far the most expensive option. However, large plants can provide a source of cuttings if you are looking to bulk up the stock quickly. If you want the cuttings to flower in their first year, try to get your plants before the end of April. As with bedding strips, don't be tempted to buy plants while there is still a risk of frost or you might lose them.

Bulbs

The main season for buying spring bulbs is from late August to October. Make sure they are sound and free of rot and go for cultivated varieties rather than species to avoid buying bulbs collected from the wild. If you miss buying them in autumn, pots of bulbs are available in early spring. March and April are the best times to find summer bulbs.

Climbers

When buying climbers look for at least three strong stems. Large plants trained on trellis are generally a poor buy as they are best cut back and retrained if they are to look attractive in containers.

Shrubs

Avoid plants which are pot-bound and go for well-shaped symmetrical plants to grow as specimens.

Check shrubs to make sure they are not pot-bound

Perennials

Most are quick growing so small plants are a good buy, as are large plants that can be split up prior to planting.

Preplanted containers

An increasing trend amongst garden centres is to offer tubs and baskets ready planted or in kit form. Kits consist of the container, compost and collection of plants needed to recreate the examples on display. Plant combinations may vary from good to bad, though prices are generally around the same or slightly less than it would cost to create the container display from separately purchased components. Worth considering if you want an instant display and need a container as well as the plants.

Many unusual tender perennials are now available as plantlets or 'tots'

Protecting plants over winter and taking cuttings

Taking cuttings

Tender perennials are exceptionally easy to root from cuttings. All you need is the tip of a shoot with a few leaves and no flowers. Insert this into a pot of compost, and with the exception of pelargoniums (geraniums), cover with a clear polythene bag. Keep at 15-20°C (65-70°F) in a light place but not in direct sunlight for a few weeks and they should root. You can use a rooting hormone powder to speed up the process, though it is not essential.

The other easy way to propagate plants with a trailing or rambling habit is by layering. Simply peg a stem down into a pot of compost and within a few weeks, the newly rooted section can be severed.

Climbers can be rooted from leaf bud cuttings. Make your top cut just above a pair of leaves and the lower cut half way between two leaf joints. For shrubs, shoot tips trimmed to just below a leaf joint are generally successful. With perennials, use the new shoots that emerge in spring.

Plants in containers tend to get better treatment than plants in the garden because they are regularly inspected along with the daily watering. This makes it easier to treat pests and diseases before they become serious and to remove dead leaves and flowers, which helps keep the plants healthy and prolong flowering. Problems can occur when pots are left to stand in trays so that the compost becomes waterlogged. Or when they are allowed to dry out. Feeding can also be neglected during the summer. Most of these problems can be overcome by following the advice on composts, watering and feeding on pages 16-17.

Overwintering tender plants

The best way to overwinter tender plants is in a heated greenhouse or conservatory at a minimum temperature of 7°C (45°F). Provided you remove any capillary matting to keep down the humidity, keep the vents open while using a paraffin or gas heater, remove all dead growth and keep the compost barely moist, plants should survive. All you need do then is give them a trim in spring so that they resume their bushy habit.

The problem in keeping plants over the winter is that they take up a lot of space. For this reason many people prefer to take cuttings in August to produce young plants to keep over the winter. Cuttings are less resistant to cold spells than mature plants, so it becomes more vital to maintain a minimum of 7°C (45°F).

If you have a greenhouse but don't heat it, you can still successfully overwinter tender plants. Cover them with a double layer of garden fleece if frost is forecast. Although there may be some losses in a bad winter, a good proportion of plants and cuttings should survive.

Take pelargonium cuttings in late summer

If you don't have a greenhouse, take cuttings or select the best plants to keep in the coolest room in the house. Cuttings need to be kept near a window but plants will survive low light levels providing they are kept cool and the compost barely moist. Most of the failures with tender plants kept indoors are due to high temperatures as the plants will struggle to grow. Watering too becomes critical as they rapidly dry out yet rot if overwatered. By spring, your plants are likely to have become very straggly. Once you can see signs of new growth, trim them hard back and use the resultant new growth to take cuttings. By early summer, the original plants should start to look bushy again and can be repotted.

The other option is keep plants in a sheltered porch or in an insulated cold frame outdoors. Fuchsias and pelargoniums can be buried in the garden to protect them from frost. To survive they need a well-drained soil and even then this method is not totally reliable. In milder areas, you may even get away with leaving tender plants outdoors. Keep the pots above ground level on a plank supported by bricks and against a house wall for added warmth. Then cover them with a double layer of garden fleece.

Overwintering hardy and semi-tender plants

Hardy plants are not at risk from frost but the roots can be damaged if the compost freezes. If this is likely, insulate the pot with a duvet made from a bin liner stuffed with shredded newspaper. Tie this so it completely covers the pot, like a jacket on a hot-water tank.

Semi-tender plants risk damage if the temperature dips below -5°C (41°F). To protect them from cold weather and searing winds, cover the tops with a double layer of horticultural fleece. With standards, it is also worth insulating the stems with pipe lagging, as they can split if the sap freezes.

Troubleshooting

Pests

Aphids Small infestations can be squashed or blasted off with water. For more serious attacks use pirimicarb, a systemic aphicide which will not harm bees or ladybirds. Alternatively, use a contact insecticide containing pyrethrum or fatty acid soap. These short-lived insecticides are approved by organic gardeners but they will kill beneficial insects as well as aphids. Fatty acid soap sprays can scorch the leaves of some plants.

Spider mite The symptoms are fine webbing occupied by tiny brown mites and mottled and yellowing leaves. The most effective insecticide is bifenthrin.

Bubble wrap helps insulate large containers

Scale insects These appear as small, limpet-like creatures on stems and the base of leaves. Some may cover themselves in a cotton-wool-like substance which is often mistaken for mildew. You need to catch them with a contact insecticide when the young are hatching – usually in June, July and August. Small infestations can be squashed with a finger nail or removed with a stiff brush. On woody stems, a cigarette lighter is an effective control.

Vine weevil The adult weevils cut characteristic scalloped holes in the leaves of plants but it is the larvae that cause most damage, completely devouring roots. Inspect new plants carefully for small white grubs before planting. If plants are attacked, water all the containers with a nematode solution. Nematodes for controlling vine weevil larvae are sold in garden centres as BioSafe or by mail order from specialist suppliers. They are only effective while the temperature remains above 12°C (55°F).

Whitefly The first sign is clouds of white insects when you shake the plant. Spray with permethrin or pyrethrum twice weekly until the infestation is under control.

Diseases

Leafspots These affect many plants but can usually be controlled by removing the worst affected leaves and spraying several times with a fungicide.

Mildew Powdery mildew commonly attacks plants subjected to drought. Spray with Nimrod-T at first signs and repeat several times at weekly intervals.

Rust This fungal disease generally appears as raised orange spots, most prominent on the undersides of the leaves. Control with Bio Systhane on roses, Tumbleblite on other ornamentals except fuchsias.

Viruses These cause streaking and mottling of the leaves and stunted and distorted growth. There is no cure and infected plants should be disposed of by burning or putting in the dustbin.

Other common problems

Frost damage Remove browned leaves and flower buds. Wait until May or June for signs of new life if the whole plant is affected. Prune back to new shoots if they appear.

Nutrient deficiency Symptoms vary greatly according to the plant but yellowing or pale leaves often indicates an iron or magnesium deficiency. Pelargonium leaves develop red tinges when they are short of nitrogen. If you suspect a deficiency, feed with a liquid fertiliser containing trace elements.

Oedema Wart-like swellings on the leaves caused by overwatering or large fluctuations in temperature. Remove badly disfigured leaves. Not a serious problem.

Waterlogging Plants may appear to wilt even though compost is wet. Remove the plant from the pot, let the roots dry out slightly and repot in fresh compost.

Wilting If plants look as if they are wilting beyond the point of no return, cut back the top growth and submerse the rootball in water until you can't see any more air bubbles. Keep in a shady spot and watch for signs of new growth.

Wind scorch Remove damaged growth and move plants to a more sheltered position.

In an unheated greenhouse, use sheets of bubble wrap to protect plants from frost

Mildew on plants is often a sign of drought

Treat rust with Tumbleblite

Scale insects should be squashed or sprayed with a contact insecticide

Use nematodes to control vine weevils

Viruses cannot be cured – dispose of infected plants

Annuals and tender perennials

Seasonal plants are the mainstay of the patio, principally frost-tender ones to provide colour from early summer through until the first autumn frosts, though there are also plants that give interest from both flowers and foliage virtually year-round.

Annuals, many of which are referred to as bedding plants, have been popular for many years, although in recent times the emphasis has shifted on to using them in all types of containers rather than for bedding schemes in borders. Colour theming has developed enormously in popularity, and whereas plants and seed used to be sold mostly in mixtures, today it is easy to buy separate colours to create specific colour schemes.

Pelargoniums provide colour throughout the summer

There have been considerable developments too in the range of annuals available. Plant breeders have developed many new forms of old favourites, breeding new strains that give improved garden performance. Factors on which a plant is assessed include: flower colour, looking particularly at new colour breaks; number of blooms per plant; flower size; length of flower production; foliage and plant habit; plus, of course, the plant's performance in a garden situation. Then there are biennials, which are hardy plants that are sown in summer to flower the following spring and which are useful for colour early in the season.

Tender perennials have really revolutionised the look of summer containers. This catch-all description refers to a diverse and beautiful group of plants that, as their name suggests, tolerate little or no frost, but which produce a superb display within a short time of planting. The blooms are varied in both shape and colour, they are usually borne over a long period, and in many cases the foliage is handsome too. Most of these plants originate from warmer countries around the world, so they do best in full sun and well-drained soil.

Many of these tender perennials are not actually

Nasturtiums have a perfect trailing habit for hanging baskets

Be bold in your use of containers and plants to create a riot of colour

'new' plants - some, in fact, arrived in Britain around two hundred years ago, and many were immensely popular with Victorian gardeners. However, the enormous surge of interest in container gardening today has brought them from the realm of specialist gardeners to the attention of a wider audience. In response to this renewed popularity, many new hybrids are being developed.

The real bonus of these plants is that, unlike annuals, they can be overwintered in a frost-free place such as a greenhouse, porch or conservatory and moved outside in late spring once the danger of frost is past. In the vast majority of cases they are easy to propagate from cuttings, so even without a tailor-made structure for overwintering it is still possible to root cuttings in small pots and keep them through the winter on a windowsill indoors.

Garden centres and nurseries tend to offer a reasonable range of tender perennials, though for a comprehensive selection it is usually best to contact a specialist nursery. A number of these nurseries supply plants by mail order, and some also have display gardens where it's possible to see established plants in their full glory. Another good place to find them is at garden shows where a number of specialist nurseries are exhibiting.

Petunias and lobelias make a stylish combination

Acalypha reptans

(*Acalypha pendula*)

Shape and size

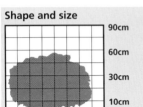

90cm
60cm
30cm
10cm

Position   Overwintering

7°C   7°C

Containers   Compost

Multi-purpose

Watering   Feeding

FEED FEED

Features calendar

Jan	Feb	Mar	Apr	May	June
					✿
✿	✿	✿			
July	Aug	Sept	Oct	Nov	Dec

Buying tips *Late spring/early summer is the best time to find plants on sale. Check for signs of pests before buying.*

Long, catkin-like flowers of acalypha

Half a dozen plants will cover a basket

Growing guide

This member of the euphorbia family is an ideal choice if you are looking for something different for a hanging basket or small tub. The long, red, catkin-like flowers are borne throughout the summer against a background of glossy, green, heart-shaped leaves. Despite its trailing habit the plant still retains a fairly compact shape. To keep it neat and bushy, pinch out the shoot tips occasionally during the growing season.

Acalypha is best planted as a single subject hanging basket so its attractive shape can be fully appreciated. It does best in partial shade and should not be allowed to dry out.

Propagation

Take cuttings in spring to increase your stocks or during the summer for overwintering.

Troubleshooting

Spider mite can be a problem, particularly in dry summers, and whitefly can be a nuisance under glass. Control with bifenthrin (Polysect) or, for whitefly, use a permethrin spray every four days.

Which variety?

Acalypha reptans is the one for patio containers. Shrubby species such as ***A. wilkesiana*** are available for conservatories, and are grown mainly for their coloured foliage.

Ageratum

Shape and size

90cm
60cm
30cm
10cm

Position

Over-wintering

Treat as Annual

Containers

Compost

Multi-purpose

Watering

Feeding

FEED FEED

Features calendar

Jan	Feb	Mar	Apr	May	June
					✿
July	Aug	Sept	Oct	Nov	Dec
✿	✿	✿			

Buying tips *Avoid unnamed varieties as they might be variable in quality and produce an uneven flowering display. Unnamed varieties are also more likely to be prone to rotting in wet weather which is a particular problem with ageratums. Look for compact plants that show no signs of fungal attack.*

'Adriatic' – a free-flowering dwarf variety

Growing guide

Ageratums are available in blue, pink or white and in a range of sizes. The dwarf varieties are best for containers because they tend to be the most uniform and free-flowering. The blue are the most striking and most popular. White ones can look unsightly if not regularly deadheaded as the flowers turn brown as they fade.

Ageratums generally perform best in fine summers and will tolerate becoming quite dry at the roots, but cannot withstand prolonged drought. They make an attractive edging for large mixed plantings and are good fillers for window-boxes, if you want a pastel scheme.

Propagation

Sow seed at 15°C (60°F) in March or early April, lightly covering the seed with compost.

Troubleshooting

Flowers, particularly the white varieties, are prone to rotting in wet weather. Mildew can be a problem if watered infrequently. Older varieties such as **'Blue Mink'** tend to have sparse flowers.

Which variety?

The following are all dwarf free-flowering varieties, growing 10-15cm (4-6in) in height.
'Adriatic' mid-blue.
'Blue Champion' mid-blue. **'Light Blue Champion'** is a paler form.
'Blue Danube' lavender blue. **'Royal Hawaii'** is similar.
'Pacific' violet-blue.

Alonsoa

Shape and size

90cm
60cm
30cm
10cm

Position   Overwintering

5°c   10°c

Containers   Compost

Multi-purpose   Grit

Watering   Feeding

FEED

Features calendar

Jan	Feb	Mar	Apr	May	June
					✿
✿	✿	✿			
July	Aug	Sept	Oct	Nov	Dec

Buying tips *A. warscewiczii is becoming more widely available, at garden centres. Other species will probably have to be obtained from a specialist nursery.*

Alonsoa acutifolia

Alonsoa warscewiczii

Growing guide

These free-flowering tender perennials bear an abundance of small, brightly coloured, saucer-shaped flowers from mid-summer through to autumn.

A. warscewiczii is the species most widely grown in containers, and it can be treated in two ways. If a reasonably bushy plant is desired, the tips can be pinched out regularly to promote branching and to maintain a more rounded, upright shape. However, if the stems are not stopped, the plant develops a lax, trailing habit, making it ideal for hanging baskets and raised containers.

Propagation

Sow seed at 15°C (60°F) in early spring. Spring-sown seed will produce plants for summer flowering. Seed of *A. acutifolia* can also be sown in mid-summer for winter flowering in a heated conservatory or greenhouse. All species can be rooted from cuttings during the summer.

Troubleshooting

Long spells of wet weather can inhibit flowering. If such conditions occur, plants will benefit from being temporarily covered with cloches or moved under cover until the weather improves.

Which variety?

A. warscewiczii (mask flower) is the best species for a hanging basket. It produces masses of small, blazing scarlet flowers from mid-summer to autumn. The variety **'Peachy Keen'** has attractive peachy-apricot blooms.
There are also two other species that are better grown as pot plants.
A. acutifolia is a bushy plant with an upright habit which bears deep red, saucer-shaped flowers from mid-summer through to autumn. A good variety for a winter pot plant under glass.
A. meridionalis is a compact, bushy plant producing sprays of small flowers in an unusual shade of salmon-pink.

Alyssum maritimum

Shape and size

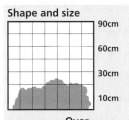

90cm
60cm
30cm
10cm

Position

Over-wintering

Treat as Annual

Containers

Compost

Multi-purpose

Watering

Feeding

FEED

Features calendar

Jan	Feb	Mar	Apr	May	June
					✿
July	Aug	Sept	Oct	Nov	Dec
✿	✿	✿			

Buying tips *Alyssum is easy to raise from seed, so it is only economical to buy plants if a very small number is required. For the best choice, look in the mail-order seed catalogues.*

Choose 'Creamery' for pastel schemes

For colour and impact 'Aphrodite' rates highly

Growing guide

At one time alyssum were available only in white. Nowadays, there is a wide choice of colours and they rival lobelias for planting around the edges of large pots, hanging baskets and window-boxes. Modern varieties form neat mounds of densely branched stems, reaching 10-15cm (4-6in) in diameter. On well-grown plants, the leaves are almost hidden by the clusters of honey-scented flowers. Alyssum prefer full sun and will tolerate occasional drying out. However, flowering can be cut short in August during a hot summer. If this happens, trim back the plants with scissors and they should produce a second flush in September.

Propagation

Sow seed from February to March at 10-13°C (50-55°F) and harden off before planting out from April onwards. Seeds can be sown directly around permanent plants in containers during March and April.

Troubleshooting

Stunted growth and white blisters on the undersides of leaves are a sign of downy mildew. Remove badly affected plants and spray the rest with fungicide to prevent the disease spreading.

Which variety?

Some of the older varieties have unsightly deadheads which can spoil the appearance of the plants unless regularly deadheaded. Some such as **'Rosie O'Day'** also have a loose habit and rather sparse flowers. The following can all be relied on to produce compact plants and good flowering display.

'Aphrodite' Bright mixture of seven colours including lilac, purple, cream, lemon and apricot. Amongst the best of the new varieties.

'Apricot' Pale creamy-apricot flowers.

'Creamery' Pale creamy-yellow flowers.

'Easter Bonnet' Mixture of purple, rose, lavender and white.

'Morning Mist' Pastel mixture of pinks, purples, cream and white.

'Oriental Night' Rich purple flowers with paler centres.

'Pastel Carpet' Mixture of white, cream, pink and violet.

'Snow Crystals' Larger than average white flowers and very compact habit.

'Wonderland' is a low-growing type available as a mixture or single colours.

Anagallis monelli

Shape and size

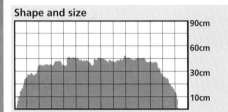

90cm
60cm
30cm
10cm

Position   Overwintering

7°c

Treat as Annual

Containers   Compost

Multi-purpose

Watering   Feeding

FEED FEED FEED

Features calendar

Jan	Feb	Mar	Apr	May	June
				✿	✿
✿	✿	✿			
July	Aug	Sept	Oct	Nov	Dec

Buying tips *Late spring/early summer is the best time to find plants on sale. Look in the alpine section if you cannot find them amongst the patio plants.*

The striking blooms of Anagallis monelli

Growing guide

An attractive plant which is related to the British native scarlet pimpernel. Its lax, spreading habit makes it a good dual-purpose plant. If grown on the level in a raised bed, a rock garden or a container, it makes a compact, ground-covering specimen. However, when grown in a hanging basket, the stems will become pendulous if left unsupported.

The slender stems are clothed with narrow, pointed, green leaves. From late spring until autumn, they are covered with small flowers in an exquisite deep shade of gentian blue with contrasting creamy stamens.

Anagallis does best in sunny positions but needs to be kept constantly moist and regularly fed.

Propagation

Sow seed at 15°C (60°F) in early spring. In addition, seed sown in mid-summer will produce good winter-flowering pot plants for the frost-free greenhouse.

Troubleshooting

Generally trouble-free if given a sunny site.

Which variety?

You may see ***Anagallis monelli*** labelled with variety names such as **'Blue Bird'** and **'Skylover'.** However, they are all the same plant.

Antirrhinum majus

Shape and size

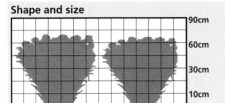

90cm
60cm
30cm
10cm

Position

Over-wintering

5°C

Treat as Annual

Containers

Compost

Multi-purpose

Watering

Feeding

FEED FEED

Features calendar

Jan	Feb	Mar	Apr	May	June
					✿
July	Aug	Sept	Oct	Nov	Dec
✿	✿	✿			

Buying tips *If buying established, pot-grown plants, buy only bushy plants that have been pinched out at an early stage. Bedding strips, on sale in April and May, are the most economical way of buying plants.*

Azalea-like blooms of 'Sweetheart'

'Chimes'

Growing guide

Antirrhinums are perennial if over-wintered in a frost-free environment, though for good, reliable performance it is preferable to raise fresh plants from seed each spring. The taller forms, growing to 60cm (24in) or more, are better for use in borders, though there is a wide choice of more compact varieties that can be used in containers. When the main flower spike has finished flowering, remove it to encourage the growth of smaller flowering spikes.

Antirrhinums do best in full sun, though they will still put on a reasonable show in light shade. They do not tolerate drying out and benefit from regular feeding. Still, humid conditions will increase the risk from diseases.

Propagation

Sow seed at 15-18°C (60-65°F) between February and April. For earlier flowering, you can also sow in September in a cool greenhouse. Light is necessary for germination so do not cover seed with compost. Sow thinly to avoid damping-off disease.

Troubleshooting

Botrytis or grey mould can affect flowers in a wet season. Pick off and dispose of infected parts as soon as possible to prevent the disease spreading.

Rust disease shows up as dark brown raised spots on leaves and stems. Throw away badly affected plants and choose resistant varieties for future use.

Trailing antirrhinums

Trailing varieties of antirrhinums have been developed for use in hanging baskets. However, the first introductions such as 'Avalanche' and 'Lampion' have proved disappointing with a rather sprawling habit, brittle stems and sparse flowers. 'Molle', with pink flowers and silvery foliage is worth trying, but still has a rather open spreading habit.

Which variety?

Most antirrhinum seeds of compact varieties are sold as mixed colours, which can be a nuisance in containers where you do not have sufficient plants to produce a balanced scheme. However, seed catalogues offer a limited range of individual colours. The following varieties grow to between 20-30cm (8-12in) high unless otherwise stated.

'Candyman Mixture' has unusually striped and flecked flowers in vivid shades of red, yellow and crimson.

'Chimes' series come in a range of colours including pink, cherry-red, rose and white, white and yellow. Height 15-20cm (6-8in).

'Lipstick Silver' has two-toned flowers of pale and deep rose-pink.

'Magic Carpet' Pastel shades of cream, yellow, pink and mauve. Rust-resistant.

'Peaches and Cream' Yellow flowers edged with salmon.

'Pixie' Mixture of white, pale yellow, pink and red. Penstemon-like flowers. Rust-resistant.

'Sweetheart' produces plants of a uniform habit with showy azalea-like flowers in red, pale and deep pink, yellow and white.

'Royal Carpet' Wide range of vivid colours. Rust-resistant.

'Tahiti' series has some unusual colours including **'Tahiti Appleblossom'** (cream and pink) and a lilac bicolour.

Arctotis

(formerly x *Venidioarctotis*)

Shape and size

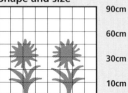

- 90cm
- 60cm
- 30cm
- 10cm

Position   Overwintering

7°C   7°C

Containers   Compost

Multi-purpose   Grit

Watering   Feeding

FEED

Features calendar

Jan	Feb	Mar	Apr	May	June
					✾
July	Aug	Sept	Oct	Nov	Dec
✾	✾	✾	✾		

Buying tips *Established plants sold in early to mid-summer tend to give the best results.*

The distinctive blooms of 'Flame'

Arctotis x hybrida 'Apricot'

Growing guide

These exceptionally showy tender perennials produce large daisy flowers which can be up to 10cm (4in) across. The flowers are borne singly on stout stems above a neat mound of divided foliage and are good for cutting. They come in a range of bright colours, mostly in shades of red and orange, though paler forms are available.

The plants need plenty of sun to flower well. For this reason, it is best to grow them individually in containers so there are no problems with shading from other plants. As the flower colours are extremely vibrant, this also enables you to group them with pots of complementary plants and avoid any severe colour clashes.

Propagation

Take stem cuttings from late spring to late summer. Seed can be sown under cover in early spring at a temperature of 18-20°C (65-70°F), though cuttings are necessary to propagate named varieties.

Troubleshooting

Arctotis dislike overwatering and good drainage is essential. Mix some sharp sand into the potting compost, as well as raising the pots off the ground to allow excess water to drain away.

Aphids can be a problem on young shoots. Spray with pirimicarb (Rapid) if necessary.

Blooms may close during the afternoon in dull, overcast weather.

Which variety?

The many colourful forms now available are all forms of **Arctotis x hybrida.**
'African Sunrise' has clear, bright orange flowers and grey-green foliage.
'Flame' has red-orange flowers and grey-green leaves.
'Midday Sun' bears orange flowers which shade to yellow in the centre, and silvery-grey foliage.
'Tangerine' has flowers which are a pale shade of apricot-orange and silver-grey leaves. **'Apricot'** is similar.
'Wine' has blooms that are an unusual shade of pinky-red, and silver-grey leaves.

Argyranthemum

(formerly *Chrysanthemum frutescens*, marguerite)

Argyranthemum

Shape and size

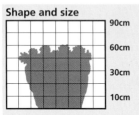

90cm
60cm
30cm
10cm

Position   Overwintering

Containers   Compost

Watering   Feeding

Features calendar

Jan	Feb	Mar	Apr	May	June
					❀
❀	❀	❀	❀		
July	Aug	Sept	Oct	Nov	Dec

Buying tips *Plants should have had their growing tips pinched out early to encourage bushy growth, so avoid thin, leggy plants. Watch out for dead leaves low down on the stems as it is a sign of earlier neglect.*

'Chelsea Girl' is grown for its finely-divided leaves

Growing guide

These tall, upright, bushy plants make ideal centrepieces in large containers where they can be surrounded by smaller, trailing plants. Pots containing single plants are also a useful addition to groups of smaller plants in containers. The most vigorous varieties are suitable for training as standards. However, the height of argyranthemums makes them unsuitable for hanging baskets.

The daisy-like flowers come in a wide range of colours and are borne in profusion from late spring through summer and into autumn; the flowers of the species tend to be smaller than those of the hybrids. Both single and double forms are available; the double forms are rather like small pompons. The fern-like foliage is pale green or grey-green, depending on the variety.

Propagation

Semi-ripe cuttings taken in late summer are most successful, though cuttings can also be taken from the soft new shoots of over-wintered plants in early spring.

Troubleshooting

Pinch out the growing tips regularly to avoid the plant becoming thin and lanky.

Which variety?

Several species and many hybrids are available.

A. gracile **'Chelsea Girl'** is grown more for its foliage, which is finely divided and an attractive shade of silver-grey, than its small, single, white flowers.

A. maderense is a species native to

Lanzarote. It bears single, lemon-yellow flowers against greyish-green foliage. Slightly spreading habit.

'Blizzard' (also known as **'Mini-Snowflake'**) is a compact grower bearing small, double, white flowers.

'Brontes' bears single, primrose-yellow flowers on a compact plant, and is neater in habit than the similar **'Jamaica Primrose'**.

'Edelweiss' is a compact plant with double, white flowers.

'Jamaica Primrose' is a single variety with large, butter-yellow flowers. Vigorous.

'Jamaica Snowstorm' (also known as **'Snowstorm'**) bears single white daisies which have a yellow centre, on a neat, compact plant of grey-green divided foliage.

'Lemon Meringue' bears double, clear lemon-yellow flowers.

'Mary Wootton' is a vigorous, double-flowered variety with deep pink flowers that are a darker shade in the centre. The blooms tend to fade to palest pink in strong sun.

'Peach Cheeks' bears pale peach blooms which are usually single, though double flowers may sometimes be borne on the same plant. Produces relatively few flowers compared to other varieties.

'Petite Pink' has a neat, compact habit, forming a cushion of foliage which is studded with many small, single pink blooms against silvery foliage.

'Pink Australian' has deep sugar-pink, double flowers, similar to **'Vancouver'** but with a neater habit.

'Powder Puff' is a compact grower bearing pale pink, double blooms.

'Rollason's Red' is an unusual colour for an argyranthemum. Its single flowers are bright red, fading to pink in strong sunshine, and with a central ring of yellow ray florets. Spreading habit. Can be shy to flower.

'Sugar Baby' has single, white, yellow-centred flowers, borne on a neat, compact plant.

'Vancouver' has double, deep dusky pink flowers.

'Jamaica Primrose' with the double, pink 'Vancouver'

33

Asteriscus maritimus
(Asteriscus 'Gold Coin')

Shape and size

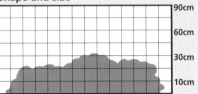

90cm
60cm
30cm
10cm

Position   Overwintering

5°c   7°c

Containers   Compost

Multi-purpose

Watering   Feeding

FEED FEED

Features calendar

Jan	Feb	Mar	Apr	May	June
					❋
❋	❋	❋	❋		
July	Aug	Sept	Oct	Nov	Dec

Buying tips *Early to mid-summer is the best time to find plants on sale.*

Asteriscus maritimus

'Gold Coin' is the popular name for these blooms

Growing guide

An attractive tender perennial with slender green leaves that contrast well with the many disc-shaped, golden-yellow flowers that are borne in profusion from mid-summer onwards. With a spreading, slightly pendulous habit, this is an ideal plant for hanging baskets and tall containers. Keep well-watered during the growing season. In winter, the compost should be just moist.

Propagation

Take cuttings in spring or mid- to late summer.

Troubleshooting

Slugs are fond of this plant, so either protect it with some form of slug bait, or grow it well out of reach of these troublesome pests in a hanging basket or a raised container.

Which variety?

Only one species is available; it is often sold under the name **'Gold Coin'**.

Begonia fuchsioides

Shape and size

90cm	
60cm	
30cm	
10cm	

Position

Overwintering

 5°c   7°c

Containers

Compost

Multi-purpose

Watering   Feeding

Features calendar

Jan	Feb	Mar	Apr	May	June
					✽
July	Aug	Sept	Oct	Nov	Dec
✽	✽	✽	✽		

Buying tips *Becoming more popular as a patio plant but most often sold as well-established specimens during the summer.*

Begonia fuchsioides

The shrub-like begonia fuchsioides

Growing guide

An unusual begonia in that it forms an upright, shrubby habit with semi-weeping stems and small red, fuchsia-like flowers. It makes an interesting curiosity in a pot of its own, but is also sufficiently free-flowering to make a centrepiece for a larger container.

It is a much tougher plant than most fuchsias or begonias as it will withstand several days of drought before it shows signs of wilting or dropping its leaves. It is equally happy as a houseplant as on the patio as it will put up with baking sun or cool conditions in dense shade.

Propagation

Easy to propagate as fuchsia from the young shoots during spring and summer.

Troubleshooting

Generally trouble-free.

Which variety?

There is only one species.

Begonia semperflorens

Shape and size

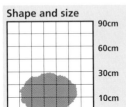

90cm
60cm
30cm
10cm

Position

Overwintering

5°C 7°C

Containers

Compost

Multi-purpose

Watering   Feeding

FEED FEED FEED

Features calendar

Jan	Feb	Mar	Apr	May	June
					✿
July	Aug	Sept	Oct	Nov	Dec
✿	✿	✿	✿		

Buying tips *Seedlings are available in early to mid-spring and can work out cheaper than buying seeds. If you do not have the facilities for growing on seedlings, look for bedding strips in May, but don't plant out until after all frosts.*

The red, pink and white flowers of 'Party Fun'

Growing guide

B. semperflorens is a dwarf species growing to 15-23cm (6-9in) high which is suited to edging containers and for window-boxes. It forms a neat, bushy plant of rounded, glossy leaves which are either fresh green or with purple or bronze tints. Flowers are either red, shades of pink, or white, and are borne on short stems from mid-summer to autumn. They thrive in sun or partial shade, but they will not tolerate drying out. At the end of the season and before the first frosts arrive, healthy plants of *B. semperflorens* can be potted up and enjoyed for a few more weeks on a cool windowsill.

Propagation

Sow seed of *B. semperflorens* in late winter at 18°C (65°C). Do not cover seed with compost as it needs light to germinate. The tiny seed can be difficult to sow thinly. Some suppliers package the seed in antistatic vials to make sowing easier and to protect the seed from damage. To stop the seed drying out, cover the pot or tray with clinging film until the seedlings are visible.

You can take cuttings from plants throughout the summer. This is a useful way to bulk up your favourite colours.

Troubleshooting

Avoid splashing water on the foliage, particularly when the plant is in full sun, as it can cause unsightly scorch marks.

Which variety?

At garden centres, plants tend to be sold by colour rather than variety. If you want to grow your own from seed, the following mixtures have all done well in *Gardening Which?* trials.

'Cocktail' Shades of pink plus white with reddish or bronze foliage.

'Party Fun' Pink, red and white with green or bronze foliage.

'Treasure Trove' Red, pink, pink and white flowers with green or bronze foliage.

Begonia x tuberhybrida

Shape and size

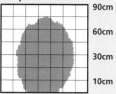

90cm
60cm
30cm
10cm

Position   Overwintering

5°C   7°C

Containers Compost   Watering   Feeding

Multi-purpose
FEED

Features calendar

Jan	Feb	Mar	Apr	May	June
					✿
July	Aug	Sept	Oct	Nov	Dec
✿	✿	✿	✿		

Buying tips

Buy named varieties as seedlings or plugs from garden centres in early spring but remember they must be kept frost-free. Later they are available in strips or in pots in flower, but do not plant out before early May. Check dormant tubers are firm and not dried out.

Begonia 'Pin-Up'

Begonia 'Non-Stop'

Growing guide

B. × *tuberhybrida* varieties grow to 30-60cm (12-24in) high. The showy, double flowers come in a wide range of colours including red, crimson, orange, apricot, yellow, pink, salmon and white. Some picotee varieties are also available, with petals edged with a contrasting colour.

Tuberous begonias can be lifted and dried off once the foliage has died back, and stored in a frost-free place over winter in soil that is kept barely moist, for repotting the following year. They can be started into growth in early spring under cover at 18°C (65°F); place the tubers hollow-side up in a tray or individual pots of compost, so the top of the tuber is not covered with compost. Once growth has started, pot the tubers up individually in 13-cm (5-in) pots.

Propagation

Sow the very fine seed in January on the surface of the compost and maintain a temperature of 18-21°C (65-70°F). Maintain high humidity around the seed to encourage germination by covering the seed tray with clinging film.

Tuberous begonias can also be propagated from stem cuttings in spring or by dividing large tubers when potting up.

Troubleshooting

Begonias are relatively trouble-free, but vine weevils can devastate a pot display if a container becomes infested. Mildew can be a problem in a wet summer.

Which variety?

'Apricot Cascade' bears double pendulous blooms, set off against bright green foliage.
'Can-Can' bears double, yellow flowers edged with red.
'Midas' bears large, double, pale yellow flowers up to 15cm (6in) across.
'Non-Stop' is a mixture of brightly coloured double blooms.
'Pin-Up' is pale pink with a dark pink margin.

Begonia: trailing varieties

Shape and size

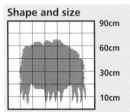

90cm
60cm
30cm
10cm

Position Overwintering

5°C   7°c

Containers   Compost

Multi-purpose

Watering   Feeding

FEED FEED FEED

Features calendar

Jan	Feb	Mar	Apr	May	June
					✿
July	Aug	Sept	Oct	Nov	Dec
✿	✿	✿	✿		

Buying tips *Buy named varieties as seedlings or plugs from garden centres in early spring but keep frost-free. They are available in strips or in pots in flower later in the year but do not plant out before early May.*

Begonia pendula

Begonia sutherlandii

Growing guide

Pendulous or cascade begonias are excellent for hanging baskets where the trailing stems and dark green foliage provide a perfect background for the large, brightly coloured blooms.

Tuberous types, such as *B. suther-landii*, can be lifted and dried off once the foliage has died back, and stored in a frost-free place over winter in soil that is kept barely moist, for repotting the following year. Start them into growth in early spring under cover at 18-21°C (65-70°F) by placing the tubers hollow-side up in a tray or individual pots of compost, so the top of the tuber is not covered with compost. Once growth has started, pot the tubers up individually in 13-cm (5-in) pots.

Propagation

Sow the very fine seed in January on the surface of the compost and maintain a temperature of 18-21°C (65-70°F). Maintain high humidity around the seed to encourage germination by covering the seed tray with clinging film.

Tuberous begonias can be propagated from stem cuttings in spring or by dividing large tubers when potting up.

Troubleshooting

Begonias are relatively trouble-free, but vine weevils can devastate a pot display if a container becomes infested. Mildew can be a problem in a wet summer.

Which variety?

B. pendula varieties are old favourites. They bear showy, large, double flowers in a range of colours including red, orange, yellow, salmon pink, white and yellow. **'Illumination'** hybrids have recently been introduced. They are very free-flowering, producing masses of flowers which are light pink or orange.
B. sutherlandii is an attractive species with lobed, bright green leaves and profuse quantities of single orange flowers. Sometimes sold under the name **'Papaya'**. However, it can be susceptible to mildew.

Bellis perennis

Shape and size

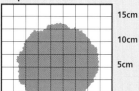

15cm
10cm
5cm

Position

Over-wintering

Containers

Compost

Multi-purpose

Watering   Feeding

FEED FEED

Features calendar

Jan	Feb	Mar	Apr	May	June
July	Aug	Sept	Oct	Nov	Dec

Buying tips *Buy trays or strips of plants in early autumn and plant them out while it is still warm enough for them to establish quickly. Alternatively, buy larger plants in early spring for instant effect.*

Double daisies are useful fillers

Bellis perennis 'Pomponette'

Growing guide

A perennial plant which is usually treated as a biennial and used to provide early spring colour. The plants form low, neat rosettes of fresh green foliage, from which rise many colourful flowers on short stems. They are ideal for containers, window-boxes and hanging baskets and make splendid companions for hyacinths or dwarf tulips.

Propagation

Sow seed thinly in a nursery bed outdoors in mid-summer. Pot the seedlings into 7.5-cm (3-in) pots when large enough to handle. Transplant to their flowering positions in early autumn, spaced 15cm (6in) apart.

Troubleshooting

Generally trouble-free.

Which variety?

Most varieties have double, pompon-type blooms.
'Carpet' Available as a mixture of red, rose-pink and white flowers, or sometimes as individual colours.
'Habenera Mixed' has red, pink and white flowers which are made up of many needle-like petals. An unusual contrast to the pompon-type flowers.
'Pomponette' Small, tightly formed blooms in red, rose-pink and white.
'Radar series' Large pompon flowers available as mixed or single colours.

Bidens

Shape and size

90cm
60cm
30cm
10cm

Position

Overwintering
 5°c
 7°c

Containers

Compost
 Multi-purpose

Watering

Feeding
 FEED

Features calendar

Jan	Feb	Mar	Apr	May	June
					🌼
July	Aug	Sept	Oct	Nov	Dec
🌼	🌼	🌼	🌼		

Buying tips *Young plantlets in early spring are the best value as they can be quickly grown on to provide a source of cuttings.*

Bidens ferulifolia

Bidens' trailing habit and daisy flowers mix well with other container plants

Growing guide

A magnificent tender perennial which has deservedly become very popular. A vigorous grower, it quickly forms a spreading mass of trailing stems covered with golden-yellow, single daisy flowers and finely divided green leaves. This versatile plant can be grown in a hanging basket to form a cascade of stems, either on its own or combined with other plants, or as ground cover in a sunny, well-drained spot. Because of the airiness of its overall growth, it also makes an excellent summer partner for container-grown shrubs such as hebes or azaleas, or with larger seasonal plants like argyranthe-mums. Its thin stems can thread through the branches of the larger plant to spangle it with yellow flowers.

Bidens thrives in a sun-baked spot. Like all plants, it is best not to let the compost dry out, but if this does happen, the plant can be rejuvenated surprisingly quickly by giving the rootball a good soaking in a bucket of water.

Propagation

Cuttings can be taken in spring or summer or the shoots can be pegged down and layered in pots of compost. Rooting takes only a few weeks. Plants can be raised from seed, though they take some time to perform well in their first season.

Troubleshooting

Generally trouble-free.

Which variety?

Two very similar species are available; they are ***B. aurea*** and ***B. ferulifolia.***

Brachyscome

Shape and size

Position

Overwintering

 5°c

 7°c

Treat as Annual

Containers

Compost

Multi-purpose

Watering

Feeding

FEED FEED

Features calendar

Jan	Feb	Mar	Apr	May	June
					✿
July	Aug	Sept	Oct	Nov	Dec
✿	✿	✿	✿		

Buying tips *Blue forms are generally available both as plantlets in early spring and plants from early to mid-summer. It may be necessary to buy other colours from a specialist nursery, or with B. iberidifolia, obtain seed from a mail-order catalogue.*

Brachyscome iberidifolia with Helichysum petiolare

Growing guide

A free-flowering plant producing many small daisy flowers amongst feathery foliage, *B. multifida* has a spreading, slightly bushy habit which makes it excellent for hanging baskets and for the edges of containers. It tends to look best in a group with other plants such as ivy-leaved geraniums where its wispy foliage and tiny flowers make a good contrast to bolder plants, rather than planted in a container on its own. *B. iberidifolia* (Swan River daisy) has slightly coarser leaves and a bushy habit up to 23cm (9in) high.

Brachyscomes thrive in a rich soil and prefer a sunny, sheltered site.

Propagation
Sow seed of *B. iberidifolia* in early spring at 18°C (65°F). Cuttings of *B. multifida* root well throughout summer.

Troubleshooting
Generally trouble-free.

Which variety?

There are two different species, one annual and one a tender perennial.

B. iberidifolia (Swan River daisy) is a half-hardy annual with an upright habit. Daisy-like flowers up to 2.5cm (1in) across, in shades of blue, rose-pink, white and lilac, are borne from mid-summer to autumn on short stems above divided green leaves. The blooms are slightly scented. **'Purple Splendour'** has deep bluish-purple flowers, **'Blue Star'** is similar, **'Blue Splendour'** has mid-blue blooms, while those of **'White Splendour'** are pure white. *B. multifida* is a tender perennial with finely divided foliage and a profusion of small flowers. The flowers of the species are mid-blue, those of **'Blue Mist'** are pale blue, **'Lemon Mist'** is pale yellow and **'Pink Mist'** has pale lilac-pink blooms.

Brassicas ornamental

(cabbage and kale)

Shape and size

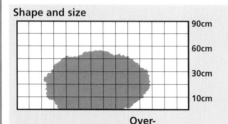

Position

Over-wintering

Containers

Compost

Watering

Feeding

Features calendar

Jan	Feb	Mar	Apr	May	June

July	Aug	Sept	Oct	Nov	Dec

Buying tips *Well-grown plants can be expensive, so it is worth looking at raising your own plants from seed if you require more than just a few.*

Ornamental kales have distinctive, crinkly leaves

Growing guide

These colourful plants with decorative foliage have rapidly become fashionable for autumn and winter displays. Leaf colours offer a wide range of variations, mostly in shades of red, pink, green and white. Plant and leaf shapes are varied too; ornamental cabbages tend to form more rounded, compact heads of foliage, while ornamental kale have a more open habit and leaves that are deeply serrated.

Although these plants are edible they have a bitter taste, so their culinary use may be best confined to that of a colourful garnish.

Propagation

Sow seed in late May or June at 15°C (60°F). Pot up seedlings individually into 10cm (4in) and then 15cm (6in) pots and keep them well watered and fed. Plants prefer cool growing conditions so keep them in light shade during the hottest months. The colours will intensify as night temperatures fall during the autumn.

Troubleshooting

Slug damage can be a problem so it is worth taking precautions at an early stage.

Also keep an eye out for traditional cabbage pests such as flea beetles, cabbage white caterpillars and mealy aphids.

Which variety?

CABBAGES

'Northern Lights' is an excellent F1 hybrid with rounded heads of leaves that are frilled at the edges and which come in a range of striking colours. Seed can be

Ornamental cabbages are as showy as most flowers

purchased either as a mixture or in separate colours of white, pink and rose.

KALE

Kale has a more open habit and feathery leaves, a tendency which is most pronounced in varieties such as **'Red Feather'**, which has bright red upper leaves and purple-red lower ones, and **'White Feather'** which is creamy-white on top and green below.

'Nagoya Mixed' also has very feathery foliage, in a mixture of red and white varieties.

Cabbages come in cream, purple and pink shades

Calceolaria

Shape and size

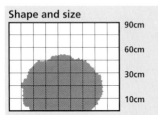

90cm
60cm
30cm
10cm

Position   Overwintering

  5°c 7°c

Treat as Annual

Containers   Compost

Multi-purpose

Watering   Feeding

FEED FEED

Features calendar

Jan	Feb	Mar	Apr	May	June
					✿
July	Aug	Sept	Oct	Nov	Dec
✿	✿	✿			

Buying tips *The perennial form is not widely available and will probably have to be obtained from a specialist nursery.*

Calceolaria 'Sunshine' forms a dense mass of flowers

Growing guide

Showy plants bearing many clusters of brightly coloured, rounded flowers. The flowers of the annual hybrids tend to be larger and much more vividly coloured than those of the tender perennial form *C. integrifolia*. Yellow is the predominant colour, though red-spotted, dark red and scarlet flowers are also available.

Calceolarias prefer a slightly acid compost and a sunny, sheltered site. They don't like to go short of water and respond to regular feeding.

Propagation

Sow seed at 15°C (60°F) from January to March. Do not cover seed with compost as it needs light to germinate. *C. integrifolia* can be propagated by cuttings during the summer.

Troubleshooting

Aphids and slugs can be a problem.

Which variety?

ANNUALS

Annual hybrids generally come in a range of seed mixtures. The following are suitable for outdoor use, though they should not be confused with other hybrids that are grown as glasshouse pot plants
'Sunset Mixed' (F1 hybrid) includes red, yellow bicolours and orange bicolours.
'Sunshine' (F1 hybrid) has golden-yellow flowers. The single colour means it can be combined easily with other plants.

PERENNIALS

C. integrifolia is a tender perennial with bright yellow flowers which are smaller and more delicate in appearance than the annual hybrids. In a mild area, it can remain outdoors all year in a sunny, sheltered spot.

Centaurea cyanus

Shape and size

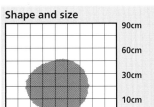

90cm
60cm
30cm
10cm

Position

Over-wintering

Treat as Annual

Containers

Compost

Multi-purpose

Watering

Feeding

FEED FEED

Features calendar

Jan	Feb	Mar	Apr	May	June
					✿
July	Aug	Sept	Oct	Nov	Dec
✿	✿	✿			

Buying tips *Plants can be raised easily and cheaply from seed. Ready-grown plants are rarely available.*

'Florence Pink'

'Florence White'

Growing guide

A popular, old cottage-garden annual with narrow leaves and colourful flowers with many slender petals. There are now several dwarf forms growing to 23-30cm (9-12in) high which are ideal for growing in containers.

Propagation

Seed can be sown under cover in the greenhouse or cold frame in September to produce sturdy plants for overwintering and early spring planting. Alternatively, sow in early spring.

Troubleshooting

Generally trouble-free, though hot summers or infrequent watering may cut short flowering.

Which variety?

'Blue Baby' has blooms that are attractive shades of mid- to deep blue.
'Florence' varieties have double, very ornamental flowers and grey-green foliage. **'Florence Pink'** is a rich pink, paler on the outside, while the blooms of **'Florence White'** are pure white.

Centradenia inaequilateralis 'Cascade'

Shape and size

90cm
60cm
30cm
10cm

Position Overwintering

  5°C 7°C

Containers Compost Watering Feeding

 Multi-purpose FEED FEED

Features calendar

Jan	Feb	Mar	Apr	May	June
					🌿
July	Aug	Sept	Oct	Nov	Dec
✳	✳	✳	🌿		

Buying tips *Buy plants early and grow on under cover so they can become established and give the best chance of flowering.*

Regard the summer blooms as a bonus

Autumn foliage colour

Growing guide

A trailing tender perennial with handsome, shiny, bronze leaves that looks stunning in a hanging basket. Saucer-shaped, vivid cerise flowers are produced in summer, but this plant can be very shy to bloom. A sheltered, sunny position will help boost flowering, though even then it is not reliable. However, it is still worth growing for its attractive leaves - look upon any blooms as a bonus. Overwintered plants can become straggly, in which case prune in early spring.

Propagation

Cuttings can be taken from early spring and throughout the summer.

Troubleshooting

Generally trouble-free.

Which variety?

There is only one species.

Cheiranthus cheiri

Shape and size

90cm
60cm
30cm
10cm

Position

Over-wintering

Containers

Compost

Multi-purpose

Watering

Feeding

FEE FEED EED

Features calendar

Jan	Feb	Mar	Apr	May	June
July	Aug	Sept	Oct	Nov	Dec

Buying tips *Plants are commonly sold bare-rooted in bundles during early autumn. While this can be an economical way of buying them, you are unlikely to have any choice of variety.*

'Scarlet Bedder'

Compact varieties of wallflower, like this 'Primrose Bedder', are ideal for containers

Growing guide

An old favourite for providing a mass of colourful, fragrant flowers in early to mid-spring. Tall forms are popular for use in beds and borders, but there are a number of compact forms that are excellent in tubs. They look particularly attractive when combined with spring bulbs such as dwarf tulips.

Wallflowers do best in a sunny position, and it is beneficial to pinch out the growing tips when plants are around 15cm (6in) high to encourage a branching habit.

Propagation

Sow seed in a prepared nursery bed outdoors in May or June. Transplant 15cm (6in) apart and grow on until autumn when they can be moved into beds or containers.

Troubleshooting

Wallflowers can be attacked by clubroot so do not plant where the disease has occurred in recent years.

Which variety?

Only compact varieties are listed below as they are most suitable for containers.

'Bedder' series are sturdy, compact plants growing 25-30cm (10-12in) high. Colours are orange, scarlet, primrose and golden-yellow, plus a mixed selection of these colours.

'Prince' series come in a range of colours including red, orange, pale and deep yellow, and purple. Height 20cm (8in).

'Tom Thumb Mixed' offers a wide range of shades. Height 15-23cm (6-9in).

Chrysanths

Shape and size

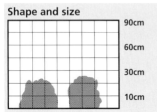

90cm
60cm
30cm
10cm

Position

Containers

Compost

Multi-purpose

Watering Feeding

FEE FEED EED

Features calendar

Jan	Feb	Mar	Apr	May	June
✿	✿	✿	✿		
July	Aug	Sept	Oct	Nov	Dec

Buying tips *Look out for them in garden centres from June onwards.*

Mini-chrysanths produce a fiery display in this chimney pot

Growing guide

Mini-chrysanthemums form tiny pompon flowers on top of 15-cm (6-in) high plants. They are ideal for providing instant colour in mid-summer up until the frosts. The orange and yellow ones create a similar effect to French marigolds, but you can also get a range of pastel and earthy shades.

When you buy them, it is best to pot four or five plants into a 15-cm (6-in) pot and move them around the patio to wherever colour is lacking. Keep well-watered and liquid-feed regularly for the best display. Plants are best discarded when they have flowered.

Propagation

Plants are generally treated to keep them dwarf so this is not worthwhile.

Troubleshooting

Generally trouble-free as temporary summer plants.

Which variety?

Generally sold as **'mini-mums' 'garden mums'** or bedding chrysanths in a range of colours.

Coleus

Shape and size

90cm
60cm
30cm
10cm

Position

Overwintering

7°c   7°c

Containers

Compost

Multi-purpose

Watering   Feeding

FEED FEED FEED

Features calendar

Jan	Feb	Mar	Apr	May	June
July	Aug	Sept	Oct	Nov	Dec

Buying tips *Go for bushy plants that you like the appearance of.*

'Wizard Mixed'

Keep coleus well fed and watered for colourful, long-lasting displays

Growing Guide

Coleus are grown for their colourful leaves which come in a myriad of bright shades and patterns. They are perennials but tend to become leggy after more than one season so are best rejuvenated by taking cuttings at least once a year.

The darker-leaved types make excellent backdrops for paler flowers in groups of containers. They can also make good specimens for the centre of a tub. The rainbow types create more of a carnival feel and look most at home amidst brightly coloured flowers.

To get the best display, keep the plants well watered and fed and pinch out the growing tips every week or two. If left to their own devices, they form rather insignificant woolly clusters of flowers and after that go rapidly downhill.

Propagation

Growing from seed is one way to get a range of different colours cheaply. Sow from February to April at 15°C (60°F). You can then select your favourite plants from which to take cuttings. Shoot tips readily root in compost or water throughout late spring and summer.

Troubleshooting

Coleus are rarely troubled by pests or diseases. Take cuttings when plants start to look past their best.

Which variety?

Mixtures such as **'Wizard Mixed'** will give you a wide range of different colours. If you have a particular planting scheme in mind go for single colours, such as **'Volcano'** bright red, or **'Scarlet Poncho'**, red with a gold edge. **'Sabre'** is a dwarf mixture growing only 15cm (6in) tall.

Convolvulus sabatius

(C. mauritanicus)

Shape and size

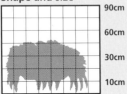

90cm
60cm
30cm
10cm

Position   Overwintering

7°c   5°c

Containers

Compost   Watering   Feeding

Multi-purpose   Grit   FEED

Features calendar

Jan	Feb	Mar	Apr	May	June
					✿
✿	✿	✿			
July	Aug	Sept	Oct	Nov	Dec

The trailing stems of convolvulus sabatius

Buying tips *Young plantlets on sale from early spring are an economical way of buying convolvulus.*

Flowers in close-up   -

Growing guide

A super trailing plant with long, slender stems clad with small, rounded, grey-green leaves. The open trumpets of flowers are satin-textured and an unusual shade of silvery-blue and are borne in profusion through summer. It makes an excellent edging plant for containers and for use in hanging baskets.

This plant loves good drainage and a sunny, sheltered site. Although it is best treated as a tender perennial and given winter protection in cold areas, it can remain outdoors in mild areas or very sheltered spots so long as the containers do not become waterlogged over winter.

Propagation

Take cuttings from sideshoots in mid- to late summer.

Troubleshooting

Generally trouble-free.

Which variety?

C.sabatius is widely available. There is also a dark form with rich, deep blue flowers.

Cosmos atrosanguineus

Shape and size

90cm
60cm
30cm
10cm

Position Overwintering

  5°c 7°c

Containers Compost Watering Feeding

 Multi-purpose FEED FEED

Features calendar

Jan	Feb	Mar	Apr	May	June
					✿
July	Aug	Sept	Oct	Nov	Dec
✿	✿	✿			

Buying tips *Plants are best bought in early to mid-summer.*

The blooms have a chocolate aroma

Growing guide

A delightful little plant bearing many small, dark red flowers, rather like those of a miniature dahlia in appearance. They are borne singly on slender stems above a rounded bush of green foliage. The fragrance of the blooms is most unusual - they have the delicious scent of dark chocolate. This plant can be overwintered in the same way as a dahlia, as it has similar, tuberous roots. Once the foliage has died back in autumn, the stems can be cut back to within 5cm (2in) of the roots, which can then be laid in a tray of soil or compost and kept barely moist through the winter in a frost-free place. In early spring, the roots can be repotted and started into growth.

Propagation

Take soft, basal cuttings from new shoots in spring.

Troubleshooting

Inspect the stored roots regularly for signs of rot, and remove any infected pieces before the rot spreads through the whole plant.

Which variety?

There is only one species. Not to be confused with annual varieties of Cosmos.

Cuphea

Shape and size

90cm
60cm
30cm
10cm

Position   Overwintering

  5°C 7°C

Containers   Compost

   Multi-purpose

Watering   Feeding

FEED FEED

Features calendar

Jan	Feb	Mar	Apr	May	June
					✿
July	Aug	Sept	Oct	Nov	Dec
✿	✿	✿	✿		

Buying tips *For a range of cupheas it is usually necessary to buy from a specialist nursery.*

Cuphea cyanaea

Cigar-like blooms of cuphea ignea

Growing guide

Bushy tender perennials with unusual tubular flowers in a range of bright colours. They were immensely popular as bedding plants during the last century, and are now beginning to make a comeback as patio container plants. Several species are extremely long-flowering and will carry on blooming if moved indoors to a warm windowsill or greenhouse in autumn. The flowered shoots can be trimmed back immediately after blooming if necessary to maintain a bushy habit. Prune overwintered plants by at least half in early spring to maintain a bushy shape.

Cupheas perform best in full sun. They respond well to regular feeding and do not like drying out.

Propagation

Sow seed from January to March at 15-18°C (60-65°F). Cuttings can be taken from sideshoots in early to mid-spring.

Troubleshooting

Generally free of pests and diseases, though spider mite can be a problem on plants under cover. Control with a systemic insecticide such as bifenthrin (Polysect).

Which variety?

C. caeciliae has dark stems and green leaves which make a striking background for the bright orange flowers.
C. cyanaea bears masses of small red flowers tipped with yellow. This species is particularly long-flowering and it will often continue blooming until the end of the year under cover.
C. hyssopifolia has tiny green leaves and masses of small, bright cerise flowers are produced on a neat, compact plant. **'Riverdene Gold'** has golden foliage that makes a lovely contrast to the pink flowers, while the blooms of **'Alba'** are pure white. Pruning of this species is not usually necessary.
C. ignea (cigar plant) is a very free-flowering species that produces many bright scarlet tubular flowers which are white at the tips.
'Variegata' has leaves which are boldly blotched with yellow.

Dianthus chinensis

Shape and size

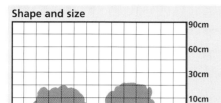

90cm
60cm
30cm
10cm

Position	Over-wintering	Containers

Compost	Watering	Feeding

Features calendar

Jan	Feb	Mar	Apr	May	June
					✿
✿	✿	✿			
July	Aug	Sept	Oct	Nov	Dec

Buying tips *You can get the best choice by buying seeds. Bedding strips, on sale in April and May, are better value than tots or individually potted plants*

'Magic Charms'

'Raspberry Parfait'

Growing guide

Indian pinks flower from mid-summer until the first frosts. They come in a range of colours including red, mauve, white and many shades of pink. Though often referred to as annual pinks, they are perennials but tend to look rather tatty in their second year unless propagated from cuttings. They need a sunny position and a well-drained compost. Regular deadheading will improve their appearance and prolong flowering. They do best in a good summer. Flowering may be delayed if the weather remains dull.

Propagation

Sow seed in March at 15°C (60°F) or take cuttings from plants in September and overwinter in a cool greenhouse or cold frame.

Troubleshooting

Waterlogging can easily kill the plants. Always use a well-drained compost and raise the container off the ground so water can drain freely.

Which variety?

The following are ideal for containers because they produce neat, uniform plants with flowers that are held well clear of the foliage.

'Carpet series' are available as a mixture or single colours. All are early flowering and produce masses of blooms on compact, dome-shaped plants. Height 20cm (8in).

'Colour Magician' is a very free-flowering variety, with blooms that turn from white to deep rose-pink. Height 25cm (10in).

'Magic Charms' is a mixture of red, pink and white. Some flowers have coloured centres. Height 20cm (8in).

'Raspberry Parfait', crimson with a darker centre, and **'Strawberry Parfait'**, rose-pink with a scarlet centre, both flower early and produce large blooms. Height 20cm (8in).

'Snowfire' has bright scarlet petals with a broad white margin. Height 20cm (8in).

'Telstar' is a mixture of white, reds and pinks. Compact and very free-flowering. Height 20cm (8in).

Diascia

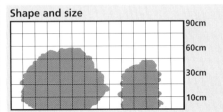

Shape and size

Position   Overwintering

Containers

Compost   Watering   Feeding

Features calendar

Jan	Feb	Mar	Apr	May	June
				✿	✿
July	Aug	Sept	Oct	Nov	Dec
✿	✿	✿	✿		

Buying tips *A few varieties may be available as young plantlets in early spring, but otherwise diascias can be found on sale right through summer.*

'Jacqueline's Joy'

Growing guide

An extremely versatile group of tender perennials that produces slender spires of long-lasting flowers throughout the summer. Most diascias are lax and spreading, so lend themselves to a wealth of uses in hanging baskets, window-boxes, shallow containers and the edges of larger containers, as well as in rock gardens or to edge a path. The long, slender flower stems will thread themselves up through a taller plant nearby, as well as tumbling downwards. They make fitting companions for bushy plants such as argyranthemums or euryops in containers, providing a garland of contrasting colour. Diascias are reasonably hardy and will often survive the winter outside, though it is always worth taking some cuttings and overwintering them under cover in case of severe frosts. Overwintered plants often do better the following year than plants which have come through the winter outside. The old stems of mature plants should be cut back in spring. Diascias prefer a sunny site, though they do reasonably well in light shade. They need good drainage but most do not tolerate drying out.

Propagation

Take cuttings from soft shoots from spring to late summer. Alternatively, peg shoots into a pot of compost, where they should root within a few weeks. You may find plants layer themselves. The species can also be raised from seed. Sow in February or March at 15°C (60°F), barely covering with compost. Grow on under glass for planting out in May or June. Pinch out shoots of young plants to encourage well-branched specimens.

Diascia barbarae

Troubleshooting

Generally trouble-free, providing compost is kept moist.

Which variety?

There is a wide range of species and hybrids to choose from. The species come in shades of pink, while the hybrids include some attractive apricot and lilac shades. Most of the hybrids are of recent introduction, bred by the grower Hector Harrison, while some of the species have been around since the last century.

SPECIES

D. barbarae bears many spikes of deep pink flowers. 30x30cm (12x12in).
D. integerrima has deep pink flowers. Reasonably tolerant of dry conditions.
D. lilacina is a dainty species

bearing 15-cm (6-in) spikes of lilac-pink flowers.
D. rigescens is more upright than spreading, growing to about 45cm (18in) high and bearing many dense spikes of coppery-pink flowers that pale slightly with age.
D. vigilis (D. elegans) produces many stems of clear pink flowers. Reasonably tolerant of dry conditions. 30x60cm (12x24in).

HYBRIDS

'Blackthorn Apricot' has clear apricot flowers. 60x45cm (24x18 in).
'Jacqueline's Joy' has large, purplish-pink flowers on a spreading plant up to 30cm (12in) high.
'Joyce's Choice' bears large salmon-apricot flowers with a coppery flush on the reverse. 30x60cm (12x24in).
'Lady Valerie' is similar to **'Joyce's Choice'**, with slightly smaller

flowers that are a stronger salmon colour.
'Lilac Mist' has a spreading habit and bears pale silvery-lilac flowers that age almost to white. 30x90cm (12x36in).
'Ruby Field' forms mats covered in spikes of coral-pink flowers. 8x15cm (3x6in).
'Salmon Supreme' has pale salmon-apricot flowers on a compact plant. 23x45cm (9x18in).
'Stella' is similar to **'Joyce's Choice'**, but with slightly pinker flowers.
'Twinkle' has rosy-lilac flowers. 45x45cm (18x18in).

Euryops

Shape and size

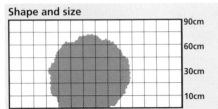

90cm
60cm
30cm
10cm

Position

Overwintering

5°C

Containers

Compost

John Innes

Watering

Feeding

FEED FEED

Features calendar

Jan	Feb	Mar	Apr	May	June
					❋
❋	❋	❋			
July	Aug	Sept	Oct	Nov	Dec

Buying tips *May be found with alpines, perennials, shrubs or patio plants at garden centres. Avoid pot-bound plants or any that are turning brown at the base.*

Euryops acraeus

Euryops pectinatus

Growing guide

These upright, bushy plants grow to 45-60cm (18-24in) high and often taller if they are more than one-year-old. Similar in habit to argyranthemums, they have a tendency to develop a short section of clear stem at the base, which makes them perfect for planting in the centre of a large container and surrounding with lower-growing plants such as diascia or osteospermum. Bright yellow, daisy-like blooms are borne singly on slender stems throughout summer, though flowering tends to be limited during long periods of dull weather. In compensation, the foliage is also an attractive feature of all the species.

Propagation

Take cuttings in mid- to late summer.

Troubleshooting

Established plants dislike root disturbance, so overwintered plants are best top-dressed with some fresh potting compost and some controlled-release fertiliser (e.g. Osmocote) rather than being repotted.

Which variety?

All species produce bright yellow flowers.
E. acraeus has attractive whorls of silvery leaves and forms a neat dome shape.
E. chrysanthemoides has glossy, bright green leaves which are rather like those of an oak tree. Flowers are smaller than *E. pectinatus*, but are borne in greater numbers.
E. pectinatus has finely divided, grey-green foliage. This species tends to flower best in the early part of the summer.

Felicia

Shape and size

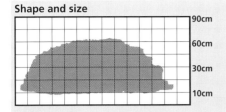

90cm
60cm
30cm
10cm

Position

Overwintering

0°c   5°c

Containers

Compost

Multi-purpose

Watering   Feeding

Features calendar

Jan	Feb	Mar	Apr	May	June
					✿
July	Aug	Sept	Oct	Nov	Dec
✿	✿	✿			

Buying tips *Plantlets or plants in small pots are a good buy in early spring. Plants in larger pots are generally available in June or July but are a lot more expensive.*

Bright blooms of Felicia amelloides

Growing guide

These neat, rounded, bushy plants produce many small, daisy-like flowers on slender stems above a mound of fresh green foliage. They are ideal as a low centrepiece to a hanging basket, window-box or a small container, or for growing on their own. Most varieties bear flowers which are a beautiful shade of sky-blue with contrasting golden centres.

Felicias can be surprisingly hardy and they often withstand several degrees of frost so long as the rootball is reasonably dry, though for safety's sake they are best over-wintered under cover in a frost-free place. However, the variegated form is less hardy than those with green leaves. Prune overwintered plants in April by trimming the whole plant lightly, removing 2.5-5cm (1-2in) of growth.

Propagation
Take cuttings from mid- to late summer.

Troubleshooting
Generally trouble-free.

Which variety?

F. amelloides is the species that is generally available, and there are also several hybrids.
'Astrid Thomas' has blue flowers which are larger than those of the species.
'Santa Anita' is similar to the above.
'Read's Blue' has similar flowers, with leaves that are more rounded than the species. **'Read's White'** has white flowers.
***F. amelliodes* 'Variegata'** has leaves which are attractively variegated with green and white; this contrasts well with its blue flowers.

Fuchsia: trailing varieties

Shape and size

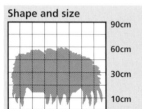

90cm
60cm
30cm
10cm

Position Overwintering

4°C   7°C

Containers

Compost Watering Feeding

Multi-purpose

FEED

Features calendar

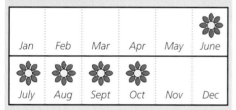

Jan	Feb	Mar	Apr	May	June
✿	✿	✿	✿		
July	Aug	Sept	Oct	Nov	Dec

Cascades of 'Cascade'

Growing guide

Trailing fuchsias are perfect for hanging baskets where their large, showy blooms can cascade freely. They can be fully appreciated at eye-level too. These varieties can also be trained as standards to form a spreading, slightly pendulous head of branches.

Propagation

As for upright varieties, see page 60.

Troubleshooting

As for upright varieties, see pages 60-61.

Which variety?

As with bush varieties of fuchsia, there is a considerable number of hybrids available, and those listed below are just a selection of the most popular ones.

'Cascade' bears single flowers, purple in the centre with soft pink sepals.

'Florabelle' is an F1 hybrid which can be grown from seed. The flowers have red sepals with purple petals, borne on shoots which branch freely so pinching out is not necessary.

'Harry Gray' has semi-double flowers which are white in the centre, with soft pink and white sepals.

'Marinka'

Growing a standard fuchsia

The following method will enable you to grow an attractive standard within six months.

1 Pot up a rooted cutting into a 13-cm (5-in) pot and insert a cane next to it. Make a paper cone with a hole in the top large enough to thread over the cane and to let through some light. Suspend the cone over the tip of the cutting using string and a paper clip as shown above.

2 As the shoot grows, tie it into the cane and keep raising the cone until the fuchsia stem reaches the desired height.

3 Remove the cone and completely remove all but the top five sideshoots.

4 Once the top five sideshoots are around 10cm (4in) long, pinch out the growing tip to get them to branch. At the same time, remove all the leaves below these sideshoots. Repeat the pinching out process to form a compact, bushy head.

'Golden Marinka' has single deep red flowers that show off well against golden foliage.

'La Campanella' has semi-double blooms, lilac in the centre with white sepals.

'Marinka' bears deep red, single flowers.

'Patio Princess' has white flowers that are veined with pink and rose-pink sepals, and is good as a weeping standard.

'Pink Marshmallow' has pale pink and white double flowers with an overall pink flush.

'Red Spider' bears single, bell-shaped, deep pink flowers with red sepals.

Fuchsia: upright varieties

Shape and size

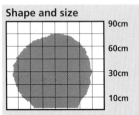

90cm
60cm
30cm
10cm

Position   Overwintering

  5°C   7°C

Containers   Compost

  Multi-purpose

Watering   Feeding

 FEE FEED ED

Features calendar

Jan	Feb	Mar	Apr	May	June
					✿
✿	✿	✿	✿		
July	Aug	Sept	Oct	Nov	Dec

Buying tips *Look out for special offers on trays of six or ten plants at garden centres. Choose compact bushy plants with unblemished leaves and plenty of roots. Larger plants are a good buy if you can find them in April as you can use these to take lots of cuttings.*

Growing guide

Fuchsias are immensely popular plants for summer containers. The blooms come in an enormous range of colours and sizes, and both single and double forms are widely available. In many cases the centre of the flower is a contrasting colour to the outside, or sepals. Upright fuchsias are easiest to grow in bush form, where they will attain a height and spread of up to 60cm (24in). They can also be trained into standards (see page 59).

Fuchsias are best grown in light shade as direct sun will scorch the leaves, bleach the flowers and turn white flowers pink. The exceptions are those with orange flowers and bronze leaves, which revel in sunny positions.

To ensure bushy, flower-laden plants, pinch out the growing tips of young plants. Flower buds should form in six to twelve weeks, though some double varieties may prove slower.

Fuchsias need to be kept constantly moist and do not like to run short of fertiliser. The best way to feed fuchsias in hanging baskets and tubs is to add controlled-release fertiliser (e.g. Osmocote) granules when planting up and supplement this with a weekly tomato feed from August onwards. Remove any seed pods that might form to prolong flowering.

Tender fuchsias can be overwintered in a frost-free place at a minimum temperature of 5°C (40°F). Trim back the shoots by half to two-thirds and keep the roots barely moist through winter. In early spring, start the plants into growth by raising the temperature to 10°C (50°F). At the same time, repot them into fresh compost and water.

Hardy varieties can be left outdoors for the winter. The top growth is likely to be killed back but will re-grow in spring. In colder areas it is advisable to insulate the container to prevent the compost from freezing. Standards should not be

Fuchsia 'Dollar Princess' is hardy enough for permanent tubs

left outdoors as you will need to train them from scratch if the top is killed.

Propagation

The vast majority of fuchsias are sold as plants, which need to be propagated by cuttings.

Cuttings can be taken from any part of the soft shoot in mid- to late summer for overwintering. You can also take cuttings from new shoots in March or April to produce plants that will flower in the same year. Two varieties can be grown from seed: these are 'Chimes' and 'Florabelle', which produce a mixture of upright and trailing varieties. Sow seed of these two varieties in January at 21-23°C (70-75°F) and grow seedlings on at 18°C (65°F).

Troubleshooting

Aphids can be a problem, especially on young growth. Spray with pirimicarb (Rapid).

Whitefly Spray with permethrin

Fuchsia 'Alice Hoffman'

bifenthrin every four days for several weeks or until no more adults appear.

Grey mould can form on white-flowered and golden-leaved varieties when grown, in a damp, sheltered spots. Remove infected shoots and place plant in a more open spot.

Rust appears as reddish-brown spots on undersides of the leaves. Spray with Nimrod-T. Discard any badly infected plants.

Which variety?

Do not confuse the tender fuchsias which are used for seasonal bedding with hardy varieties that can be planted in the border and left outside all year. There is a considerable range of tender hybrids available, and the following are just a few of the most popular ones.

'Alice Hoffman' is a hardy variety with semi-double flowers with white centres and pinky-red sepals.

'Ballerina' has single blooms, white in the centre with red sepals.

'Chimes' is an F1 hybrid which can be raised from seed to produce a mixture of upright and trailing plants with a range of flower colours.

'Dollar Princess' bears double blooms with dark blue centres and swept-back, scarlet-red sepals. This variety is hardy and good as a standard.

'Pink Spangles' produces semi-double blooms with white centres and horizontal dark pink sepals.

'Thalia' is a particularly handsome variety that is different to most hybrids, in that its deep orange-red flowers are longer, slender and borne in clusters. The dark purplish-red foliage is very attractive. More tender than most and needs full sun.

'Winston Churchill' has double flowers, purple in the centre with red sepals.

Fuchsia 'Thalia'

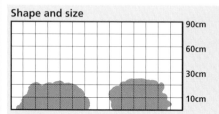

Gazania

Shape and size

90cm
60cm
30cm
10cm

Position   **Overwintering**

  7°C 5°C

Containers   **Compost**

  Multi-purpose

Watering   **Feeding**

  FEED FEED

Features calendar

Jan	Feb	Mar	Apr	May	June
					✿
✿	✿	✿			
July	Aug	Sept	Oct	Nov	Dec

Buying tips *For a wide range of gazanias, it is usually necessary to go to a supplier specialising in tender perennials.*

'Cream Beauty'

'Tiger'

Growing guide

This showy tender perennial bears large daisy flowers up to 8cm (3in) across on stout stems above a neat mound of slender leaves. The flowers are predominantly in vivid colours such as bright yellow and orange, though new hybrids are available in softer shades including pink and cream. Nearly all are single-flowered forms though there is a double-flowered variety, 'Yellow Buttons'. The foliage is silver or green. Gazanias thrive in a very sunny spot, preferring well-drained soil, and they do particularly well in a seaside environment. With a neat, low-growing habit of 23-30cm (9-12in) high and a spread of up to 30cm (12in), they are ideal for containers and window-boxes.

Propagation

Take cuttings in July or August to propagate named varieties. Seed can be sown in January or February at 15°C (60°F).

Troubleshooting

Generally trouble-free, though grey mould may be a problem if long spells of wet weather occur.

Which variety?

The varieties which are generally available are all forms of **Gazania x hybrida.**

'Aztec' has cream petals, each one marked with a bold maroon central band, and silver foliage.

'Bicton Orange' has golden petals with a central orange stripe, and silver foliage.

'Blackberry Ripple' has creamy-pink petals with a purple central stripe, and silvery leaves.

'Blaze of Fire' bears bright orange flowers with petals that turn gold at the tips, and green foliage.

'Christopher Lloyd' has deep pink flowers – an unusual colour amongst gazanias – and green foliage.

'Cream' bears soft, pure cream flowers against silvery-grey leaves.

'Evening Sun' has cream petals that deepen to orange and brown in the centre, and green foliage.

'Lemon Beauty' has large, soft orange flowers and silvery-grey leaves.

'Sunbeam' bears deep orange flowers which are darker in the centre, and silver foliage.

'Tiger' has rusty-brown flowers which are darker in the centre, and silvery foliage.

'Yellow Buttons' has double flowers, measuring about 5cm (2in) across, and silvery foliage.

Glechoma hederacea 'Variegata'

Shape and size

90cm
60cm
30cm
10cm

Position

Over-wintering

Containers

Compost

Watering

Feeding

Features calendar

Jan	Feb	Mar	Apr	May	June
July	Aug	Sept	Oct	Nov	Dec

Close-up of foliage

Buying tips *Buying young plantlets in early spring is an economical way of purchasing this quick-growing plant. There is no need to buy more than one as it is so easy to propagate.*

Growing guide

Although this trailing plant is a hardy perennial, it is widely used in hanging baskets and window-boxes to complement seasonal flowering plants. It forms long trails of slender stems clothed with kidney-shaped, toothed leaves which are attractively variegated with green and white. Small clusters of lilac-blue flowers are often borne in the leaf axils in summer, though the ornamental foliage is this plant's main attraction. The stems can grow up to 90cm (36in) long, so it needs plenty of hanging space in order to be shown to its best advantage. It thrives equally well in sun or partial shade.

Propagation

Stems of the plant can easily be layered throughout summer. Cuttings can be taken in spring and summer.

Troubleshooting

It becomes very straggly if allowed to dry out. Trim plants hard back if this happens.

Which variety?

Only one species and variety is generally available. It was formerly known as *Nepeta hederacea 'Variegata'*.

Helichrysum petiolare

Shape and size

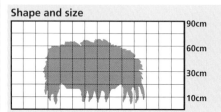

90cm
60cm
30cm
10cm

Position

Overwintering

4°C

7°C

Containers

Compost

Multi-purpose

Watering

Feeding

FEED

Features calendar

Jan	Feb	Mar	Apr	May	June
				🌿	🌿
July	Aug	Sept	Oct	Nov	Dec
🌿	🌿	🌿	🌿		

Buying tips *Young plantlets available in early spring are an economical way to buy this vigorous plant.*

Helichrysum petiolare 'Variegatum'

Helichrysum petiolare 'Limelight' with fuchsias and impatiens

Growing guide

This attractive foliage plant is widely used in summer plantings to complement flowering plants. The range of leaf colours includes silver, lime-yellow and variegated, so it makes an excellent partner for bright colours such as blue, red or orange flowers. With a spreading, freely branching habit, it is ideal for hanging baskets, window-boxes and the edges of containers. The plant is reasonably vigorous and sometimes it may be necessary to trim the shoots to restrict its overall growth. The species *H. petiolare* is most vigorous of all and is best in larger containers. For smaller containers, including hanging baskets and window-boxes, it is usually better to opt for one of the varieties with smaller or variegated leaves as they are more compact in habit.

A lot of people have trouble with overwintering these plants success-fully. The trick is to trim the plants back to leave at least 15cm (6in) in spring and keep them just moist but never wet. In late February or March, give them a bit of extra warmth to encourage new growth from which you can take cuttings.

Propagation

Take cuttings of sideshoots from spring to late summer.

Troubleshooting

Trim back plants occasionally to keep them well-branched and remove blemished leaves. Neglected plants can be rejuvenated by cutting hard back.

Which variety?

H. microphyllum (now ***Plecostachys serpyllifolia*** has tiny silver leaves and a neat, compact habit.

H. petiolare has rounded, silver-grey leaves on a vigorous, spreading plant.

'Goring Silver' has silvery leaves that are smaller than those of most of the species.

'Limelight' (sometimes called **'Aureum'**) has lime-yellow foliage.

'Roundabout' has small leaves which are variegated with grey and gold.

'Variegatum' has leaves which are variegated with gold and olive green.

Heliotropium

Shape and size

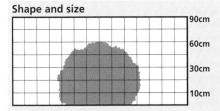

				90cm
				60cm
				30cm
				10cm

Position   Overwintering

Containers   Compost

Watering Feeding

Features calendar

Jan	Feb	Mar	Apr	May	June
❋	❋	❋			
July	Aug	Sept	Oct	Nov	Dec

Buying tips *Most garden centres stock only one or two varieties, so if you want a wider selection contact a specialist supplier.*

'White Lady'

Heliotropium 'Lord Roberts' with Verbena 'Silver Anne'

Growing guide

The bushy plants of heliotropium are popular for the sweet fragrance of their flowers. The tiny blooms are borne in clusters 8cm (3in) or more across from spring through to late summer. Flower colours are mostly shades of purple or blue, though a white form is also available. The foliage is handsome too, with dark green leaves that are attractively wrinkled. The plant forms an upright, rounded bush up to 60cm (24in) high with a spread of up to 45cm (18in). Heliotrope can be grown in a pot on its own, or used as a centrepiece in a large container. It can also be trained as a standard from cuttings taken in mid-summer; grow the rooted cuttings up a cane, removing all lateral shoots, then pinch out the growing tip once the plant has reached the desired height. Heliotrope is also excellent for perfuming a conservatory. Plants can be overwintered at a minimum temperature of 7°C (45°F) and repotted in March. At the same time, pinch out shoot tips to encourage bushy growth.

Propagation

Take cuttings in late summer or early autumn. Seed can be sown in February or early March at 16-18°C (60-65°F).

Troubleshooting

Mostly trouble-free, though whitefly can be a problem under glass. Combat with a systemic insecticide every four days for several weeks.

Which variety?

There are several hybrids which are generally available. All bear sweetly scented flowers.

'Chatsworth' has deep mauve flowers borne on a plant which is a little more upright in habit than most. Recommended for training as a standard.

'Gatton Park' bears purple flowers.

'Lord Roberts' has blooms which are mid-purple.

'Princess Marina' has very dark purple flowers and dark foliage.

'White Lady' has pale, silver-mauve flowers which fade in the sun to white.

Impatiens

Shape and size

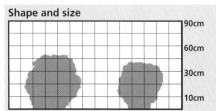

90cm
60cm
30cm
10cm

Position   Overwintering

5°C   7°C

Containers

Compost   Watering   Feeding

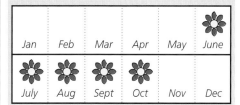

Multi-purpose   FEED FEED FEED

Features calendar

Jan	Feb	Mar	Apr	May	June
✿	✿	✿	✿		✿
July	Aug	Sept	Oct	Nov	Dec

Buying tips *As impatiens need to be sown early at high temperatures, buying ready-germinated seedlings in early to mid-spring can be particularly good value. This tends to apply to single-flowered varieties, as double ones are generally only available as plants later in the season.*

'Super Elfin Pink' and 'Cherry'

Variegated and double-flowered 'Dapper Dan'

Growing guide

Busy lizzies are popular and versatile plants for providing masses of summer flowers. The vast majority of hybrids have single flowers and they come in a wide range of colours, varying from soft shades such as lilac, pale pink and white, to vibrant colours like red, orange, burgundy and cerise. Multi-coloured forms with a central white star are also available.

Impatiens thrive in full shade, which makes them particularly useful for brightening up dull corners. They also do well in sun but it is preferable to avoid very hot sites. With a low-growing, slightly spreading habit, they are excellent for all containers including hanging baskets, window-boxes, hanging flower bags and pouches, as well as in borders. Busy lizzies look equally attractive planted on their own or combined with other plants.

Plants like to be permanently moist. They will drop their flower buds and then their leaves if allowed to dry out. Regular feeding is also beneficial to produce the best quality plants.

Towards the end of the season, healthy plants can be lifted, potted up and brought indoors where they will carry on flowering for a number of weeks. Plants can be overwintered at a minimum temperature of 7°C (45°F) though if you can keep them at 13°C (55°F) they will carry on flowering all winter indoors. However, plants treated in this way can easily become leggy and unsightly by the spring. If this is the case, take cuttings and discard the main plant. Specimens kept in cooler conditions are best repotted in mid-spring.

Propagation

Sow seed at 21-25°C (70-75°F) from January to March. Sow the seed on the surface of the compost as light is needed for germination. Cover pots or trays with clinging film until seedlings appear, to prevent the seeds from drying out. Cuttings from the stem tips can be rooted at virtually any time of year.

Troubleshooting

Aphids can be a problem, particularly on plants grown under cover. Over-watering causes older leaves to turn yellow and fall.

Which variety?

There is a huge range of hybrids available in a wealth of colours, and new varieties are being developed all the time. In many cases the seed is offered as a mixture as well as individual colours.

'Accent' hybrids come in a wide range of colours, including white, pale pink with a darker eye, apricot, salmon, coral, orange, violet, red, and white-starred forms. The foliage is a fresh green.

'Deco' hybrids offer a range of bright colours including orange, pink, violet and red. The flowers are enhanced by bronzed foliage and red stems.

'Expo' hybrids produce very large flowers on compact plants and are tolerant of varied weather conditions. There is a considerable range of colours available.

'Mega Orange Star' has larger than average blooms that are bright orange with a central white star. Performs exceptionally well in a wide range of weather conditions.

'Super Elfin' series F1 hybrids come in a wide range of bright, showy colours. With many of the varieties, the flowers have a darker central eye.

'Swirl' hybrids have attractive picotee flowers – paler in the centre with a darker edge. Colours are pink, coral and peach.

'Tempo' hybrids bear large flowers up to 4-5cm (1-2½in) across, in colours including white, blush pink, lavender, apricot, scarlet and burgundy.

'Deco' hybrids

Double-flowered impatiens

Double-flowered impatiens have been introduced comparatively recently; they have pretty blooms that resemble those of a miniature rose, and some have the bonus of variegated foliage too.

Varieties with double flowers generally grow slightly larger than single-flowered ones, reaching about 30-38cm (12-15in) in height and spread. The varieties listed below have green foliage unless otherwise stated. Those with variegated leaves are particularly ornamental.

'Ballerina' has soft pink flowers.

'Blackberry Ice' has bright purple flowers and leaves which are variegated grey-green and white.

'Dapper Dan' bears bright red flowers against green and gold foliage.

'Madame Pompadour' bears blooms which are a bright, glowing pink.

'Orange Sunrise' has bold orange flowers and foliage which is dark olive-green.

'Peach Ice' has soft peachy flowers and leaves which are variegated with grey-green and white.

'Raspberry Ripple' has bicoloured, red and white flowers.

'Salmon Princess' bears deep salmon-pink blooms.

'Snowflake' has small white flowers and is more compact than other varieties.

Impatiens: New Guinea hybrids

Shape and size

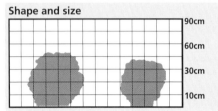

90cm
60cm
30cm
10cm

Position   Overwintering

5°c   7°c

Containers   Compost

Multi-purpose

Watering   Feeding

FEED FEED

Features calendar

Jan	Feb	Mar	Apr	May	June
					✿
✿	✿	✿	✿		
July	Aug	Sept	Oct	Nov	Dec

Buying tips *New Guinea impatiens are generally sold as established pot plants and can be found on market stalls and in florists, as well as garden centres. Varieties are often not named.*

Many hybrids have coloured foliage

New Guinea hybrids make good specimens

Growing guide

New Guinea impatiens form larger plants than the normal types, growing to around 23-38cm (9-15in) in height. The foliage is more ornamental too; the leaves are bigger and they are often attractively bronzed or a dark, glossy green. New Guinea hybrids are excellent in containers and as individual pot plants. Unlike single-flowered impatiens, they need a sunny position. Regular feeding is particularly important to promote good flowering.

Troubleshooting - see page 67

Propagation

Take cuttings from spring through to late summer

Which variety?

There is a considerable range now available, though the colours on offer tend to be the brighter, more vibrant ones such as reds, pinks and purples.

'Anaea' has red flowers and glossy green leaves.
'Ambrosia' bears orange-red flowers and has bronze leaves.
'Aruba' has dark lilac-purple blooms and bronze foliage.
'Grenada' has bright salmon flowers with bronze foliage.
'Isis' has salmon-orange flowers and variegated foliage.
'Kallima' bears glowing pink blooms against dark green leaves.
'Lanai' bears clear red flowers against dark green leaves.
'Martinique' has clear, cherry-red flowers and dark green foliage.
'Spectra' varieties come in a range of colours including pink, orange, scarlet and cerise. This variety can be grown from seed, though expect flower colour and leaf marking to be very variable.
'Tahiti' has soft pink flowers with a darker eye, and dark green foliage.
'Tango' bears large flowers in a vivid shade of tangerine-orange. They are shown off well against the glossy, dark green leaves.

Lantana

Shape and size

90cm
60cm
30cm
10cm

Position   Overwintering

  7°C   7°C

Containers   Compost

      Multi-purpose

Watering   Feeding

Features calendar

Jan	Feb	Mar	Apr	May	June
					🌼
🌼	🌼	🌼			
July	Aug	Sept	Oct	Nov	Dec

Buying tips *You can often find them amongst the plantlets on sale in March and April. Larger plants can be found from early to mid-summer.*

Lantana camara 'Cocktail'

Lantana camara 'Aloha'

Growing guide

These tender evergreen shrubs are generally grown as patio plants for their summer display. The rounded flower heads, each one made up of many small florets, are produced in abundance all summer. The blooms have a slight fragrance and are attractive to butterflies. Most have a rounded habit and are ideal in pots on their own or as part of a larger planting in tubs. The spreading types make attractive hanging basket plants.

Most varieties have dark green leaves which are toothed at the edges. They are all evergreens so should be kept growing through the winter. Keep the plants just moist in good light at a minimum temperature of 7°C (45°F). If the plants become straggly, prune them hard back in spring.

They like a sunny, sheltered position and will withstand occasional drying out though not neglect.

Propagation

Take cuttings from mid- to late summer.

Troubleshooting

Generally trouble-free.

Which variety?

Most plants are hybrid forms of *Lantana camara* and are generally sold by flower colour rather than variety. The flowers come in yellow, orange, red, pink and white. You may also come across the following named forms.

'Aloha' has pale green foliage attractively variegated with creamy-yellow which sets off its bright yellow flowers.

'Cocktail' has blooms which change colour from yellow to red as they age.

L. montevidensis has a low spreading habit, growing 15cm (6in) tall and up to 90cm (36in) across. It produces many clusters of rosy-lilac flowers through the summer. White and yellow forms are also available.

WARNING: ALL PARTS OF THE PLANT ARE POISONOUS

Lobelia: bush types

Shape and size

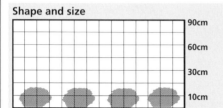

90cm
60cm
30cm
10cm

Position   Overwintering

5°C

Treat as Annual

Containers

Compost   Watering   Feeding

Multi-purpose

FEED FEED

Features calendar

Jan	Feb	Mar	Apr	May	June
					✿
✿	✿	✿			
July	Aug	Sept	Oct	Nov	Dec

Buying tips *The best way to buy plants is as seedlings in March or April or as bedding strips in May.*

Lobelia 'String of Pearls'

Lobelia 'Sapphire'

Growing guide

These lobelias form tight mounds up to 15cm (6in) high and are covered with tiny flowers. They are best used as edging plants in containers and raised beds, where they can be planted to contrast with other flower colours.

Lobelias prefer partial shade and need to be kept well-fed and constantly moist. In full sunshine, they tend to finish flowering prematurely in a hot summer. If this happens, trim them hard back and you should get a second flush of flowers. Similarly, neglected plants may stop flowering and should be given the same treatment.

Propagation

Sow seed from January to March at 18°C (65°F). Do not cover the tiny seed as it needs light to germinate. To prevent the seed from drying out place a sheet of clinging film over the pot or tray until the seedlings are visible. Prick out the tiny seedlings in clumps of about half a dozen, as they are too small to handle individually.

Although generally thought of as annuals, you can also take cuttings from lobelias in summer to produce plants that will flower early the following year. For best results, trim back a plant in July and take cuttings from the new shoots when they are around 5cm (2in) long and before they flower.

Troubleshooting

The tiny seedlings are subject to damping off disease. Avoid this problem by reducing humidity around the seedlings; sow thinly to encourage air movement and water from the bottom by standing pots or trays in water until the surface of the compost darkens. Using a copper fungicide (e.g. Bordeaux Mixture) when watering is another preventive measure.

Which variety?

The range of colours includes white, carmine-red and lilac, though the many different shades of blue tend to be the most popular and the most reliable. Some varieties have flowers with a distinctive white eye.

'Cambridge Blue' has clear, sky blue flowers.

'Crystal Palace' has deep blue flowers and bronzed foliage.

'Mrs Clibran' bears deep blue flowers with a white eye.

'Riviera Blue Splash' is white with a blue throat.

'Riviera Lilac' has lilac-pink flowers.

'Riviera Sky Blue' is a pretty shade of mid-blue, slightly deeper than **'Cambridge Blue'**.

'Riviera White' has pure white flowers.

'Rosamund' has carmine-red flowers with a distinctive white eye.

'String of Pearls' is a mixed variety which includes blue, red and white flowers.

Lobelia: trailing varieties

Shape and size

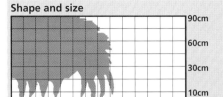

90cm
60cm
30cm
10cm

Position   Overwintering

5°C

Treat as Annual

Containers

Compost   Watering   Feeding

Multi-purpose

FEED FEED

Features calendar

Jan	Feb	Mar	Apr	May	June
					✿
July	Aug	Sept	Oct	Nov	Dec
✿	✿	✿			

Buying tips *Young plantlets or tots of L. richardii are often available from February to April. Others are best purchased as seedlings or bedding strips.*

'White Fountain'

Lobelias in a mixed basket

Growing guide

Trailing lobelias add a light, airy look to containers and are ideal for covering the edges of hanging baskets, window-boxes and large pots and tubs. In combinations, its slender stems can easily grow through other plants to fill in gaps. Lobelias can also look very attractive when grown on their own, particularly in hanging flower bags or pouches, where their growth will quickly hide the rather unsightly material of the bag itself.

As with the bush forms, trailing lobelias do best in light shade as they tend to finish flowering prematurely in August if exposed to direct sunshine in a hot summer. Trimming the plants hard back with scissors may result in a second flush of flowers in September.

Propagation

As with bush varieties, *L. richardii* can be propagated by cuttings in spring or late summer.

Troubleshooting

As for bush varieties.

Which variety?

Most varieties are grown as annuals, though there is a perennial species.

ANNUALS

'Cascade' varieties offer a colour selection that includes blue, red, lilac and white.
'Fountain' varieties come in light blue, crimson, lilac, rose and white.
'Regatta' varieties start flowering early, at least two weeks before **'Fountain'**; varieties include white, rose/white eye, lilac and several shades of blue.
'Sapphire' bears deep blue flowers with a distinctive white eye.

PERENNIALS

L. richardii is a perennial species that bears many single blue flowers. It performs well even in hot summers, often continuing after seed-raised forms have become exhausted. **'Kathleen Mallard'** bears double, mid-blue flowers.

Lotus

Shape and size

90cm
60cm
30cm
10cm

Position   Overwintering

7°C   7°C

Containers   Compost

Multi-purpose | Grit

Watering   Feeding

FEED

Features calendar

Jan	Feb	Mar	Apr	May	June
					✿
✿	✿	✿			
July	Aug	Sept	Oct	Nov	Dec

Buying tips *Large plants are a better buy as they are more likely to flower. Look for specimens with lots of shoots. Avoid those with yellowing or pale greenish tinges to the foliage.*

Lotus berthelotii x maculatus

Lotus maculatus

Growing guide

These attractive plants form a cascading curtain of slender stems which can grow up to 90cm (36in) long. For this reason they are best in a hanging basket or a raised trough where the stems have sufficient space to fall without interruption. The feathery grey-green or silver foliage is particularly handsome, and indeed in cooler areas it is best to think of this plant primarily for its foliage effect, as flowers are only freely produced in a long, hot summer. Lotus need good drainage but are reasonably drought-tolerant and do not require a lot of fertiliser. Apply a liquid feed no more than once a month during the growing season.

The dark red or orange blooms are unusually shaped and are produced in claw-like clusters; blooms are more likely to be produced on two-year-old plants. For this reason, it is best to try and overwinter plants without cutting them back. Keep plants barely moist during winter.

Propagation
Take cuttings of sideshoots from early to mid-summer.

Troubleshooting
Foliage can look tatty if allowed to dry out for long periods. Trim back if this happens.

Which variety?

Three species are commonly available, though the similarity of their names can lead to some confusion.
L. berthelotii produces long stems clad with fine, needle-like, silver leaves and bears dark red flowers.
L. berthelotii x maculatus has pale green leaves and flowers which are a mixture of red and yellow.
L. maculatus has pale green leaves and orange/yellow flowers.

Lysimachia

Shape and size

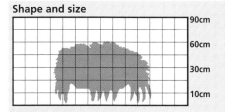

Position

Overwintering

Containers

Compost   Watering   Feeding

Features calendar

Jan	Feb	Mar	Apr	May	June
					✽
July	Aug	Sept	Oct	Nov	Dec
✽	✽	✽			

Buying tips L. nummularia *is very easy to propagate, so one plant can soon produce a large number.*

The species is plain green

Lysimachia nummularia 'Aurea'

Growing guide

These trailing plants with handsome foliage and golden-yellow flowers are ideal for hanging baskets, window-boxes and container edges. *Lysimachia nummularia* 'Aurea' (golden creeping Jenny) is actually a hardy perennial, though it is widely used in summer displays for its pale yellow foliage. It is particularly useful for concealing the sides of damaged or unattractive containers, as it soon forms a curtain of leafy stems.

L. nummularia 'Aurea' does best in light shade or shade. It will grow in full sun providing you keep the containers well-watered, though the leaves may become bleached by strong sunshine. *L. congestiflora*, on the other hand, is a tender perennial that prefers a sunny position but will tolerate light shade.

Propagation

The easiest way to propagate *L. nummularia* 'Aurea' is to peg down shoots into pots of compost. Layers should root within a few weeks and can be detached from the parent plant and potted up anytime through the growing season. Take cuttings of *L. congestiflora* in mid- to late summer.

Troubleshooting

Generally trouble-free provided plants do not run short of water.

Which variety?

L. congestiflora (also known as **L. lyssii** and sometimes called **L. 'Lissy'**) does well on its own in a hanging basket, where it forms a neat, pendulous plant clothed with heart-shaped green leaves and studded with clusters of yellow flowers.

L. congestiflora 'Outback Sunset' is similar to the above, but with striking gold and green variegated foliage.

L. nummularia 'Aurea' develops long, slender, trailing stems clad with small, rounded, pale yellow leaves. Single, bright yellow flowers are borne in summer.

Marigolds

Shape and size

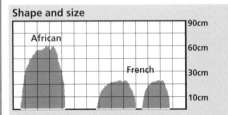

Position

Over-wintering

Treat as Annual

Containers

Compost

Multi-purpose

Watering

Feeding

Features calendar

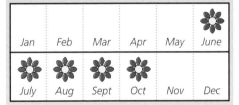

Jan	Feb	Mar	Apr	May	June
July	Aug	Sept	Oct	Nov	Dec

Buying tips *French marigolds are best grown from seed or bought as seedlings or bedding strips. With African marigolds, it is worth buying larger plants to ensure a long flowering period.*

French marigold 'Orange Boy'

Growing guide

The flower heads of these popular bedding plants are vividly coloured, mostly in shades of yellow and orange. They are borne on neat, upright plants above divided green leaves that emit a pungent smell when bruised. African marigolds have the largest heads, up to 10cm (4in) across. Those of French marigolds are smaller but often borne in greater numbers.

Although most widely used for bedding in borders, marigolds are ideal in containers and window-boxes. French marigolds thrive in all weathers, will withstand occasional drying out and can be relied on to flower all summer. African marigolds do best in a hot summer.

Propagation

African marigolds take 12 weeks or more to flower so are best sown in February. French marigolds flower in 6 to 8 weeks and can be sown in April or early May. Germinate at 15-18°C (60-65°F).

Troubleshooting

Grey mould can be a problem in prolonged spells of wet weather. Remove and destroy infected parts of the plant and spray with Bio Supercarb Systemic Fungicide to prevent the disease spreading if the attack is severe.

Which variety?

Many different varieties of both African and French marigolds are available. The following are particularly recommended for containers.

AFRICAN MARIGOLDS

These varieties all have large ball-shaped flowers and include Afro-French hybrids.

'Discovery' hybrids are most compact of all, growing up to 25cm (10in) high. The blooms are around 8cm (3in) across, in bright orange or yellow.

'Excel' hybrids have large blooms in orange, golden-orange, lemon-yellow and primrose-yellow. Height 25-35cm (10-14in).

'Inca' hybrids have flowers up to

African marigold 'Inca Orange'

African marigold 'Vanilla'

10cm (4in) across in gold, orange and bright yellow. They are bushy and compact, up to 30cm (12in) high.

'Vanilla' is a new colour with blooms that are a soft shade of creamy-yellow. Height 30-35cm (12-14in).

FRENCH MARIGOLDS

'Alamo' series flower early, producing large double flowers on compact plants. Height 20-25cm (8-10in). Varieties include include **'Alamo Flame'** (orange/red), **'Alamo Harmony'** (maroon/orange crest), **'Alamo Orange'** (bright orange) and **'Alamo Yellow'** (deep yellow).

'Boy' series form compact plants with double flowers. Height 16-20cm (6-8in). Varieties include **'Golden Boy'** (golden-yellow), **'Harmony Boy'** (gold with red crest), **'Orange Boy'** (deep orange) and **'Yellow Boy'** (lemon-yellow). **'Boy O'Boy'** is a mixture of these varieties.

'Disco' is a good selection of single-flowered varieties. Height 20-25cm (8-10in). They include **'Disco Flame'** (red/orange bicolour), **'Disco Orange'** (warm orange), **'Disco Red'** (dark red edged with gold) and **'Disco Yellow'** (lemon-yellow).

'Gate' series have crested, double flowers in bright yellow and orange, as well as mahogany-red edged with gold. They are good performers with flowers up to 8cm (3in) across. Height 15-25cm (6-10in).

'Jacket' varieties have brilliantly coloured, crested flowers in orange or yellow. Height 20-25cm (8-10in).

'Naughty Marietta' bears large, single flowers of golden-yellow with a maroon blotch at the base of each petal. Height 30-35cm (12-14in).

French marigold 'Boy O'Boy'

Melianthus major

Shape and size

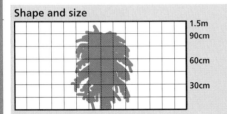

1.5m
90cm
60cm
30cm

Position

Over-wintering

 5°c

Containers Compost

Multi-purpose

Watering Feeding

FEED FEED

Features calendar

Jan	Feb	Mar	Apr	May	June
				🌿	🌿
🌿	❀	❀	🌿		
July	Aug	Sept	Oct	Nov	Dec

The finely divided leaves of Melianthus major

Buying tips *Once a difficult plant to obtain, it is now being grown more widely though it may still be necessary to buy from a specialist nursery.*

Growing guide

A large and spectacular plant that provides handsome foliage. The leaves are deeply divided and serrated, gently curved, and an attractive shade of grey-green. In very mild areas this plant can survive outside all winter, where it can reach a considerable size – up to 1.8m (6ft) high with a spread of 1.2m (4ft) or more – but in a container it is generally much smaller, though still impressive. It is best overwintered in an unheated greenhouse or conservatory, and any excess or untidy growth can be pruned back in early spring. The foliage is its main attraction, though sprays of greenish flowers with maroon bracts may be borne in late summer on stems that were produced the previous year. It prefers a site in sun or light shade.

Propagation
Sow seed in early spring. Cuttings can be taken in mid-summer.

Troubleshooting
Generally trouble-free.

Which variety?

Only one species is widely cultivated.

Myosotis

Shape and size

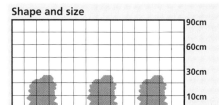

90cm
60cm
30cm
10cm

Position

Over-wintering

Treat as Annual

Containers

Compost

Multi-purpose

Watering

Feeding

FEED

Features calendar

Jan	Feb	Mar	Apr	May	June
			✹	✹	
July	Aug	Sept	Oct	Nov	Dec

Buying tips *Buy plants in late summer or early autumn and plant as soon as possible so they can establish before winter.*

Forget-me-nots and variegated hosta

The bright blooms of 'Victoria Rose'

Growing guide

Forget-me-nots are old favourites for spring colour because of their many sprays of dainty azure-blue flowers with distinctive yellow eyes. They are very easy to grow, generally self-seeding widely if the seed heads are allowed to mature before the plants are pulled up. Traditionally, blue has always been the most popular flower colour, though pink and white forms are also available. The white-flowered form makes a very pretty contrast to the blue varieties. Forget-me-nots are good for use in containers, window-boxes and bed edges. They do well in most situations, but flourish best in partial shade.

Propagation

Sow seed thinly in trays or in a nursery bed between May and early July. Pot up young plants into final containers in September or October.

Troubleshooting

Powdery mildew is a common problem, especially on plants which have finished flowering or are allowed to dry out at the roots. Pull up and burn or dispose of infected plants.

Which variety?

There are a number of hybrids which have a neat, compact habit and are ideally suited for containers.

'Blue Ball' has rich indigo-blue flowers on a neat, rounded, compact plant.

'Blue Basket' has an upright, neat habit and dark blue flowers.

'Dwarf Indigo' is deep blue.

'Pompadour' has large, deep rose-pink flowers.

'Victoria Blue' bears deep blue flowers.

'Victoria Rose' is an attractive shade of pink.

'Victoria White' bears pure white flowers.

'Victoria Mixed' offers a selection of pink, white and blue.

Nemesia

Shape and size

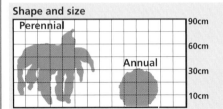

Perennial					90cm
					60cm
		Annual			30cm
					10cm

Position   Overwintering

7°C   7°C

Containers   Compost

Multi-purpose

Watering   Feeding

FEED FEED

Features calendar

Jan	Feb	Mar	Apr	May	June ❀
❀ July	❀ Aug	❀ Sept	Oct	Nov	Dec

Buying tips *For the best choice of annual varieties, buy seed from a mail-order supplier. The perennial varieties are sold as young plantlets or tots in March and April, or in small pots in May and June.*

The annual 'Carnival Mixed'

The spreading 'Innocence'

Growing guide

This varied group of plants offers a wide range of flower colours for summer display. The annual varieties generally have vividly coloured flowers and an upright habit which makes them ideal for tubs and window-boxes. The tender perennial forms produce an abundance of small pastel blooms on each stem, and have a more lax, spreading habit suited to hanging baskets, as well edging for larger containers.

Annuals tend to stop flowering after around eight weeks, but will often produce a second display in late summer if cut back hard after the first flush. The perennial forms will flower continuously throughout the summer if you deadhead them regularly. Nemesias prefer a reasonable amount of sun and do not like to run short of water, particularly the annuals.

Propagation

Sow seed of annual varieties at 15-18°C (60-65°F) in March or April. Take cuttings of tender perennials from spring to late summer.

Troubleshooting

Generally trouble-free providing plants do not dry out.

Which variety?

ANNUALS

'Carnival Mixed' contains a mixture of bright flower colours including red, blue and yellow.
'Galaxy Mixed' is a compact and free-flowering mixture with colours that include blues and pinks.
'KLM' has attractive and unusual bicoloured flowers; the top petals are rich blue and the lower ones are creamy white. They are the colours of the Dutch national airline, hence the name. Flower size is smaller and more dainty than other annual varieties.
'Orange Prince' bears vivid orange blooms on compact plants.
'Red Ensign' has bicoloured flowers which are white and dark red.

TENDER PERENNIALS

N. caerulea has lilac-mauve flowers with a yellow centre.
N. caerulea **'Elliott's Variety'** has light blue flowers with a yellow eye.
N. caerulea **'Joan Wilder'** bears mauve blooms with a yellow eye.
N. caerulea **'Woodcote'** is a deep violet blue with a yellow centre.
N. denticulata **'Confetti'** has pale, silvery-pink blooms which are scented.
N. **'Innocence'** bears pure white flowers; it has a yellow eye that stands out particularly well.

Nicotiana

Shape and size

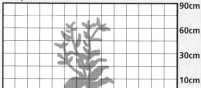

				90cm
				60cm
				30cm
				10cm

Position   Over-wintering

Treat as Annual

Containers   Compost

Multi-purpose

Watering   Feeding

FEED

Features calendar

Jan	Feb	Mar	Apr	May	June
					✿
✿	✿	✿			
July	Aug	Sept	Oct	Nov	Dec

'Domino Lime Green'

'Domino Mixed'

Growing guide

These plants are popular for their summer colour and have large flowers borne on tall stems above light green leaves. The whole plant is sticky to the touch. If the day is extremely hot, the flowers may close up but will re-open in the evening. The blooms of some varieties give off a strong, sweet scent in the evening; those with white flowers tend to have the strongest fragrance. To enjoy them to the full plant scented forms near house doors and windows and around seating areas. Many species and hybrids grow at least 60-90cm (24-36in) tall, which tends to limit their use to borders and large containers, though recently several more compact varieties have been introduced. These have a neat, bushy habit with many blooms borne on short, stout stems that do not need any form of support. Most of these compact varieties tend not to be scented.

Nicotianas are generally tough plants that will tolerate occasional drying out and do well in sun or light shade. Plants may survive the winter outdoors to flower a second year.

Propagation

Sow seed at 18°C (65°F) from mid-February to March. Do not cover seed as it needs light to germinate.

Troubleshooting

Aphids can be a problem, particularly on young plants. Spray infestations with pirimicarb (Rapid).

Which variety?

'Domino' hybrids are compact and branch well from the base. The flowers stay open all day, even in the heat, and this variety also tolerates light shade. The seed is available as mixed colours and several individual colours, including white, lime-green, salmon-pink, red, pink with a white eye, and 'Domino Picotee', which is white, edged with rose-pink. Unfortunately, these varieties are not scented. Height 25-30cm (10-12in).

'Havana Appleblossom' has flowers which are white in the centre surrounded by rose-pink, with darker colour towards the edges. It is an excellent performer in a wide variety of weather conditions. Slight evening scent. Height 38cm (15in).

'Havana Lime Green' similar to above with lime-green flowers and marginally stronger scent

'Hippy Mixed' is the first strongly scented dwarf type, introduced in 1996. Slightly taller than the others at 50-60cm (20-24in).

'Starship' hybrids include red, pink, burgundy and lime-green. Height 30cm (12in).

Nierembergia repens 'Mont Blanc'

Shape and size

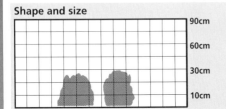

90cm
60cm
30cm
10cm

Position   Overwintering

7°C

Treat as Annual

Containers   Compost

Multi-purpose

Watering   Feeding

FEED FEED

Features calendar

Jan	Feb	Mar	Apr	May	June
					✿
July	Aug	Sept	Oct	Nov	Dec
✿	✿	✿			

'Mont Blanc' planted en masse

Buying tips *Nierembergia is not often sold as plants, so it is usually necessary to raise your own stock from seed.*

Growing guide

A delightful annual which bears many little, white, cup-shaped flowers with yellow centres, against dark green foliage. It has a neat yet spreading habit that makes it ideal for hanging baskets, flower pouches, window-boxes and containers. It loves a sunny site and performs particularly well in hot summers. Deadheading is very beneficial to encourage the production of new flowers.

Propagation

Sow seed in February or March at 18°C (65°F). Although normally grown as an annual, you can also take cuttings in June or July to produce plants that will flower the following year.

Troubleshooting

Slugs can be a problem, especially with young plants.

Which variety?

'Mont Blanc' is most widely available and is the best performer. However, there is also the form **'Purple Robe'** with purple, yellow-centred flowers.

Nigella damascena

Shape and size

90cm
60cm
30cm
10cm

Position

Over-wintering

Treat as Annual

Containers

Compost

Multi-purpose

Watering

Feeding

FEED FEED

Features calendar

Jan	Feb	Mar	Apr	May	June
					✽
✽	✽				
July	Aug	Sept	Oct	Nov	Dec

Buying tips *Grow from seed, which is widely available in late winter and spring.*

'Persian Jewels'

Nigella 'Miss Jekyll Blue'

Growing guide

An easy-to-grow annual with feathery foliage, saucer-shaped flowers and attractive seed heads, *Nigella damascena* is useful for sowing in a tub around a permanent shrub to provide summer colour or in a pot on its own. The flowers mostly come in blue or white, though pink and mauve shades are also available.

They like a sunny position and should be kept moist in order to prolong flowering.

Propagation

Sow seed direct in containers in March or April, covering lightly with compost. Alternatively, for larger and earlier flowering plants, sow in pots or trays in a cold frame or cool greenhouse in September.

Troubleshooting

Generally trouble-free.

Which variety?

'Miss Jekyll Blue' Large, semi-double, bright-blue flowers.
'Persian Jewels' Mixture of semi-double pink, mauve, purple, blue and white flowers.
'Persian Rose' Rose-pink flowers.
N. hispanica Slightly scented blue flowers with red stamens.

Osteospermum

Shape and size

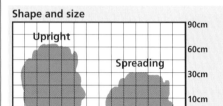

Position   Overwintering

Containers

Compost   Watering   Feeding

Features calendar

Jan	Feb	Mar	Apr	May	June
					✿
✿	✿	✿			
July	Aug	Sept	Oct	Nov	Dec

Buying tips *As there is such a wide range available now, it might be best to wait until plants are in flower to see the exact colours before buying.*

Osteospermum 'Whirligig'

Growing guide

A diverse group of plants that has become very popular in recent years; as a result many new varieties are available. They produce large, daisy-like flowers about 5-8cm (2-3in) across which are borne individually on short stems. A few have variegated foliage, and others have distinctive petals which are spoon-shaped. Pinks and purples tend to be the dominant colours, though there are white and yellow varieties too.

Although they have a long flowering season, from early summer until the frosts, the blooms have a tendency to be produced in flushes, and plants can be shy to bloom in periods of dull, cool weather. Osteospermums have two main growing habits; those which are upright and reach a height of about 45cm (18in), while others have a lax, spreading habit and grow to 20cm (8in) high with a spread of 45cm (18in). Both types thrive in containers, though obviously the habit dictates whether they are used in the centre of the pot or around the edges. Osteospermums need a site in full sun to flower well.

Established plants can be kept over winter in a frost-free greenhouse, though they often survive outside all year in mild areas.

Propagation

Cuttings can be taken through the growing season from late spring to early autumn. Late summer is the best time to take cuttings for over-wintering.

Troubleshooting

Generally trouble-free.

Osteospermum ecklonis 'Prostratum' is one of the hardiest varieties

Which variety?

UPRIGHT VARIETIES

'Blue Streak' has white flowers with a blue centre. The petals are bluish on the reverse side.

'Buttermilk' has creamy-yellow flowers with contrasting dark centres.

'James Elliman' bears deep purple flowers.

'Pink Whirls' has deep pink flowers with unusual spoon-shaped petals.

'Sunny series' includes magenta, pink and white varieties. All are compact plants.

'Whirligig' has spoon-shaped white petals and the flowers have a contrasting dark centre.

'Zulu' bears deep yellow flowers.

SPREADING VARIETIES

O. ecklonis **'Prostratum'** has white flowers that are bluish-purple underneath. Hardier than most.

'Bodegas Pink' has leaves which are edged with cream and soft pink flowers with darker centres.

'Brickell's Hybrid' (also called **'Chris Brickell'**) has soft pink flowers.

'Canington Roy' has lilac-mauve blooms that shade to white in the centre.

'Gweek Variegated' has cream and green foliage and purple flowers.

'Port Wine' has deep maroon-purple flowers.

'Silver Sparkler' has attractive cream and green variegated foliage. The flowers are pure white with a darker eye.

'Weetwood' bears white flowers with a dark centre.

Osteospermum 'Stardust'

Pansy

Shape and size

90cm
60cm
30cm
10cm

Position

Over-wintering

Containers

Compost   Watering   Feeding

Features calendar

Jan	Feb	Mar	Apr	May	June
✿	✿	✿			✿
July	Aug	Sept	Oct	Nov	Dec

Buying tips *Pansies are often sold in flower in individual pots. However, bedding strips are a more economical way to buy them. These are generally available from March to May and in September.*

'Imperial Antique Shades'

Growing guide

Pansies are superb for providing colour in containers almost year-round. Winter-flowering varieties will bloom on and off during mild spells throughout the coldest months of the year, but they can be grown to flower during any period. The other types are best suited for spring and summer flowering.

To ensure a good display of flowers, keep containers well watered at all times but never let the compost get waterlogged. Regular deadheading will increase the quantity and period of flowering. They do not like intense heat and do best in light shade during the summer.

Propagation

Sow seed at 15°C (60°F) in February to March for summer flowers, in May for winter blooms, or in September for a spring display. You can also propagate them from cuttings, or earthing up around the plants so that the individual stems take root.

Troubleshooting

Fungal diseases can attack pansies and kill the whole plant, particularly in wet conditions. Always use fresh compost when growing pansies.

Which variety?

FOR SPRING AND AUTUMN FLOWERS

'Chalon Giants Mixed' have ruffled blooms that give the effect of double flowers. They come in shades of lilac, violet, mahogany and yellow, with blotched centres. **'Imperial'** series bear medium to large flowers in a range of attractive shades: **'Imperial Antique Shades'** range from apricot to rose, **'Imperial Frosty**

'Jolly Joker'

Rose' is rosy-purple and white, while **'Imperial Lavender Shades'** range from palest lavender to deep lavender-purple.

'Jolly Joker' has flowers which are a startling combination of orange and purple.

'Padparadja' is an unusual colour, with blooms that are uniform, bright, glowing orange.

FOR WINTER FLOWERS

'Ultima' series offer a good colour selection including some unusual shades, such as **'Ultima Chiffon'**, a pretty creamy-white with a bold rose blotch, and **'Ultima Sherbet'** which is similar but has its white area tinged with rose-pink.

'Universal' series come in a huge range of colours including reds, blues, yellows and whites. Some have plain 'faces', others have a dark central blotch, and yet more have a coloured central blotch.

'Imperial Frosty Rose'

Papaver nudicaule

Shape and size

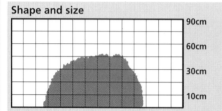

90cm
60cm
30cm
10cm

Position	Over-wintering	Containers
	Treat as Annual	

Compost	Watering	Feeding
Multi-purpose Grit		FEED FEED ED

Features calendar

Jan	Feb	Mar	Apr	May	June
✿	✿	✿			
July	Aug	Sept	Oct	Nov	Dec

Buying tips *Plants are rarely available. You may need to get seed from a mail-order supplier.*

The range of colours of Papaver nudicaule

Growing guide

This is a spectacular specimen plant for the patio, with blooms resembling tissue-paper up to 8cm (3in) across on tall leafless stems. *P. nudicaule* is best grown in a pot on its own and moved to a prominent position once the flowers are in bud.

They revel in a well-drained compost and should be kept regularly watered and fed. To produce the largest blooms, pinch out the first flower stems that grow in order to get bigger plants.

This is the only poppy which survives as cut flowers. Pick the blooms while they are in bud and dip them straight into boiling water before putting them into a vase.

Propagation

Sow seed in autumn and keep in a cold frame over the winter. Alternatively, sow in February or March at 13°C (55°F) and treat as a bedding plant. Pot up seedlings into their final containers while they are still very small as larger plants will resent root disturbance.

Troubleshooting

Be prepared for some losses when transplanting. Otherwise generally trouble-free.

Which variety?

Most varieties contain a mixture of flowers in shades of pink, salmon, apricot, yellow and red on 60-cm (24-in) stems.

'Artist's Glory' Extra large blooms on 40-cm (16-in) stems.

'Champagne Bubbles' Large flowers on 45-cm (18-in) stems.

'Garden Gnome' A dwarf variety growing only 30cm (12in) tall. All bright colours.

'Summer Breeze' Orange, yellow and white flowers. The best one for spring sowing to produce flowers the same year.

Parochetus communis

Shape and size

90cm
60cm
30cm
10cm

Position	Over-wintering	Containers
	5°C	

Compost	Watering	Feeding
Multi-purpose / Grit		FEED

Features calendar

Jan	Feb	Mar	Apr	May	June
✳	✳	✳	✳	✳	✳

July	Aug	Sept	Oct	Nov	Dec
✳	✳	✳	✳	✳	✳

Buying tips *Plants are generally available in late spring or early summer. Sometimes found amongst the alpines.*

Not the most elegant trailing plant

The flowers are best viewed close up

Growing guide

A handsome and unusual trailing plant for a hanging basket which is ornamental in both flowers and foliage. The leaves are clover-like in shape and a superb shade of dark green; they make an ideal background for the blue, pea-like flowers.

This plant excels in a hanging basket on its own as the long, slender stems will dangle down and come together underneath the basket to form a heart-shape.

Parochetus prefers partial shade and does not like drying out at the roots. Plant can be overwintered in a frost-free greenhouse. It is evergreen, so keep it moist but not waterlogged throughout the winter.

Propagation
Stems can be layered at any time throughout the growing season.

Troubleshooting
Generally trouble-free.

Which variety?

There is only one species.

Pelargonium: upright types

Shape and size

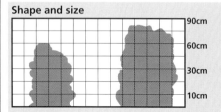

90cm
60cm
30cm
10cm

Position Overwintering

7°C   7°C

Containers

Compost Watering Feeding

Multi-purpose

FEED FEED FEED

Features calendar

Jan	Feb	Mar	Apr	May	June
					✸
✸	✸	✸	✸		
July	Aug	Sept	Oct	Nov	Dec

Buying tips

Raising plants from seed tends to be costly as they need early sowing, and the seed of F1 hybrids can be expensive. Buying seedlings in early spring can be much more economical. Alternatively, look for larger plants in April, from which you can take cuttings.

'Morval'

Growing guide

Pelargoniums, or geraniums as they are popularly known, are one of the most widely grown plants for containers and baskets. Their brightly coloured flowers, neat, compact habit and resistance to drought make them ideal for containers, window-boxes and the centre of hanging baskets.

Most of the varieties sold nowadays are F1 hybrids and are free-flowering. They love sunshine and will survive if you forget to water them occasionally. However, they do like regular feeding and develop reddish tinges to the leaves if they are going hungry. Plants will grow in light shade but tend to be a bit leggier with fewer flowers.

Single-flowered varieties drop their petals, so, unlike double varieties it does not spoil the whole of the cluster. With double-flowered varieties, deadheads look unsightly, especially on white forms, and may rot in wet weather. Both types should be deadheaded regularly to prolong flowering.

Plants can be overwintered in a frost-free place. If they are potted up individually and kept on a warm windowsill, flowers will often be produced right through the winter. Despite popular advice, plants do not need to be trimmed back for the winter unless you are short of space. Do, however, remove dead leaves to avoid disease problems.

Propagation

Take cuttings in early spring to provide plants for the current season, or in mid- to late summer to produce young plants for over-wintering. When removing the lower leaves on the cutting, take care to also remove the stipule or 'ruff' at the base of each leaf. Do not cover cuttings with polythene as they are prone to rotting.

An even simpler way to propagate most modern hybrids is to heap up compost around the base of the stems. After a few weeks, each stem should root and can be potted up individually to produce a new plant.

Seed can be sown from January to

'Mrs Henry Cox'

'Multibloom Mixed'

'Orange Appeal'

Regal pelargoniums

These have big serrated leaves with no zoning and large showy flowers. Although sometimes sold as patio plants, they are very prone to nutrient deficiencies and whitefly attacks and are best regarded as collectors' plants.

early April. Germinate at 21°C (70°F) and grow plants on at 13°C (55°F).

Troubleshooting

Modern varieties are generally trouble-free. Watch out for mildew and grey mould on older types.

Which variety?

MODERN VARIETIES

The following are all F1 hybrids, and can be grown from seed or bought as plants in garden centres.

'Century' series come in a wide range of colours, including pink, red, scarlet, violet-rose and white. Most have attractively zoned foliage.

'Maverick Star' is a new variety with unusually coloured flowers. The heads are larger than average, and the flowers are blush-pink with a distinctive rose-pink eye, The petals are a deeper pink at the edges.

'Multibloom' series produce lots of flower stems on compact plants, though the individual flowers are less showy than other types. Colours include rose-pink, lavender-pink, red, salmon-pink, bright scarlet, scarlet with a white eye, and white. They are easy to grow from seed, blooming about two weeks earlier than most.

'Orange Appeal' has large, showy flowers which are pure, bright orange.

'Raspberry Ripple' has salmon-pink flowers that are heavily flecked with red to give a distinctive and unusual effect.

'Video' series form short bushy plants and are ideally suited to containers. There are four colours: red, salmon, pink, and white with a pink blush.

OLDER VARIETIES

Some of the older varieties are still well worth growing for their attractive foliage. These are raised from cuttings and are mostly available from specialist nurseries.

'Caroline Schmidt' has silver-edged leaves and small, double red flowers.

'Dolly Vardon' has cream, green and red foliage and small, single scarlet flowers.

'Freak of Nature' bears white leaves edged with green and single red flowers.

'Morval' produces golden foliage with a chestnut zoning and pale pink, double flowers on dwarf plants.

'Mrs Henry Cox' (**'Henry Cox'**) has green leaves with brown and red markings and a yellow margin. Salmon-pink, single flowers.

Pelargonium: scented-leaf types

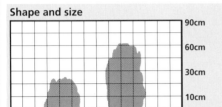

Shape and size

90cm
60cm
30cm
10cm

Position   Overwintering

Containers   Compost

Watering   Feeding

Features calendar

Jan	Feb	Mar	Apr	May	June
					✿
July	Aug	Sept	Oct	Nov	Dec
✿	✿	✿			

'Lady Plymouth'

Pelargonium quercifolium

Growing guide

Scented-leaf pelargoniums have leaves that give off a strong and pleasant scent when crushed. The majority of varieties have foliage which is lemon-scented, though there are also types that smell of peppermint, pine, balsam and apple. The foliage is the main feature of these plants, not just for its scent but also because, in many cases, the leaves are attractively shaped or variegated. In some cases the flowers are very ornamental too.

Scented-leaf pelargoniums are most frequently seen as windowsill pot plants where they can be appreciated year-round, but they also make excellent plants for patio containers. This is particularly so in the case of plants which are at least two years old as they will have formed a reasonable-sized bush of handsome foliage. The leaves make an interesting addition to pot-pourri when dried, and the plants also go well with a grouping of herbs.

Scented pelargoniums will tolerate drought for short periods and it is best to let the compost become almost dry between waterings. Use liquid fertilisers sparingly at half the strength recommended for other plants. Repot overwintered plants in March or April. If plants get too big or leggy, you can trim them hard back to within a few centimetres of the base. Deadhead and pick off dead leaves regularly throughout the growing season.

Propagation
Take cuttings in early spring or mid- to late summer. These root best in a mixture of sharp sand and compost; use a rooting hormone to speed up the process. Shade cuttings for the first week but do not cover.

Troubleshooting
Generally trouble-free.

The pine-scented 'Fragrans'

Which variety?

The following is a selection of the most popular types.

'Attar of Roses' has large, rounded, rose-scented leaves and pale pink flowers. 45x45cm (18x18in).

'Citriodorum' is lime-scented, with handsome mauve flowers. 30x30cm (12x12in).

P. crispum has densely packed leaves that are toothed at the edges, and have a lemon fragrance. The form **'Variegatum'** has white-margined leaves and pale mauve flowers. 60x60cm (24x24in).

'Filicifolium' has fern-like leaves which are deeply and finely divided. They have a balsam-like fragrance. 30x30cm (12x12in).

'Fragrans' has small, sage-green leaves with scalloped edges, and small white flowers. The leaves have a pine scent. 30x30cm (12x12in).

'Graveolens' has large, deeply lobed leaves that have a strong lemon scent. It also bears small rose-pink flowers. Pinch out growing tips regularly to keep it bushy. 90x90cm (36x36in).

'Lady Plymouth' bears deeply lobed leaves which are attractively variegated with pale green and white. It has a pungent lemon scent. 60x60cm (24x24in).

P. odoratissimum produces rounded, fresh green leaves that have a strong apple scent. Tiny white flowers are produced on long trailing shoots. These are best trimmed off if they become bare and unattractive. Ideal for hanging baskets. 20x45cm (8x18in).

P. tomentosum has large, velvety, grey-green leaves that have a strong peppermint scent. Small white flowers are produced in succession throughout the summer.

'Chocolate Tomentosum' has brown blotches in the centre of the leaves. Sprawling habit. 45x60cm (18x24in).

P. crispum 'Variegatum'

Pelargonium: trailing types

Ivy-leaved types

Shape and size

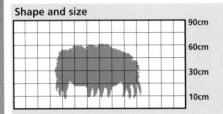

90cm
60cm
30cm
10cm

Position · Overwintering

  7°C 7°C

Containers

Compost   Watering   Feeding

Features calendar

Jan	Feb	Mar	Apr	May	June
					✿
July	Aug	Sept	Oct	Nov	Dec
✿	✿	✿	✿		

Buying tips *Most trailing pelargoniums are only available as plants, though there is an increasing range of young plantlets being offered from late winter to mid-spring.*

The striking 'Rouletta'

Growing guide

The habit of trailing pelargoniums is very informal, with spreading stems that tumble loosely over the edges of a hanging basket, window-box or raised container. The stems can grow up to 90cm (36in) long. Clusters of single flowers are borne on short stems. There is a wide range of flower colours, though the colours are generally a little less vivid than those of the upright types.

Propagation

As for upright pelargoniums, see page 88.

Troubleshooting

Ivy-leaved types are susceptible to oedema, which shows as corky growths or blisters on the leaves. Overwatering or fluctuations in water supply is a principal cause of this problem. Remove unsightly leaves.

Which variety?

SEED-RAISED VARIETIES

'Breakaway' varieties have stems which branch out horizontally from a container, only trailing when they reach a reasonable length. However, they are excellent for hanging baskets as the flowers face downwards. Red and salmon-pink forms are available.

'Summer Showers' is the first ivy-leafed geranium available as seed. It is a single-flowered mixture of red, pink, lavender, magenta and white flowers.

'L'Elegante'

'Mini Cascade Red'

The old favourite 'Beauty of Eastbourne'

CONTINENTAL TRAILING GERANIUMS

'Balcon' (also called **'Decora'** or **'Cascade'**) varieties are popular for use in window-boxes and balconies on the Continent. The flower clusters are fairly small but are borne in great profusion on loosely trailing stems. Colours include lilac, pink, red and white.

IVY-LEAVED PELARGONIUMS

P. peltatum is a traditional ivy-leaved geranium which is available in a wide range of varieties. The small flowers are borne in clusters of five to seven blooms. There is a good selection of colours including red and purple, also many shades of pink, mauve and white, as well as a number of attractive bicolours. Recommended varieties include:

'Beauty of Eastbourne'; cerise-red **'Crocodile'**, grown primarily for its foliage which has a yellow mesh pattern; **'L'Elegante'**, with white single flowers and cream-edged leaves; **'Mini Cascade Red'**, compact with single red flowers; **'Rouletta' ('Mexicana')**, with striking white petals edged with cerise on semi-double blooms; and **'Snow Queen'**, which has double white flowers with tiny red centres.

93

Penstemon

Shape and size

90cm
60cm
30cm
10cm

Position Overwintering

0°C   5°C

Containers Compost Watering Feeding

Multi-purpose

FEED FEED

Features calendar

Jan	Feb	Mar	Apr	May	June
					✿
✿	✿	✿			
July	Aug	Sept	Oct	Nov	Dec

Buying tips

A limited range is available in early spring as plantlets. Otherwise look for larger specimens from early summer. Check out the alpine section of the garden centre as well as the patio plant area.

Penstemon pinifolius

Penstemon 'Garnet'

Growing guide

Penstemons range from tall border plants to dwarf rock plants. Those that grow around 45-60cm (18-24in) in height make attractive patio plants.

They form long spikes of delicate, tubular flowers and are much loved by bees. Most of the hybrid varieties produce their main display from June or July until August, with a lesser flush on the sideshoots in early autumn.

The varieties recommended below will withstand frosts down to -5°C (23°F) but will be killed if they become waterlogged over winter. Ensure pots are not standing in trays or areas where water can collect. Raise the pot above ground level on bricks or 'pot feet' to allow free drainage.

In spring, cut back the old foliage and either repot the plant or replace some of the old compost with new.

Pot plants in an equal mixture of potting compost and sharp grit and keep them well-watered through the summer.

Propagation

Take cuttings from leafy sideshoots from late spring onwards. Remove the lower leaves and treat with a rooting hormone. Keep the cuttings in a cold frame or cool greenhouse over the winter.

Troubleshooting

Generally trouble-free.

Which variety?

'Appleblossom' has pink and white flowers from June to August.
'Evelyn' bears pale pink flowers from June to August.
'Garnet' produces wine-red flowers from July to September.
P. pinifolius has small red flowers from June to September. Dwarf rock garden species. 20x15cm (8x6in).

Perilla

Shape and size

90cm
60cm
30cm
10cm

Position   Overwintering

7°C   5°C   Treat as Annual

Containers   Compost

Multi-purpose

Watering   Feeding

FEED

Features calendar

Jan	Feb	Mar	Apr	May	June
July	Aug	Sept	Oct	Nov	Dec

Buying tips Not commonly seen as plants. Seed is available from major mail-order suppliers.

A young plant of Perilla frutescens

Growing guide

This plant is grown for its reddish-purple leaves, which are oval and serrated. Its upright habit makes it a good centrepiece in a tub planted with pink, pale blue and white flowers.

Perilla will produce spikes of small tubular flowers during the summer but these are rather insignificant compared to the foliage. As a bonus, the leaves are aromatic when crushed or after rain. To ensure bushy plants, pinch the tips out several times while the plants are growing.

They like sunshine and will tolerate minimal watering and feeding.

Propagation

Sow in March at 15°C (60°F) and treat as a bedding plant.

Troubleshooting

Generally trouble-free.

Which variety?

P. frutescens, with oval serrated leaves, is most readily available, but there are different forms with various degrees of leaf convolutions.

Petunia: trailing types

Shape and size

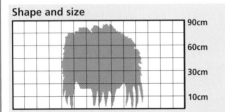

	90cm
	60cm
	30cm
	10cm

Position · Overwintering

7°c   7°c

Containers · Compost

Watering · Feeding

Features calendar

Jan	Feb	Mar	Apr	May	June
					✿
July	Aug	Sept	Oct	Nov	Dec
✿	✿	✿	✿		

Buying tips

Buying young plantlets in early spring is an economical way to obtain these vigorous plants.

Surfinia 'Pink Vein'

Growing guide

Trailing petunias have recently become enormously popular, mostly due to the introduction of Surfinia petunias, a range of exceptionally vigorous, trailing varieties that develop stems up to 1.2m (4ft) long and bear masses of flowers. Trailing petunias are perfect for hanging baskets, free-standing jardinières and tall pots where their stems can cascade unobstructed.

Owing to their growth rate, it is advisable to grow these petunias in a container on their own, rather than mixed in with other plants. These trailing petunias also make excellent ground cover as they quickly spread to form a prostrate mass of flowers and foliage, or will tumble over the edge of a raised bed.

Propagation

Take cuttings of perennials from spring to late summer. Seed-raised varieties are grown as for ordinary petunias.

Troubleshooting

Supply of Surfinias was a problem at one stage when imported plants were discovered to have come from virus-infected mother plants. As a result, many of the plants on sale were infected with a virus. This is a potential problem with all the perennial varieties raised from cuttings. Aphids should be carefully controlled as they can spread some virus diseases from other plants.

Which variety?

SUPERCASCADES

These seed-raised varieties were named after a North American mountain range rather than their

'Purple Wave' produces a stunning flower display

habit. They have very large blooms and form horizontal stems up to 60cm (24in) long before they start to flop. **'Supercascade Improved Mixed'** is the best of the bunch, containing ten plain colours.

CASCADIAS

Cascadia varieties bear many blooms on a vigorous, trailing plant which develops stems to around 60cm (24in) long. Colours are mostly pinks and purples, including **'Champagne and Cherie'** (bright purple), **'Chaplin'** (blue-purple), **'Charme'** (soft pink) and **'Charisma'** (deep pink with white edge). **'Casablanca'** is pure white.

SURFINIAS

These perennial varieties are available in a wide range of colours. **'Blue Vein'** has pale blue flowers boldly veined with deep blue. **'Hot Pink'** bears large, very bright pink flowers which are lightly veined with purple. **'Pastel Pink'** has large, soft pink flowers.

'Pink Mini' bears many small, deep cerise-pink blooms. **'Pink Vein'** has soft pink flowers that are heavily veined with dark pink.

'Purple' bears large, bright purple flowers. **'Purple Mini'** bears many small, magenta-purple blooms. **'Violet Blue'** has deep blue flowers. **'White'** is pure white.

OTHERS

'Million Bells' is a semi-trailing perennial that forms a bushy mass of spreading stems which are smothered with small, bell-shaped flowers. They look superb planted in old chimney pots and tall containers. Two colours, blue and pink, are presently available. Both have a handsome golden eye that is more prominent in the case of the blue form. Being small, the flowers have good weather resistance.

'Purple Wave' only grows to around 15cm (6in) high but has a spread of up to 1.2m (4ft). It makes a stunning display of large, vivid purple flowers. Being a seed-raised variety, viruses are unlikely to prove a problem.

Petunia: upright types

Shape and size

90cm
60cm
30cm
10cm

Position   Overwintering

7°C   7°C

Containers

Compost   Watering   Feeding

Multi-purpose   FEED FEED FEED

Features calendar

Jan	Feb	Mar	Apr	May	June
					✿
July	Aug	Sept	Oct	Nov	Dec
✿	✿	✿			

Buying tips *Buying pots of ready-grown seedlings in early spring is an economical way to buy petunias.*

'Fantasy', also known as 'Junior Petunia'

Growing guide

Petunias are popular bedding plants with large, exuberant, brightly coloured flowers from 5-10cm (2-4in) across. The majority of varieties bear single flowers, although there are a number with double blooms that are exceptionally showy. The overall colour range is extensive; as well as plain colours in many shades of red, purple, pink, blue, cream and white, there are flowers veined with a darker shade of the same colour, some with a bold central white star or splash and others that have coloured margins.

With a compact, bushy habit and above average drought-tolerance, these petunias are excellent for use in all sorts of containers.

Those with larger blooms tend to be more susceptible to damage by wind and rain. However, strains have been developed that are more weather-resistant.

Petunias revel in a hot, sheltered position. They will tolerate drying out occasionally but respond well to regular feeding, watering and daily deadheading.

Propagation

Sow seed in March at 15-18°C (60-65°F). Mix the fine seed with silver sand to make it easier to sow thinly.

Troubleshooting

Aphids can be a problem on young plants. Spray with pirimicarb (Rapid) if necessary. Virus diseases may occur, with symptoms including mottling and distortion of the foliage. Infected plants should be destroyed.

Petunia 'Frenzy' with Cordyline behind

Which variety?

SINGLE FLOWERS

'Aladdin' hybrids have ruffled petals and come in a range of nine colours as well as a mixture.

'Dream' hybrids come in pink, salmon, magenta, deep purple, red and white, with large rain-proof flowers.

'Express' hybrids produce large blooms in an enormous range of colours including starred and veined varieties as well as pure colours.

'Frenzy' hybrids bear flowers in a variety of colours including creamy yellow, uncommon among petunias. The veined forms such as **'Satin and Silk'** have particularly good weather resistance.

'Ice' hybrids bear single flowers which are boldly coloured in the centre of the petals and broadly edged with white on the edges. Colours are violet-blue, cherry-red, deep red and rich purple.

'Joy' hybrids display a mixture of seven colours, including pink with a white throat, and two star patterns. Reliable and weather-resistant.

'Mirage Reflections' are a mixture of five closely matched pinks, plus purple and red, all with large, veined blooms.

DOUBLE FLOWERS

'Duo Dolly Mixed' bear showy double flowers on well-branched plants. Colours available include burgundy, red/white bicolour, rose-pink, salmon and pale blue. Reasonably weather-tolerant, but best in a sheltered spot.

Phlox, dwarf

Shape and size

90cm
60cm
30cm
10cm

Position

Overwintering

Treat as Annual

Containers

Compost

John Innes

Watering

Feeding

FEED

Features calendar

Jan	Feb	Mar	Apr	May	June
					❀
❀	❀	❀			
July	Aug	Sept	Oct	Nov	Dec

Buying tips *Dwarf varieties are rarely sold as plants. Seed is available from mail-order seed suppliers.*

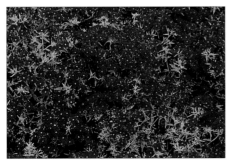

'African Sunset' grows to 10cm (4in) tall

'Tapestry' contains a good mix of colours

Growing guide

The new generation of dwarf phloxes extend the range of plants for containers in light shade. The flowers have a sweet fragrance, come in a wide range of colours and the plants grow no more than 25cm (10in) high.

Dwarf phloxes will flower well even through a hot summer, though they can become a bit leggy by September. They do best in a John Innes compost as they can become too lush in peat-based composts. It is important to keep them well-watered but be sparing with any fertiliser. A slow-release fertiliser applied at the start of the season is more than adequate. Too much fertiliser will result in taller plants that are more likely to flop and have fewer flowers.

Propagation

Sow in March at 15°C (60°F). Grow on as a bedding plant.

Troubleshooting

Generally trouble-free, given the right growing conditions.

Which variety?

'African Sunset' bears deep red flowers on 10-cm (4-in) plants.
'Bright Eyes' has pink, mauve, purple and cream shades, some with a contrasting eye.
'Chanal' produces double apple-blossom-pink blooms on 20cm (8in) tall plants.
'Coral Reef' flowers are a pastel mixture of pink, apricot, cream and yellow.
'Of Sheep' has blooms a pastel mixture ranging from creamy white to pastel orange with some bicolours.
'Tapestry' bears flowers of a pink, mauve, cream and yellow shade, most with a contrasting eye.

Plectranthus forsteri 'Marginatus'

Shape and size

90cm
60cm
30cm
10cm

Position

Overwintering
 7°C
 7°C

Containers

Compost
 Multi-purpose

Watering

Feeding
 FEED

Features calendar

Jan	Feb	Mar	Apr	May	June
July	Aug	Sept	Oct	Nov	Dec

Buying tips *Buying young plantlets in early spring is an economical way to purchase this thriving plant as you can then increase your stock from cuttings.*

Attractive variegated foliage of Plectranthus forsteri 'Marginatus'

Growing guide

A vigorous trailing plant that is useful for providing foliage interest in hanging baskets and tall containers. It produces stems that can grow up to 1.8m (6ft) in length, though it is generally best to pinch out the growing tips to encourage slightly shorter and more branching growths. The rounded leaves are attractively variegated with green and white, and they can be used as an excellent foil for many plants that have brightly coloured flowers.

Propagation

Cuttings can be taken from spring to late summer. Pinched-out shoot tips will root within a week or two.

Troubleshooting

Generally trouble-free.

Which variety?

P. forsteri **'Marginata'** is the variety sold as a patio plant. Other forms of plectranthus, such as *P. australis* (Swedish ivy), are sold as houseplants.

Polyanthus

Shape and size

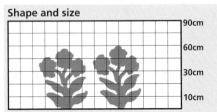

90cm
60cm
30cm
10cm

Position

Over-wintering

Containers

Compost Watering Feeding

Features calendar

Jan	Feb	Mar	Apr	May	June
July	Aug	Sept	Oct	Nov	Dec

Buying tips *Polyanthus are widely sold in all sorts of outlets but most will be un-named varieties and may not prove reliably hardy in outdoor containers. Garden centres are generally the best places to find hardy types. They tend to be on sale as green plants or strips in autumn.*

'Crescendo' is one of the best hardy polyanthus

Growing guide

For a splash of colour in the late winter and spring, you cannot beat polyanthus for their rainbow shades. If you find them too brash, there is also a selection of single colours, though they are not always easy to find in garden centres.

The key to success with polyanthus is to keep them moist at all times and to give them an occasional liquid feed. They prefer light shade but will cope with a sunny position while they are in flower. Move them to a shadier position for the summer though.

They are ideal for all sorts of containers. Pots of polyanthus can be added to tubs containing permanent plants to provide seasonal colour. Bright mixtures tend to look best with evergreens or on their own. Single colours make suitable companions for spring bulbs.

Propagation

Sow seed in May or June at 15-18°C (60-65°F). Temperatures above 18°C (65°F) will reduce germination. The seed should be sown on the surface as it needs light to germinate. Cover pots or trays with clinging film. After 7 to 12 days, the seed should have started to germinate. Cover with a thin layer of ground vermiculite and replace the clinging film until the seedling shoots appear.

A much simpler way of propagating plants is to split them up after flowering and plant them in an out-of-the-way part of the garden for retrieval in the autumn.

Troubleshooting

Birds like to peck off the flower heads, though this is likely to be less of a problem with containers next to the house. Slugs and snails like the new leaves. Again this is less of a problem in pots. Plants that do not flower are usually a result of sowing too late at too high a temperature.

Which variety?

A lot of varieties are bred for the gift market and are not hardy. The following are all outdoor types.

'Crescendo' is the best of the hardy types, available as bright mixtures or single colours.

'Husky' bears large flowers in a mixture of colours on tough plants.

'Rainbow' is a short-stemmed variety in mixed colours, orange and red and lemon and gold combinations and some single colours.

Portulaca

Shape and size

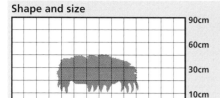

90cm
60cm
30cm
10cm

Position   Overwintering

Treat as Annual

Containers   Compost

Multi-purpose   Grit

Watering   Feeding

FEED

Features calendar

Jan	Feb	Mar	Apr	May	June
					✿
July	Aug	Sept	Oct	Nov	Dec
✿	✿	✿			

Buying tips *Most commonly encountered as bedding strips in April and May. Plants are rarely seen for sale at other times of the year.*

Portulaca 'Sundial Peppermint'

Growing guide

This succulent annual produces pretty, cup-shaped flowers in a range of bright colours throughout the summer. Its red stems and cylindrical green leaves tend to develop into a sprawling tangled habit but it has the virtue of being almost completely drought-resistant. In fact, you should not water it until the leaves look slightly shrivelled.

It thrives in a sunny position and well-drained compost. The flowers of older varieties close up during dull weather, but the newer F1 forms put on a good show in a poor summer. Single and double forms are available, the latter having rose-like blooms. It is best grown on its own as it does not like being shaded by other plants.

Propagation

Sow at 18°C (65°F) during March. Do not cover the seed as it germinates best in light. Treat as a bedding plant.

Troubleshooting

Seedlings are prone to damping off. Water compost from below, always use fresh compost and sow as thinly as possible. As an added precaution, use a copper fungicide (e.g. Bordeaux Mixture) when watering.

Aphids can be a serious menace. Spray with pirimicarb (Rapid) if necessary. Wash off sticky residues and sooty mould.

Which variety?

Available in mixtures of yellow, orange, red, purple, pink and white, with either single or double flowers.
Names like '**Special Mixed**' and '**Improved Double Mixed**' are likely to be old types which close up in dull weather.
'**Cloudbeater**' is claimed to flower well in all weathers.
'**Sundial**' has larger double flowers, which should stay open for most of the day.

Pyrethrum ptarmiciflorum

Shape and size

90cm
60cm
30cm
10cm

Position   Overwintering

5°C

Treat as Annual

Containers

Compost   Watering   Feeding

Multi-purpose

FEED

Features calendar

Jan	Feb	Mar	Apr	May	June
July	Aug	Sept	Oct	Nov	Dec

Buying tips *Not commonly sold as plants. Order the seed from a mail-order catalogue.*

The feathery leaves of pyrethrum ptarmiciflorum "Silver Feather'

Growing guide

There are two types of pyrethrum foliage for containers. *Pyrethrum ptarmiciflorum* 'Silver Feather' has bright silvery foliage and is similar to *Senecio maritimus* 'Silver Dust', but with finer, lace-like leaves. It makes a good filler for tubs and baskets, especially when combined with pale blue or pink flowers to create pastel effects. *Pyrethrum aureum* 'Golden Moss' forms mats of yellow, moss-like foliage. It has long been used in parks for carpet-bedding schemes but is equally suited to covering the sides of wire baskets. As a single subject for a shallow bowl, it makes a dramatic contrast at the base of a taller pot containing a plant with large foliage.

Both *P. ptarmiciflorum* and *P. aureum* are short-lived perennials and will produce daisy-like flowers in their second year, though by then the plants tend to become a bit messy and are best replaced.

Propagation
Sow from February to March at 15°C (60°F). You can also take cuttings in spring from plants kept over the winter.

Troubleshooting
Generally trouble-free.

Which variety?

P. aureum **'Golden Moss'** has yellow or golden foliage, forming a mat. Height 10cm (4in). *P. ptarmiciflorum* **'Silver Feather'** produces bushy plumes of silver, lace-like foliage. Height 20cm (8in).

Salvia

Shape and size

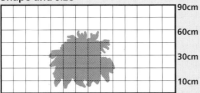

90cm
60cm
30cm
10cm

Position

Over-wintering

Treat as Annual

Containers

Compost

Multi-purpose | Grit

Watering

Feeding

FEED FEED FEED

Features calendar

Jan	Feb	Mar	Apr	May	June
					✿
✿	✿	✿			
July	Aug	Sept	Oct	Nov	Dec

Buying tips *Late spring is the best time to buy plants, though seedlings are often available in early spring.*

Salvia farinacea 'Victoria'

Salvia coccinea 'Lady in Red'

Growing guide

S. splendens, with its intensely bright scarlet spikes of flowers, has long been a favourite for bedding in borders and, to a lesser extent, in containers. Red remains by far the most popular flower colour, though recent developments have seen the introduction of forms with white, salmon, lavender, coral and purple flowers. For something a little more subtle, *S. farinacea* is an excellent tender perennial that is usually grown as a half-hardy annual, with many blue or white slender flower spikes, borne above fresh green foliage. Salvias grow to 20-45cm (8-18in) high so they are best used in containers, with the more compact types suited to window-boxes. They prefer a sunny site.

Propagation
Sow seed at 18-21°C (65-70°F) in February or March.

Troubleshooting
Generally trouble-free.

Which variety?

S. FARINACEA VARIETIES
These are available in several colours, mostly shades of blue.

'Rhea' is the most compact form, with blue-mauve flowers. Height 35cm (14in).

'Strata' is an excellent variety with greyish flower spikes on which the blue flowers stand out well. It performs to a particularly high standard. Height 45cm (18in).

'Victoria' has flowers which are a handsome shade of mid-blue. Height 45cm (18in).

'White' bears pure white blooms. Height 40cm (16in).

S. SPLENDENS VARIETIES

'Blaze of Fire' is bright scarlet. It has a compact habit, growing to around 23cm (9in).

'Phoenix Mixed' is a blend of scarlet, purple, lavender, dark and light salmon flowers. Height 30cm (12in).

'Sizzler' series include burgundy-red, lavender, deep purple, salmon and white forms. Height 25-30cm (10-12in).

S. COCCINEA VARIETIES

'Coral Nymph' is a compact form with a free-branching habit up to 20cm (8in) tall.

'Lady in Red' is similar in habit to 'Coral Nymph', with light scarlet flowers.

Scaevola aemula

Shape and size

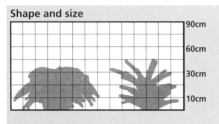

					90cm
					60cm
					30cm
					10cm

Position   Overwintering

  7°C 7°C

Containers

Compost   Watering   Feeding

Multi-purpose   Grit   FEED

Features calendar

Jan	Feb	Mar	Apr	May	June
					✿
✿	✿	✿			
July	Aug	Sept	Oct	Nov	Dec

Scaevola aemula 'Blue Wonder'

Scaevola aemula

Growing guide

This pleasant trailing plant has become very popular within a short time. Handsome blue, fan-shaped flowers with a central golden eye are borne on long, trailing stems, making this an ideal plant for a hanging basket. However, it also does well in window-boxes and container edges. Scaevola thrives in a sunny site, though it flowers reasonably well in light shade.

Propagation

Take cuttings in spring or mid- to late summer.

Troubleshooting

Generally trouble-free.

Which variety?

Several varieties of **S. aemula** are available:

'Blue Fan', 'Blue Wonder' and **'New Wonder'** all produce similar flowers of a vivid shade of light violet-blue.

'Petite' has tiny, pale blue flowers.

Senecio maritimus

(formerly Cineraria maritima, dusty miller)

Shape and size

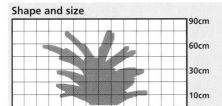

90cm
60cm
30cm
10cm

Position   Overwintering

5°c
5°c
Treat as Annual

Containers   Compost

Multi-purpose

Watering   Feeding

FEED

Features calendar

Jan	Feb	Mar	Apr	May	June
				🌿	🌿

July	Aug	Sept	Oct	Nov	Dec
🌿	🌿	🌿	🌿		

Senecio maritimus makes a suitable underplanting for standards

Buying tips **'Silver Dust'** *is widely sold as bedding strips during April and May. You may need to grow other varieties from seed.*

Senecio maritimus 'Silver Dust'

Growing guide

These silvery-grey foliage plants are the perfect companions for almost any flowers, toning down bright colours and adding style to pastels. You can use them in tubs, window-boxes or hanging baskets, where they are ideal for edgings or fillers.

They are remarkably drought-tolerant and require little feeding. Light shade is no problem for the plants, but for the best foliage colour, you need to grow them in sun.

The plants are perennials and will survive outdoors in sheltered gardens through a mild winter. However, they tend to become tall and straggly in their second year if not regularly trimmed back. Yellow flowers are also produced in the second year.

Propagation

Sow seed from February to April at 15°C (60°F). You can also take cuttings in spring or summer.

Troubleshooting

Generally trouble-free.

Which variety?

'Cirrus' has rounded greyish-silver leaves. Height 30cm (12in).

'Silver Dust' has finely cut, lace-like leaves in a bright silver. Height 15cm (6in).

Soleirolia soleirolii

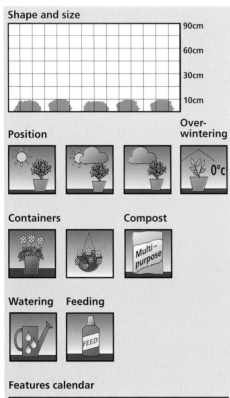

Shape and size

Position

Over-wintering

Containers

Compost

Watering   **Feeding**

Features calendar

| Jan | Feb | Mar | Apr | May | June |
| July | Aug | Sept | Oct | Nov | Dec |

Buying tips *Commonly found amongst the houseplants. Mini-plants sold for terrariums are a good buy.*

Soleirolia creates a green mat beneath a container-grown shrub

Growing guide

Formerly known as *Helxine*, this creeping plant forms a luxuriant mass of tiny, fresh green leaves. It thrives in conditions from sun to deep shade, and it is particularly useful for dark, shady corners. Although it is a flat-growing, carpeting plant, the stems root as they spread and it can be grown over low domes of wire netting filled with moss and compost to create an unusual display. It can also be grown in hanging baskets.

To build up stock quickly, buy small plants in early spring and plant them in seed trays, spaced well apart. Their growth will soon spread and these larger plants can be divided. In mild areas they can survive outside all year, though it is best to overwinter containers in a frost-free place.

Propagation
Detach rooted parts of the plant and pot them up separately from early spring through to late summer.

Troubleshooting
Generally trouble-free, but take care not to let this plant escape into the border or the lawn in mild areas as it can be very hard to eradicate. The plant will die back if allowed to dry out.

Which variety?

S. soleirolii has fresh, mid-green leaves.
'Aurea' (also called **'Golden Queen'**) has leaves which are an attractive shade of greeny-gold.
'Variegata' (also called **'Argentea'** and **'Silver Queen'**) is variegated with white and green.

Solenopsis axillaris

(also known as Isotoma and Laurentia)

Shape and size

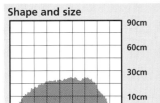

90cm
60cm
30cm
10cm

Position Overwintering

7°C 7°C

Containers Compost

Multi-purpose

Watering Feeding

FEED FEED

Features calendar

Jan	Feb	Mar	Apr	May	June
					✿
July	Aug	Sept	Oct	Nov	Dec
✿	✿	✿			

Buying tips *Early summer is the best time to buy established plants.*

Front to back: Solenopsis, Zantedeschi, Iceland Poppy and mini-chrysanths in chimney pot

The star-shaped blooms complement the delicate foliage

Growing guide

This eye-catching and versatile plant forms a cushion of feathery-green foliage covered with masses of star-shaped flowers. The blooms give off a delicate fragrance in the evenings. It can be used in hanging baskets or containers, and is best planted on its own to form a balanced mound of foliage, rather than being mixed with other plants.

It does best in a sunny, reasonably sheltered position.

Propagation

Take cuttings from early spring to late summer. Seed can be sown in January at 15°C (60°F) to produce plants that flower from mid-summer onwards.

Troubleshooting

Generally trouble-free.

Which variety?

S. axillaris bears flowers that are an attractive shade of blue-mauve. **'Alba'** has pure white flowers, and there is also a pink-flowered form.

Sphaeralcea munroana

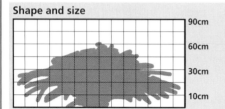

Shape and size

90cm

60cm

30cm

10cm

Position   Overwintering

  7°C 7°C

Containers   Compost

  Multi-purpose Grit

Watering   Feeding

  FEED

Features calendar

Jan	Feb	Mar	Apr	May	June
					❋
July	Aug	Sept	Oct	Nov	Dec
❋	❋	❋			

Buying tips *Plants are generally available from early summer onwards.*

The handsome foliage and delicate blooms of Sphaeralcea

Growing guide

A pretty trailing plant producing long stems clad with greyish-green, finely cut leaves. The foliage makes an excellent background for the flowers, which are a becoming shade of pinky-mauve and mallow-like in appearance. It is excellent in containers, though as the plant's habit is rather open it is best combined with other plants to give the container a balanced appearance. Sphaeralcea thrives in a well-drained soil in full sun.

Propagation

Take cuttings in early spring or mid- to late summer.

Troubleshooting

Generally trouble-free.

Which variety?

In addition to the species, there is a pale pink form with blooms of a delicate shade of shell-pink.

Sutera cordata

(also known as Bacopa)

Shape and size

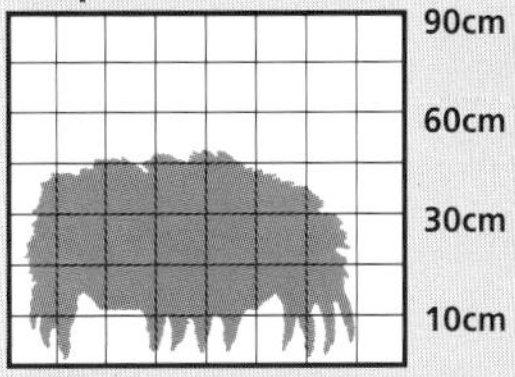
90cm
60cm
30cm
10cm

Position / Overwintering

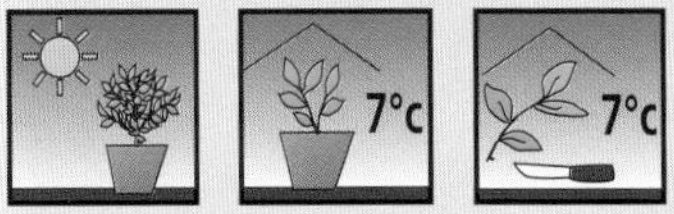
7°C
7°C

Containers

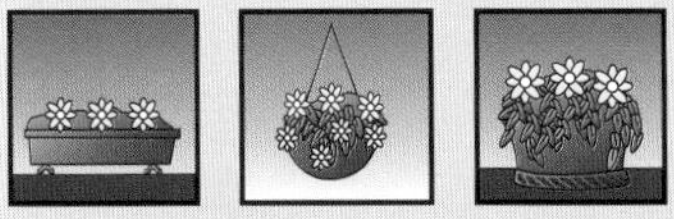

Compost / Watering / Feeding

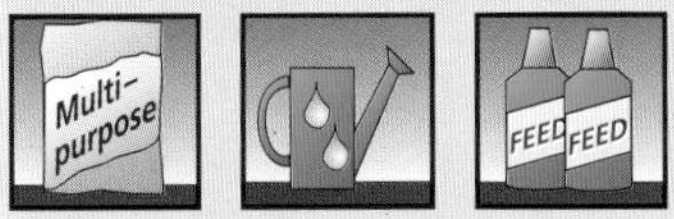
Multi-purpose
FEED
FEED

Features calendar

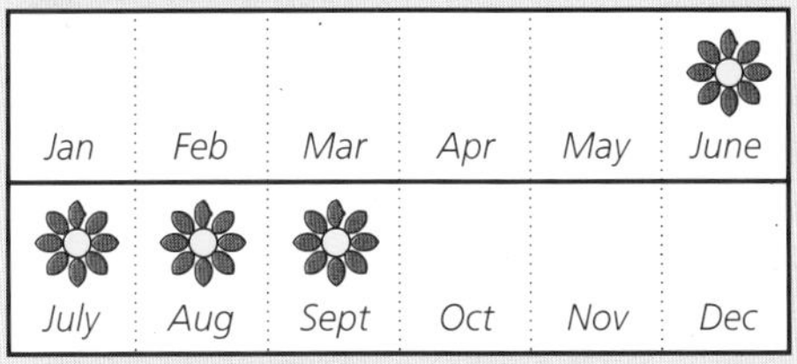
Jan
Feb
Mar
Apr
May
June
July
Aug
Sept
Oct
Nov
Dec

Buying tips *Young plantlets are generally available in early spring, larger plants from late spring to early summer.*

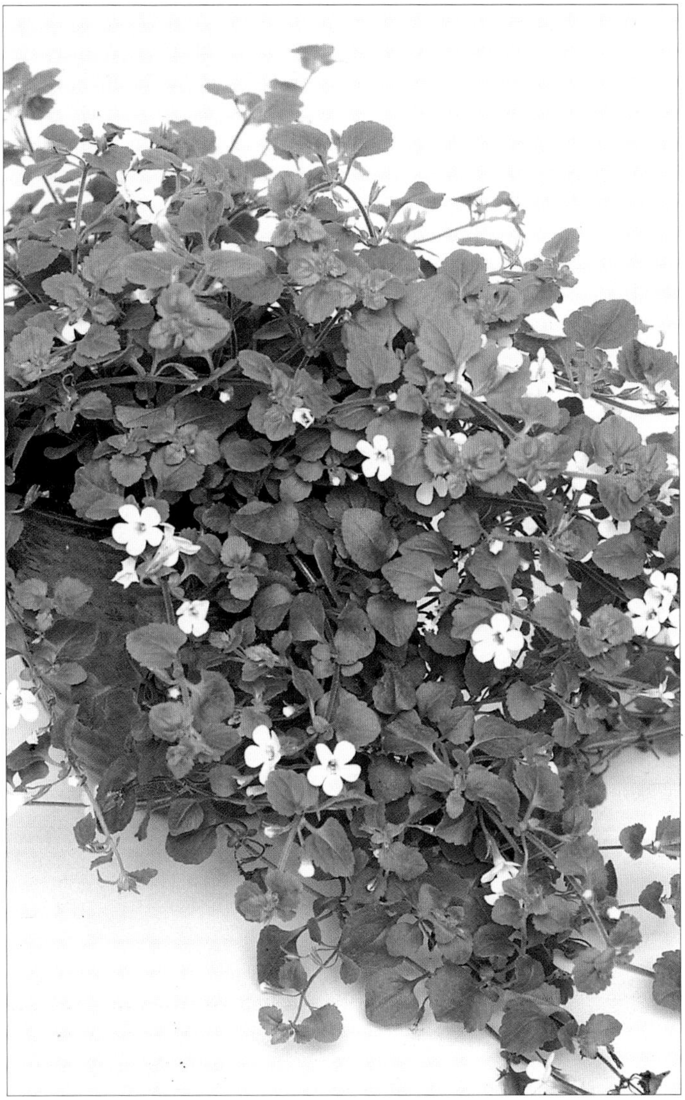

Sutera cordata 'Snowflake'

Growing guide

This plant is a recent introduction which has quickly become very popular. The stems trail, forming a dense mass of tiny, rounded, mid-green leaves that make a contrasting background to the profuse quantities of small flowers that are borne throughout summer.

It is an excellent plant for hanging baskets, window-boxes and container edges, and it forms a neat, well-balanced plant if grown on its own in a hanging basket.

Propagation

Take cuttings in early spring or late summer.

Troubleshooting

Generally trouble-free.

Which variety?

'Lilac Pearls' bears tiny lilac-mauve flowers.

'Snowflake' has pure white flowers that stand out particularly well against the foliage.

Tagetes signata
(T. tenuifolia)

Shape and size

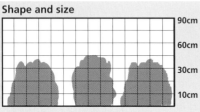

90cm
60cm
30cm
10cm

Position

Over-wintering

Treat as Annual

Containers

Compost · Watering · Feeding

Multi-purpose · FEED FEED

Features calendar

Jan	Feb	Mar	Apr	May	June
					✿
✿	✿	✿			
July	Aug	Sept	Oct	Nov	Dec

Buying tips *Not as widely sold as French marigolds, but you should be able to find plants in strips during March and April.*

Tagetes are ideal for less formal groupings

Tagetes 'Lemon Gem' beneath African marigolds

Growing guide

Tagetes are very similar to French marigolds, except they grow marginally taller and have larger numbers of smaller flowers. Their slighter, looser habit makes them better suited to less formal groupings.

They are reasonably drought-tolerant, though perform best if regularly fed and watered. A sunny position is ideal but you should still get a good display in light shade.

Propagation
Sow seed from March to April at 15°C (60°F).

Troubleshooting
Generally trouble-free.

Which variety?

Tagetes signata bears many small flowers. Varieties include **'Golden Gem'** with dainty, star-like, golden flowers, **'Lemon Gem'**, which has larger, lemon-yellow blooms and **'Tangerine Gem'** with yellow-orange flowers. Height 30cm (12in).

Tropaeolum majus

Shape and size

1.2m
90cm
60cm
30cm

Position

Over-wintering

Treat as Annual

Containers

Compost

Multi-purpose

Watering

Feeding

FEED

Features calendar

Jan	Feb	Mar	Apr	May	June
					✹
July	Aug	Sept	Oct	Nov	Dec
✹	✹	✹			

Buying tips *Perennial varieties are available from early spring onwards. Single plants in pots are often available in early summer, but as nasturtiums are so easy to grow from seed, they are not good value.*

'Gleam' hybrid

'Hermine Grashoff'

Growing guide

These are old favourites that produce bright summer flowers and grow easily. With a lax, spreading habit, nasturtiums are excellent for containers and hanging baskets. Traditionally, flower colours were vivid and bright and, although these are still popular, they have been joined by a range of pastel shades. They excel in full sun, and it is best to feed in very limited amounts as too much fertiliser encourages foliage at the expense of flowers. Nasturtiums self-seed easily which is usually a welcome habit – if not, the seedlings can easily be pulled up. Perennial varieties can be overwintered in a frost-free place.

Propagation

Seed germinates readily and can be sown direct where plants are to flower. For an early start, seed can be sown under cover in an unheated greenhouse from March onwards. Perennial varieties need to be propagated from cuttings taken from spring to late summer.

Troubleshooting

Blackfly and cabbage-white caterpillars can be a problem. In the early stages, small infestations can be pinched out by hand. Larger numbers can be controlled with a contact insecticide.

Which variety?

The following varieties are annuals unless otherwise stated.

'Strawberries and cream'

'Alaska' has unusual variegated foliage, its large leaves liberally splashed with white. This attractive foliage makes it a particularly good choice for containers. Mixed colours include gold, scarlet and cream.

'Empress of India' has orange-red flowers with a darker throat.

'Hermine Grashoff' is an old perennial variety with double orange flowers.

'Gleam Hybrids' have long, trailing stems up to 1.2m (4ft) long. Colours include red, orange and yellow.

'Jewel' series have a compact habit with flowers that include gold, deep yellow, orange and crimson.

'Peach Melba' bears creamy-apricot flowers.

'Red Wonder' is a perennial variety with dark green foliage that goes well with its dark red blooms.

'Salmon Baby' is salmon with darker flecks.

'Strawberries and Cream' has flowers with creamy-yellow petals that are boldly blotched with red at the base.

'Tom Thumb' is a compact variety growing to 23cm (9in) high and up to 38cm (14in) across. Flowers are borne in a range of vibrant colours including red, orange and yellow.

'Whirlybird' series have bright flowers in colours including cherry-red, dark red, orange, scarlet, gold and tangerine.

(*See also* Climbers for tubs, page 151.)

Verbena

Shape and size

Position   Overwintering

Containers

Compost   Watering   Feeding

Features calendar

Jan	Feb	Mar	Apr	May	June
July	Aug	Sept	Oct	Nov	Dec

Buying tips *Most trailing varieties cannot be grown from seed. Young plantlets, available from early spring, are a good buy. By early summer, you will generally find single plants in pots.*

'Silver Anne'

'Peaches and Cream'

Growing guide

Verbenas were immensely popular with the Victorians and these colourful plants are now making a comeback. There are bush and trailing forms, both of which are excellent for containers. The trailing types are particularly suited to hanging baskets and container edges, where they combine well with other plants. Pink and red forms look especially good with geraniums and fuchsias. The flowers are borne in flattened or rounded heads composed of many small blooms. Virtually all trailing types are tender perennials that are best bought as plants and propagated by cuttings, whereas bush types are annuals that can be raised from seed. Verbenas thrive in a sunny site.

Propagation

Sow seed of bush types from January to March on the surface of the compost and cover with a thin layer of fine grade vermiculite. Keep in the dark at 21°C (70°F) until the seeds germinate (at least two weeks). All types can be propagated from cuttings in spring and summer.

Troubleshooting

Mildew can be a problem, particularly if plants have been placed under stress due to prolonged drought or starvation. Spray with Nimrod-T before the disease spreads. Discard severely affected plants.

'Pink Parfait'

'Sissinghurst'

Which variety?

TRAILING VARIETIES

'Aphrodite' (also called **'Carousel'**) has striking, bicoloured flowers which are deep purple with a central white stripe on each petal.

'Blue Cascade' has soft blue flowers.

'Foxhunter' bears bright red blooms.

'Imagination' is spreading rather than trailing, though its loose, open habit makes it suitable for a hanging basket. It produces small heads of violet-blue flowers. This variety is raised from seed.

'Lawrence Johnston' bears large, bright red flowers.

V. x maonettii has mauve- and white-striped flowers.

'Pink Parfait' has larger than average blooms that are an attractive and unusual mixture of light and dark pink.

'Silver Anne' bears large, soft pink flowers which have a light fragrance.

'Sissinghurst' has compact cherry-red flowers.

'Tapien Purple' and **'Tapien Pink'** are new varieties that produce a mass of vigorous growth yet still remain compact. Profuse quantities of deep pink or deep violet-purple flowers are produced.

'White Cascade' and **'White Knight'** both bear pure white blooms.

BUSH VARIETIES

'Amour' series are a group of varieties with a neat, compact, branching habit, growing to 20-30cm (8-12in) high. Large, rounded heads of flowers are produced in a range of colours including pale pink, rose-pink, purple, and scarlet with a white eye.

'Blue Lagoon' has a neat, compact habit. It produces heads of handsome, deep true-blue flowers.

'Romance' series have a slightly spreading habit. Colours include rose, scarlet, white, pink/white and violet.

'Novalis' series come in a range of colours including some with a distinctive white eye. These are deep blue, rose-pink, red and scarlet. Plain colours include white, scarlet and rose-pink.

'Peaches and Cream' bears very attractive flowers in unusual pastel shades of coral, yellow, orange and salmon. It has a compact, upright habit.

Viola

Shape and size

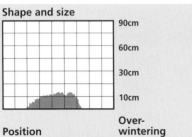

90cm
60cm
30cm
10cm

Position

Over-wintering

Containers

Compost   Watering   Feeding

Features calendar

Jan	Feb	Mar	Apr	May	June
					✿
July	Aug	Sept	Oct	Nov	Dec
✿	✿	✿			

Buying tips *Not as widely sold as pansies. Late spring and early autumn are generally the best times for a wide choice.*

'Johnny Jump-Up'

Growing guide

Violas have daintier flowers than pansies and are more tolerant of hot conditions and occasional drying out. They are all low-growing, which makes them ideal for all containers including hanging baskets and window-boxes. The hybrid types are the most showy and are the best choice for containers. Like pansies, deadhead them regularly for best results.

Propagation

Sow seed in July in trays placed in a shaded cold frame or a sheltered spot in the garden. Plants can be transplanted into their flowering site in early autumn or early spring. For summer flowers, sow seed at 15°C (60°F) in March. Cuttings of basal shoots can also be taken in July. Earthing up around the plants will encourage each individual stem to root.

Troubleshooting

Fungal diseases can attack violas and kill the whole plant, particularly in wet conditions. Always use fresh compost when growing violas.

Which variety?

'Arkwright Ruby' bears large blooms that are a deep ruby-crimson with a darker central blotch.
'Baby Lucia' has pale blue flowers, like those of a miniature pansy.
'Bowles Black' bears flowers that are an exceptionally dark shade of purple that appears almost black, with a tiny, contrasting yellow eye.

'Princess Yellow'

'Chantryland' is an attractive shade of apricot.

'Cuty' is an unusual bicolour with white, yellow-eyed blooms and purple upper petals.

'Johnny Jump-Up' has small flowers that are an attractive mixture of purple, lavender and bright yellow.

'Princess' series are a range of neat, compact varieties offering a fine colour selection including violet-blue, deep purple, lavender with yellow/white centre, purple with gold centre, blue and cream.

'Prince Henry' is an old favourite with very dark purple-violet flowers.

'Prince John' has blooms that are pure golden-yellow.

'Sorbet' series offer some unusual colours. They include **'Sorbet Blueberry Cream'** (light blue fading to cream in the centre), **'Sorbet Lemon Chiffon'** (pale yellow upper petals, darker below), **'Sorbet Yellow Frost'** (yellow with blue upper petals) and **'Sorbet Purple Duet'** (dark purple above, paler below). A mixture is also available.

'Velour' series are a cross between a pansy and a viola, with medium-sized flowers. Colours include shades of blue, purple with a yellow eye and pure golden-yellow.

'White Perfection' bears pure white flowers.

Zebrina pendula

Shape and size

90cm
60cm
30cm
10cm

Position

Overwintering   Containers

 7°C
 7°C

Compost   Watering   Feeding

Multi-purpose

FEED FEED

Features calendar

Jan	Feb	Mar	Apr	May	June
July	Aug	Sept	Oct	Nov	Dec

Buying tips
Look in the houseplant section at garden centres. Small plants are a good buy as they grow very quickly.

Take cuttings from houseplants to grow in hanging baskets

Zebrina pendula 'Quadricolour'

Growing guide

Although most commonly grown as houseplants, zebrinas make interesting additions to summer hanging baskets. They can also be planted beneath specimens in tubs to provide foliage colour.

Outdoors, they will grow in sun or shade. They tend to become straggly with neglect, so water and feed regularly and pinch out the tips of the stems to encourage them to become more branched.

Propagation
Pieces of stem pushed into the compost will take root within days.

Troubleshooting
Generally trouble-free.

Which variety?
Zebrina pendula has silver-striped leaves which are red on the underside.
'Discolor' is similar to the above but with coppery, green leaves.
'Purpusii' has dark green leaves which develop a strong purple flush in good light.
'Quadricolour' has red, white and pink bands on the leaves.

Zinnia

Shape and size

90cm
60cm
30cm
10cm

Position

Over-wintering

Treat as Annual

Containers

Compost

Multi-purpose

Watering

Feeding

FEED FEED FEED

Features calendar

Jan	Feb	Mar	Apr	May	June
❀	❀	❀			
July	Aug	Sept	Oct	Nov	Dec

Buying tips *Zinnias are not widely available as plants. They are most likely to be sold in florists as established pot plants. Defer your buying decision until you have an idea how the summer will turn out.*

'Star White'

'Dreamland Pink'

Growing guide

Zinnias produce bright, dahlia-like blooms on short, stocky plants. The flower size ranges from tiny single blooms to doubles over 10cm (4in) across. They thrive in hot, sunny conditions and are likely to be a disappointment in a cool, damp summer. The flowers are very prone to rain damage, and the plants are more likely to succumb to diseases in humid conditions.

They like a compost with plenty of nutrients but will not suffer if you forget to water them occasionally. However, regular neglect will put the plants under stress and make them more vulnerable to mildew.

Zinnias are best grown as a single subject in containers, partly because they tend to out-dazzle other flowers and partly because they do not like being crowded out.

Propagation

Sow seed at 21°C (70°F) in March or April. Grow on at minimum of 13°C (55°F).

Troubleshooting

Seedlings are prone to damping off. Water from below and use a copper fungicide (such as Bordeaux Mixture) when sowing. Prick out the seedlings at an early stage into individual pots and keep the greenhouse well ventilated to prevent grey mould becoming a problem. Mildew often strikes plants that are watered erratically. Spray with a fungicide as soon as the first signs of mildew appear.

Which variety?

The following are short-growing hybrid varieties, the best choice for containers.

'Dreamland' series have large double flowers. They come in red, yellow, pink, coral and ivory. Height: 20cm (8in).

'Envy' has double lime-green blooms. Height: 60cm (24in).

'Peter Pan' series are similar to 'Dreamland' but in a wider range of brighter colours.

'Small World' series have rounded double blooms. The very tight petals make the flowers more rain-resistant. Height: 35cm (14in).

'Star' series have many tiny single blooms on bushy plants. They are more disease- and weather-resistant than most. Height: 30cm (12in).

Colourful bulbs for containers

Many types of bulbous plants are ideal candidates for containers. They provide trouble-free, colourful displays in spring, summer and autumn. Although most bulbs are sun-lovers, some will thrive in a shady spot provided it gets some sun or at least good light. Shade-loving bulbs tend to be native to cool, damp areas and so need to be kept moist at all times, particularly during hot weather after flowering.

Narcissus brighten up a pot of skimmias and periwinkles

For impact, especially early in the season, try planting bulbs en masse. Cram bulbs into containers as tightly as possible. Small bulbs can be planted so that they are touching, but those with large flowers need space for the flowers to unfurl. Unfortunately, such displays tend to be short-lived, but can be extended a little by planting in layers – the deeper bulbs flowering later. Some bulbs produce multiple flowers which help fill out the display. Good candidates are tulips like 'Toronto' and dwarf daffodils such as 'Hawera' and 'Tête à Tête'.

Bulbs are a good way to cheer up permanent planting displays in large containers when the main specimen is looking dull. Choose bulbs that will not multiply too quickly; for instance, species crocuses will last several years without dividing, whereas daffodils may need to be lifted and split every two years.

Summer-flowering types can form effective focal points for larger containers. For example, the Indian shot plant (canna) produces vividly coloured blooms above lush, tropical-looking foliage to give an exotic feel to your patio. Dahlias too are perfect for the summer patio. Choose dwarf varieties that grow up to 60cm (24in).

Although bulbs can be grown in quite small pots, for permanent displays you will have to opt for one at least 20cm (8in) deep as bulbs need to be kept moist when growing without getting waterlogged. Before planting put a 2.5-cm (1-in) layer of coarse gravel or crocks in the base to aid drainage. Containers without drainage holes will need to be deeper and have a drainage layer in the base at least 5cm (2in) in depth. For temporary displays, any well-drained compost would be suitable, but for permanent containers use a soil-based compost such as John Innes No. 2. As a rough guide plant bulbs with their 'noses' at least two bulb depths below the compost surface.

Deadhead spring-flowering bulbs after they have bloomed, leaving flower stems and leaves to die down naturally. Annual displays can be tipped out of their pots and stored in a dry shed or garage to free the container for bedding

Early tulips and late daffodils

Iris danfordiae and I. reticulata with ivies

A collection of bulbs in pots makes a bright spring feature

displays. Store shade-loving bulbs in moist peat as they will shrivel up and die if allowed to dry out. Bulbs in permanent displays can look unsightly after flowering unless you cover up the fading leaves with bedding plants. Summer-flowering bulbs are tender and need to be kept in trays or boxes filled with peat in a frost-free place.

Creating a succession of colour

There are two simple ways you can create a continuous flowering display on your patio. Plant up several plastic pot liners with displays that follow on from one another, then simply swap over the liners as the plants come into bloom. You can get a similar effect in a single container by planting bulbs that flower at different times. This method is particularly useful for permanent planting schemes. For example, the display pictured left and above started with *Iris reticulata* 'Violet Beauty', *Iris danfordiae* and *Anemone blanda* in February, followed by Narcissus 'Tête à Tête' and Crocus 'Snowstorm'. *Hyacinthus* 'Carnegie' extends the display into April.

Narcissus adds spring colour to winter grouping of heather and ivies

Bulbs in hanging baskets

You can get an eye-catching display of bulbs in a basket provided you choose short-stemmed varieties and keep the compost moist at all times. Iris, dwarf narcissi, crocuses and grape hyacinths can all look good, especially when combined with trailing ivies to give a contrast in colour and texture.

Crocus 'Snowstorm' and Narcissus 'Tête à Tête'

Canna

Shape and size

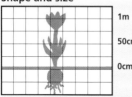

1m

50cm

0cm

Position

Over-wintering

Containers

Compost

Watering

Feeding

Features calendar

Jan	Feb	Mar	Apr	May	June
					🌼

July	Aug	Sept	Oct	Nov	Dec
🌼	🌼	🌼			

Canna x generalis 'Lucifer'

Buying tips

In spring look for firm, fleshy rhizomes with no signs of rotting or drying out. If buying plants, choose specimens with several stems, as these will produce more flowers and be ready for dividing next year.

Growing guide

Although canna lilies are, strictly speaking, herbaceous plants, they have tough, fleshy rhizomes. You will find rhizomes for sale alongside summer-flowering bulbs in the spring, and plants during the summer. All cannas produce tall stems of vividly coloured flowers above large, banana-like leaves, which are either green, bronzed or purple. The flowers come in bright colours, including pink, yellow, orange and scarlet and they create an exotic feel to a sunny patio.

Cannas range in height from 75cm (30in) for compact varieties such as the 'President' up to 2-m (7-2ft) giants such as *Canna indica*.

Plant in a 20-cm (8-in) pot (or larger), keep well-watered throughout the summer and apply a weekly liquid feed. Remove the stems once they start to die off in autumn and keep the rhizomes in frost-free conditions over winter. They need to be kept moist but not wet.

For earlier flowering, you can pot up the rhizomes in February or

March and grow on at a minimum temperature of 15°C (60°F). The plants should be hardened off before being placed outside in late May or early June. Alternatively, repot the plants in April or May and resume normal watering once the frosts have passed.

Propagation

Established plants can be divided in spring when the shoots are visible. Split the rhizome into sections, each with a shoot and roots, and pot up individually in 15-cm (6-in) pots. Keep at a minimum of 10°C (50°F).

Cannas can also be raised from seed, though the seedlings are likely to be different to the parent. Soak the seed in warm water for 24 hours before sowing and germinate at 21°C (70°F).

Troubleshooting

Generally trouble-free, though slugs can sometimes damage the roots and the leaves.

Which variety?

Most of the plants on sale will be hybrids (varieties of **C. x generalis**), most of which grow 0.9-1.2m (3-4ft) tall. Garden centres commonly sell them by colour but good, named varieties to look out for are:
'Lucifer', which bears red flowers with yellow margins and purple leaves.
'Evening Star' has bright pink flowers and green leaves.
'Orange Perfection' produces muted orange flowers and green leaves.
'President' boasts bright red flowers and green leaves.
'Wyoming' has bronzed-yellow flowers and bronze leaves. 1.5m (5ft) tall.

Cannas create a lush foliage effect

Crocus

ns running vertical label

Crocus

Shape and size

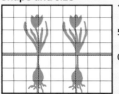

10cm
5cm
0cm

Position

Over-wintering

Containers

Compost   Watering   Feeding

Features calendar

Jan	Feb	Mar	Apr	May	June
	❁	❁	❁		
July	Aug	Sept	Oct	Nov	Dec

Buying tips *Mixed crocuses are often sold in packs of 50 or more corms, which is usually an economical way to create a splash of colour. However, if you wish to create a particular colour scheme, you may have to buy them in smaller packs.*

'Snow Bunting'

Crocus 'Yellow Mammoth' creates a seasonal splash

Growing guide

These popular and reliable dwarf bulbs flower from February to April and are just the ticket for providing a cheerful splash of early spring colour in containers. As they only grow to around 10cm (4in) high, they can be planted in most containers including window-boxes, alpine troughs, shallow bowls and hanging baskets, as well as around the edges of larger pots and raised beds. In addition to the spring-flowering crocuses that are listed below, there are also a number of autumn-flowering crocus species, though they are more suited to border cultivation as they produce their leaves in spring. Crocuses thrive in a sunny site. Plant them from September to October as soon as the bulbs are available.

Propagation

Small cormlets are produced and can be separated from the parent corm when the leaves are dying back. The larger cormlets can be planted direct in the flowering site for the next year, and tiny ones can be planted in nursery rows to grow on for a year.

Troubleshooting

Mice can damage planted corms during winter. Birds may peck at the young flowers.

Which variety?

Crocuses come in a range of colours, predominantly purple, blue, yellow and white. The selection opposite is of showier varieties which do well in pots. For a long display, plant both the early- and later-flowering types.

124

The early-flowering 'Cream Beauty'

'Whitewell Purple'

FEBRUARY TO MARCH

The following are hybrids of **Crocus chrysanthus** with many small flowers up to 8cm (3in) high.

'Advance' is an unusual combination of yellow on the inside of the blooms and mauve on the outside.

'Blue Pearl' is light blue with a dark yellow base to the flowers, the colour slightly paler on the inside.

'Cream Beauty' is creamy-white with a darker throat.

'Fuscotinctus' is an early-flowering variety, often blooming as soon as January. It has deep yellow flowers which are striped with bronze.

'Ladykiller' is white with purple outer petals.

'Snow Bunting' is white with a yellow throat.

'Whitewell Purple' has lilac-mauve flowers.

'Zwanenburg Bronze' is a dark bronze-yellow with distinctive pale margins to the petals.

MARCH TO APRIL

The following garden hybrids have large blooms around 10cm (4in) in height. Sometimes they are sold in separate colours rather than as named varieties.

'Enchantress' is a light mauve-purple.

'Joan of Arc' (**'Jeanne d'Arc'**)has pure white flowers.

'Pickwick' is pale lilac striped with a deeper shade of mauve.

'Purpureus Grandiflorus' does especially well in pots, bearing masses of glossy, deep purple blooms.

'Remembrance' is a particularly good performer, producing masses of soft purple flowers with contrasting golden stamens.

'Yellow Mammoth' bears deep golden flowers.

Dahlia

Shape and size

40cm
20cm
0cm

Position

Over-wintering

5°c

Containers

Compost

Multi-purpose

Watering

Feeding

FEE FEED EED

Features calendar

Jan	Feb	Mar	Apr	May	June
✿	✿	✿			
July	Aug	Sept	Oct	Nov	Dec

Buying tips *Tubers are on sale from February to April. Choose ones that are plump and firm to the touch, without any signs of rot.*

Dahlias provide valuable summer colour

Growing guide

These popular and brightly coloured flowers are widely grown in borders and often enjoyed as cut flowers, though there are also a number of dwarf varieties that can be used to provide valuable summer and autumn colour in containers. The flowers come in a variety of colours and shapes, ranging from ornate and vividly coloured blooms to simple, single-flowered types in softer colours.

To overwinter tubers, wait until the first frosts have blackened the foliage, cut back the stem to within a few centimetres of the ground and dig up the tubers carefully, taking care not to spear them with the fork. Gently knock off the soil and stand them upside-down in a dry place for several days so any moisture can drain away. Then place the tubers in trays or boxes, cover with compost or soil, and store in a frost-free place. Keep the soil barely moist to prevent the tubers from shrivelling. Check them periodically through the winter for signs of rot and remove any diseased tubers immediately.

Tubers can be started into growth in late winter and hardened off before planting out in May, or they can be planted directly outside in April or May. Dahlias prefer an open, sunny site.

Propagation

Cuttings can be taken in spring from new shoots which grow from the tubers. If you want to take cuttings, it is best to pot up the tubers in February or March and keep them in a warm place at around 13°C (55°F) to encourage plenty of new shoots.

Troubleshooting

Aphids can be controlled with pirimicarb (Rapid). Earwigs often eat holes in leaves and flowers; control by tucking pots of straw or balls of newspaper among the foliage overnight and destroying the pests in the morning. Grey mould can occur in wet summers; remove and destroy affected parts. Virus diseases cause stunting, distorting and yellowing of foliage, and affected plants should be destroyed.

Which variety?

The following are dwarf varieties that grow to a maximum height of 60cm (24in).

Dwarf anemone dahlias have attractive flowers with a double, pompon centre. They mostly come in single colours including red, orange, yellow and white. Height: 60cm (24in).

Lilliput dahlias bear many small, single flowers and grow to around 30cm (12in) high. Varieties include: **'Bambino',** cream; **'Maid Marian',** rose-pink; **'Red Riding Hood',** orange-scarlet variety.

Eucomis bicolor

Shape and size

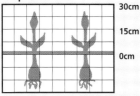

30cm
15cm
0cm

Position

Overwintering

 7°C

Containers

Compost

John Innes

Watering

Feeding

FEED FEED

Features calendar

Jan	Feb	Mar	Apr	May	June
July	Aug	Sept	Oct	Nov	Dec

Eucomis bicolor prior to flowering

Buying tips *Although Eucomis is becoming more popular, it may be necessary to buy it from a specialist mail-order bulb supplier.*

Growing guide

An unusual plant for both flower and foliage interest, eucomis produces large heads of flowers on stout spikes any time from mid-summer to early autumn, above a basal tuft of broad, green leaves. The flower spike is around 30cm (12in) long and consists of many densely packed, tiny blooms which are green edged with purple. The stem is also heavily splashed with purple.

Eucomis prefers a sunny, sheltered site and needs to be overwintered in a frost-free place. However, as the bulb is dormant during winter, light is not important during this period. Plant the bulbs in spring about 10cm (4in) deep in well-drained compost. They require plenty of water during the growing season.

Propagation
Established clumps can be divided in spring.

Troubleshooting
Generally trouble-free.

Which variety?

Only the species is generally available.

Hyacinthus

Shape and size

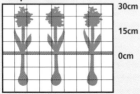

30cm
15cm
0cm

Position	Over-wintering	

Containers

Compost **Watering** **Feeding**

Features calendar

Jan	Feb	Mar	Apr	May	June
July	Aug	Sept	Oct	Nov	Dec

Buying tips *Do not confuse bulbs that have been specially treated for indoor forcing with those for planting outside. The latter are often called bedding hyacinths.*

Hyacinths, tulips and grape hyacinths

The pebbles and 'Gypsy Queen' make a superlative planting

Growing guide

With their large heads of brightly coloured flowers, hyacinths are reliable and showy performers for containers and unsurpassed for fragrance. They grow to around 15-23cm (6-9in) tall, with flower spikes around 10-15cm (4-6in) long, and bloom during April and May. Their large blooms look best in a formal setting and they are excellent in pots by themselves, or in troughs and window-boxes combined with other seasonal plants that also have a neat habit, such as polyanthus.

The flowers come in a range of colours, among which blue tends to be the most popular, though there are also red, pink, white and yellow forms. Plant 10-13cm (4-5in) deep in autumn, up to the beginning of November, in a sunny site. Take care when handling the bulbs as they can occasionally cause skin rashes.

Propagation

Seed can be harvested as soon as it ripens and sown in trays in a cold frame. However, hybrids do not come true from seed and plants take 3-5 years to flower.

Troubleshooting

Root rot shows as black and decaying roots. Bulb rot shows as a grey rot that soon destroys the bulb. Virus diseases show as pale spots and stripes on the leaves. In all three cases, dig up and burn or throw out infected bulbs.

Which variety?

The following is a selection of the most popular hybrids.
'Amsterdam' Rosy-red.
'Blue Giant' Large, silvery-blue.
'Blue Jacket' Dark blue.
'Carnegie' Pure white.
'City of Haarlem' A soft primrose-yellow (an unusual colour among hyacinths).
'Delft Blue' Mid-blue.
'Gypsy Queen' Yellow flushed with apricot.
'Lady Derby' Light shell-pink.
'Pink Pearl' Dark pink.
'Violet Pearl' Dark bluish-pink.

Iris reticulata

Shape and size

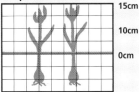

15cm
10cm
0cm

Position

Over-wintering

Containers

Compost

Multi-purpose   Grit

Watering

Feeding

FEED FEED

Features calendar

Jan	Feb	Mar	Apr	May	June
	🌼	🌼			
July	Aug	Sept	Oct	Nov	Dec

Buying tips *Dry bulbs are widely available in early autumn. Also look for pots of bulbs in bud at garden centres during February.*

Iris danfordiae

Small pot of Iris reticulata reflects the blue of the pansies

Growing guide

These dainty little dwarf bulbs grow to a maximum height of 15cm (6in) and are perfect for containers such as shallow pans, troughs and window-boxes. Plant them in raised containers as the colourful blooms are produced in late winter and early spring. Most have beautiful markings on the petals, and the flowers can be fully appreciated at close quarters.

A drawback with these irises is that they form wiry leaves after the flowers fade, which can look unattractive. One solution is to grow them in 10-cm (4-in) pots and sink the pots into tubs or window-boxes while the bulbs are in flower. Plant 10–15 bulbs per pot for a good display. For best results, grow them in compost mixed with an equal volume of sharp sand.

Propagation

Mature clumps of bulbs can be divided in autumn.

Troubleshooting

Generally trouble-free provided they do not get waterlogged. *I. danfordiae* bulbs may break into smaller bulblets after flowering and these can take two years or more to produce flowers.

Which variety?

I. danfordiae has bright yellow flowers with lower petals that are attractively spotted with brown. The sweetly scented blooms are produced from February to March. This species is best planted fresh each year, using mature, newly purchased bulbs. Height 15cm (6in).

I. reticulata bears deep purple-blue, scented flowers with petals that are beautifully marked with gold. It flowers from February to March. After flowering, the slender leaves can grow up to 45cm (18in) high before dying back, but they are generally not obtrusive. Height 15cm (6in)

HYBRIDS

These include the following. All flower in February or March and grow to around 10cm (4in) high.
'Cantab' has mid-blue, yellow and white flowers.
'Clairette' is pale sky-blue with darker lower petals.
'Harmony' is sky-blue with yellow markings.
'J. S. Dijt' bears scented, reddish-purple flowers with gold markings.
'Natascha' has ivory-white, scented flowers veined with green and marked with yellow.

Lilium

Shape and size

60cm
30cm
0cm

Position

Over-wintering

Containers

Compost

Multi-purpose

Watering   Feeding

FEED FEED

Features calendar

Jan	Feb	Mar	Apr	May	June ✽
July ✽	Aug ✽	Sept ✽	Oct	Nov	Dec

Buying tips *Lily bulbs are on sale in autumn and spring, though it is often best to plant in spring to avoid any potential problems with waterlogging or pest damage. Bulbs should be firm with fleshy white roots. Avoid dry-looking bulbs with shrivelled roots.*

'Connecticut King'

The eye-catching 'Stargazer'

Growing guide

The tall, waxy-petalled blooms of lilies can add an air of luxuriance to your patio in summer. By selecting some of the many varieties that also exude a heady fragrance, you can further enhance the atmosphere.

Flower colours cover a considerable range, from pearly whites and soft pastels to fiery reds and oranges. As lilies like to have their heads in the sun and their roots in the shade, they are perfect for patios where they can be grown in pots and surrounded by other containers. With tall stems around 0.6-1.2m (2-5ft) high, they stand well above many other container plants to make an excellent contrast.

Plant lilies on their own in groups of three. Solitary planting means that they can be brought forward at their peak and taken off show as soon as the blooms finish. Plant stem-rooting lilies 15-20cm (6-8in) deep and basal-rooting lilies 5cm (2in) deep.

Place scented lilies next to seats, doorways and windows where their fragrance can be fully appreciated.

Plant lilies in autumn or spring. Good drainage is important, particularly with autumn-planted bulbs. Lilies can remain in their pots for 3-4 years before they need separating and repotting, though it is important to stand the pots in a sheltered spot over winter to prevent waterlogging and frost damage. Topdress each spring with some fresh potting compost and a controlled-release fertiliser.

Propagation

Scale propagation is one way to increase species and hybrids. In autumn or spring, pull off healthy scales from the parent bulb and sink them halfway in pots or trays containing a 50/50 mixture of potting compost and sharp sand. Place them in a cold frame until top growth appears, at which point the scales can be potted individually and grown on for 1–2 years before planting out. Lilies can also be propagated from seed, though named hybrids do not come true from this method and it takes a number of years to produce flowering plants. One of the easiest lilies to raise from seed is *Lilium regale*, which can flower from seed in 2–3 years. Collect seed when ripe, usually in early autumn, and sow immediately in pots or trays of compost mixed with sharp sand to improve drainage. Stand the pots in a cold frame, and put down slug killer as young seedlings are very vulnerable to attack.

Troubleshooting

Lily beetle is an increasing problem, particularly in southern areas. The

Lilium regale – one of the easiest to grow

orange-brown larvae can be found under leaves and in the axils, covered in dark slime. The adult beetles are bright red and very conspicuous. Control measures involving hand-picking the larvae are generally best as they hatch over a long period, though a systemic insecticide can be used where hand control is not practical.

Slugs adore lilies and the newly emerging shoots are particularly vulnerable to attack. As well as putting down slug killer, the new stems can be surrounded with tall collars made from cut-down mineral water bottles.

Which variety?
HYBRIDS

Asiatic hybrids bear large blooms on sturdy stems 0.9-1.2m (3-4ft) high. They flower early, blooming in June and July, and include some of the brightest colours available.
'Connecticut King' Bright yellow.
'Côte d'Azur' Rose-red.
'Grand Cru' Gold with a distinctive red throat.
'Gran Paradiso' Orange-red.
'Orange Triumph' Bright orange.

Oriental hybrids have flowers with the petals mostly spread open so the stamens are more prominent, and the petals are sometimes spotted with a darker colour. August is the main flowering time. All are fragrant, some exceptionally so. Unless otherwise stated, the following varieties all grow to around 1.2m (4ft).
'Casa Blanca' Brilliant white.
'Hit Parade' A delicate shade of blush pink.
'Imperial Silver' and **'Kyoto'** have large white flowers spotted with dark pink.
'Journey's End' Red petals edged with white.
'Noblesse' White petals that are pink at the tips with a gold central band.
'Mona Lisa' Soft pink. 60cm (24in).
'Stargazer' Crimson edged with white. 60cm (24in).

Trumpet hybrids bear long, slender trumpets of flowers and are generally very fragrant. Height 1.2-1.5m (4-5ft).
'African Queen' Deep apricot.
'Golden Splendour' Golden yellow.
'Pink Perfection' Deep pink.

SPECIES

L. longiflorum bears long, slender trumpets of pure white, fragrant flowers in July and August. Height 60cm (24in).
L. regale is one of the easiest to grow and an excellent choice for first-time lily growers. It has a glorious scent that spreads over a wide area. The white blooms, borne in July and August, are streaked with purple on the outside and have prominent golden stamens.
'Album' has pure white flowers.

Lilium longiflorum

Mirabilis jalapa

Shape and size

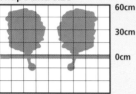

60cm
30cm
0cm

Position

Overwintering

Treat as Annual

5°C

Containers

Compost

Multi-purpose

Watering

Feeding

FEED FEED

Features calendar

Jan	Feb	Mar	Apr	May	June
✽	✽	✽			
July	Aug	Sept	Oct	Nov	Dec

Buying tips *Check that packaged tubers are firm to the touch with no sign of rot.*

White form of mirabilis

The flowers open in the afternoon

Growing guide

An upright, bushy plant that grows to around 60cm (24in) in height and is excellent for growing in a container on its own. It is ideal for people who are out at work during the day as the many small, trumpet-shaped flowers tend not to open until mid-to late afternoon – hence the common name of four o'clock plant. However, if the weather is cool and dull, they may open earlier.

The sweetly-scented flowers come in a range of vibrant colours including red, crimson, pink, yellow and white. This plant does best in a sheltered, sunny site. Plant the tubers in April. In autumn, before the first frosts, the tubers can be lifted and stored in a frost-free place over winter.

Propagation
Sow seed in trays at 18°C (65°F) in February or March. Prick out seedlings into small pots, grow on and harden off before planting out in late May.

Troubleshooting
Generally trouble-free.

Which variety?

Only the one species is generally available.

Muscari

Shape and size

20cm
10cm
0cm

Position

Over-wintering

Containers

Compost   Watering   Feeding

Features calendar

Jan	Feb	Mar	Apr ✿	May ✿	June
July	Aug	Sept	Oct	Nov	Dec

The deep blue spikes of grape hyacinths

Buying tips *Grape hyacinths are often sold in packs of 50 or 100 bulbs, which is an economical way to create a large splash of colour.*

Grape hyacinths with Primula Wanda

Growing guide

Grape hyacinths, with their short, dense spikes of deep blue flowers, are a familiar sight in many gardens where they tend to spread freely. Loose clumps of narrow, deep green leaves appear in autumn, though the flowers are produced in April and May. As this plant has a lax habit, it is ideal in hanging baskets and window-boxes where a more natural appearance is desired. Grape hyacinths do best in sun but tolerate light shade, in any reasonably well-drained soil. Plant the bulbs as early as possible, preferably by the end of September. For use in containers, plant the bulbs so that they are almost touching. This will give you a bold display and there will be less tendency for the stems to flop.

Propagation

Established clumps of bulbs can be divided and replanted immediately as soon as the leaves turn yellow, or in autumn. Plants will often self-seed.

Troubleshooting

Generally trouble-free.

Which variety?

Muscari armeniacum is the most widely grown species. It bears spikes of blue flowers up to 15cm (6in) high. There are also double-flowered and white forms.

Narcissus

Shape and size

40cm
20cm
0cm

Position

Over-wintering

Containers

Compost   Watering   Feeding

Multi-purpose

FEED

Features calendar

	Jan	Feb	Mar	Apr	May	June
		✿	✿	✿	✿	
	July	Aug	Sept	Oct	Nov	Dec

Pot of daffodils highlight unplanted urn

Dwarf daffodils with skimmia and variegated periwinkles

Growing guide

The cheerful flowers of daffodils and narcissi are an essential ingredient of the spring garden. Strictly speaking, all daffodils are correctly called narcissi, though the term daffodil is generally used to describe those taller varieties with large, single flowers. Plants with smaller or multi-headed blooms are popularly referred to as narcissi. The bright flowers are borne from early to mid-spring; they come in shades of yellow, though there are also white and cream varieties, and some with a contrasting orange cup in the centre of the flower. A number of varieties are also sweetly scented, particularly the multi-headed narcissi.

One of the most important points to consider is the degree of exposure to wind that your containers will receive, as plant sizes range from compact dwarf varieties 10cm (4in) high, to tall, large-flowered daffodils up to 45cm (18in) high. Of the taller plants, those with double flowers are par-ticularly susceptible to wind damage. Taller varieties are best in deep pots, both for stability and to give sufficient depth of soil over the large bulbs. Dwarf varieties can be used in window-boxes, hanging baskets, shallow pots and troughs.

Daffodils and narcissi look good combined with other seasonal plants with contrasting colours, such as grape hyacinths, polyanthus and pansies. They also go well with foliage plants such as variegated ivy, and the dwarf types are ideal for underplanting shrubs in tubs.

As they need plenty of time to make root growth, daffodils and narcissi are best planted by the end of September. If you want to wait until spring to plant your arrangements, plant up clumps in 10-cm (4-in) pots which can later be sunk into larger containers.

Propagation

Once they have finished flowering, plant them out in the garden or an old growing bag until the leaves die down naturally. At this stage, clumps of established bulbs can be lifted and divided for replanting in autumn.

Troubleshooting

Basal rot shows as yellow, wilted leaves, and inspection reveals soft, rotting bulbs. Narcissus fly sometimes infests bulbs; symptoms show as limited leaf growth that appears late, and white maggots can be found in the bulbs. Stem and bulb eelworm shows as weak growth and twisted or streaked leaves; further inspection reveals soft bulbs. In all cases, dig up and burn or throw out infected bulbs.

Which variety?

The following are a selection of the most popular varieties which are suited to pots. Many other dwarf types are offered by specialist mail-order bulb suppliers.

CYCLAMINEUS HYBRIDS

These charming little bulbs bear attractive flowers with swept-back petals. They have short, sturdy stems and are ideal for containers. They flower early, generally from February or early March to the beginning of April. Heights range from 10-30cm (4-12in).

'February Gold' Bright yellow.
'Jack Snipe' Creamy-yellow petals and a deeper yellow cup.
'Jenny' Creamy-white.
'Peeping Tom' Bright yellow with long trumpets.
'Tête-à-Tête' Tiny, bright yellow flowers.

Buying tips *Dwarf varieties tend to be sold in prepacks. Check the packs as best you can for firm bulbs and uniformity of size. Alternatively, look for pots of bulbs in bud during early spring. With species bulbs, buy those of cultivated origin. This should be clearly stated on the packet. Bulbs collected from the wild not only damage native habitats but are generally of poorer quality.*

Narcissus 'Tête-à-Tête' and Tulipa 'Red Riding Hood'

Narcissus 'Peeping Tom'

DWARF SPECIES

N. canaliculatis bears dainty, sweetly scented flowers in April and May. Several blooms are borne on each stem, the white petals are swept back and contrast with the golden cup. Height 15cm (6in).
N. triandrus varieties flower in April and May; one of the best is **'Thalia'** with multi-headed stems of white flowers. Height 30cm (12in).

JONQUILS

Their multi-headed stems of flowers, borne in April and May, are renowned for their sweet fragrance. Heights range from 20-45cm (8-18in).
'Baby Moon' is one of the smallest, with deep yellow flowers.
'Pipit' bears yellow flowers; the cup becomes creamy-white with age.
'Sun Disc' produces deep yellow

flowers that are an unusual disc shape.
'Waterperry' has white blooms with an apricot-pink cup.

TAZETTAS

This group also has multi-headed stems of flowers which are sweetly scented, though the blooms are generally larger than those of the Jonquil group and so they need a more sheltered position to avoid wind and damage. Flowering time is March and April and heights range from 20-45cm (8-18in).
'Cheerfulness' is an old favourite with very fragrant, creamy-white double blooms.
'Geranium' bears white flowers with a red cup.
'Hawera' is one of the smallest with creamy-yellow flowers and reflexed petals.
'Minnow' is a dainty dwarf with pale yellow flowers that have darker cups.
'Yellow Cheerfulness' has bright yellow, double blooms.

TRUMPET DAFFODILS

A wide range of daffodils bear single flowers on tall stems around 38-45cm (15-18in) high. Colours range from plain yellow and white to varieties that have a cup in a contrasting colour to the petals. These varieties are generally more suited to beds and borders, though they can be grown in containers provided the site is sheltered, as the tall stems are easily blown over and snapped. Cover bulbs with at least 10cm (4in) of compost.

Tulipa

Shape and size

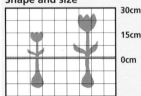

Position

Over-wintering

Containers

Compost

Watering

Feeding

Features calendar

Jan	Feb	Mar ✿	Apr ✿	May ✿	June
July	Aug	Sept	Oct	Nov	Dec

Buying tips *Choose firm bulbs with their outer brown tunics still in place, avoid dried-up or damaged ones. Superficial mould is nothing to worry about. Dry bulbs are available in autumn or spring. Buy in bud for a long display.*

'Red Riding Hood'

'Pinocchio' - one of the compact Greigii hybrids

Growing guide

Of all the spring bulbs, tulips offer perhaps the greatest variety of colour and interest over a long period. There are many different types that can provide a succession of flowers over several months, and some have attractive foliage into the bargain. Height, flower colour and shape vary enormously and there is a tulip to suit most tastes, from simple, single-flowered dwarfs in plain colours to varieties with dramatically frilled and vividly coloured blooms. Most tulips are suitable for containers, though it is best to avoid the taller types such as the Darwin hybrids and the May-flowering single tulips, as they can easily be damaged by wind. Tulips are best planted late in the season from mid-October to the end of November, as bulbs planted earlier tend to be more susceptible to disease. Good drainage is also particularly important for tulips for the same reason.

Propagation

Tulips can be propagated from seed and offsets. Seed is more difficult and only species come true using this method. Offsets procured at the base of the bulb can be separated and graded by size before replanting in August. Large offsets can be planted in their flowering position and may flower the folowing year. Smaller ones will take two or three years to bloom. All will come into flower quicker if fed fortnightly with a weak tomato feed throughout the growing season.

Troubleshooting

Planting at the correct time and ensuring adequate drainage can minimise the risk of potential problems. Tulip fire and grey mould are fungal diseases that show as grey blotches on the foliage and stunted growth; further inspection reveals rotting bulbs. Dig up and dispose of any infected plants. The same goes for virus diseases that show as streaked, mottled or distorted foliage. Tulip bulbs are often eaten by animal pests such as mice and pheasant.

Which variety?

The following groups are particularly suited to containers because of their compact habit. There are also many other, taller tulips that can be grown in large tubs, beds and borders.

EARLY DOUBLE TULIPS

This group has showy, double flowers in a range of brilliant colours, borne on sturdy stems 25-30cm (10-12in) in March and April. Varieties include:
'Electra' Deep cherry-red.
'Monte Carlo' Deep yellow.
'Peach Blossom' Deep rose-pink flowers flushed with yellow.
'Schoonoord' White blooms.
'Willemsoord' Red petals with distinctive white edges.

'Johann Strauss'

Dwarf 'Cape Cod' is ideal for containers

GREIGII HYBRIDS

These compact, sturdy plants have leaves that are attractive and boldly streaked. The flowers are borne on 20-25cm (8-10in) stems in April. Varieties include:
'Cape Cod' Orange-red striped with yellow.
'Oratorio' Deep pink flowers.
'Pinocchio' Red flowers with white edges to the petals.
'Red Riding Hood' Bright red.
'Toronto' Rose-pink and bearing two or three flower heads on each stem.

KAUFMANNIANA HYBRIDS

One of the earliest hybrids to flower, blooming from mid-March onwards. Most varieties have leaves that are attractively streaked and mottled with a darker colour. Some varieties have flowers of a more open shape which are sometimes described as 'waterlily' tulips. They range from 15-25cm (6-10in) in height. Varieties include:
'Chopin' Lemon yellow flowers with a black base.
'Fritz Kreisler' An unusual bicolour with flowers that are rose-pink inside with a yellow base.
'Johann Strauss' Creamy-yellow petals striped with red on the outside.
'Scarlet Baby' Deep red with a yellow throat.
'Shakespeare' Orange flowers.

Climbers for tubs

Although climbers generally do best in borders, a few are also ideal for growing in containers. With the wide range of pots and supports now available, it is easy to create a pillar of attractive flowers or foliage to make a superb patio feature, either on its own or as a centrepiece to a group of containers. Where there is no border soil at all, such as with a concrete or paved patio, growing climbers in containers is the only way to clothe bare walls with an eye-catching curtain of foliage. From a practical point of view, climbers can be used for screening to create privacy and to cover ugly walls, fences and other objects including drainpipes.

If you want to grow a fairly vigorous climber, such as ivy or the Chilean glory vine, then you will need a container at least 50cm (20in) in depth and diameter. Annual climbers will grow happily in a 25-cm (10-in) pot and most perennials should do well in a 45-cm (18-in) pot. If you choose a smaller container, your plant will require watering and feeding more regularly and the growth of the climber is likely to be restricted. If the container is to occupy a sunny position, opt for one made of wood, stone or concrete rather than plastic, because plastic tends to get too hot in summer and fails to provide enough root insulation during the winter. Be aware that terracotta containers can be prone to frost damage during the winter and will require a lot more watering at other times, unless you line the sides with polythene before planting – make sure you do not cover the drainage holes, however. Raising the tub on flat pebbles or purpose-made 'pot feet' should also help to improve drainage. Add a 5-cm (2-in) layer of crocks in the bottom of containers without drainage holes before planting.

Choosing the right compost is also important. Soil-based John Innes

Scented honeysuckle trained up trellis

brands are heavy and so provide much-needed stability. They also maintain their structure for longer than peat-based composts so are useful for permanent climbers. Multipurpose compost is ideal for raising annual climbers from seed. Even for acid-loving plants you would be better off using a good John Innes compost than a specially formulated ericaceous one.

There are several different ways to support container-grown climbers. Bamboo canes are cheapest of all, and they can be placed in a container and tied together to form a tripod or pyramid shape. Alternatively, tie the canes in a fan or trellis shape to your own design

using garden raffia or thin wire. There are a number of ready-made supports that can be purchased, varying from fan- and bell-shaped wooden trellis frames to those topped with attractive rounded finials or obelisks made of wrought iron or a similar material. There are even trellis supports that are specially designed to fit around a drainpipe. Remember, however, that free-standing climbers in pots may get top-heavy, especially in late spring after they have put on a new flush of growth. So it is important to match the size of container with the height of support and vigour of the climber, particularly on an exposed site.

Climbers against walls

Contrary to popular opinion, even vigorous climbers will not cause damage to sound walls. They can, in fact, act as an insulating layer which protects the wall against the elements. However, large, self-clinging plants, which include some ivies, climbing hydrangea and Virginia creeper, can cause problems if the mortar is loose or crumbly. These climbers are also unsuitable for pebble-dash walls as their weight can pull the rendering away from the brickwork.

In these situations, grow twining or other non-clinging types of climber on wires stretched on vine eyes, or on trellis panels. If the walls need regular painting, it is a good idea to hinge the trellis on to wooden battens fixed securely to the wall.

Many climbers can be grown in pots, though it is best to opt for those which are relatively compact in habit as vigorous plants can soon shoot up to leave a mass of unattractive, bare stems at the base. For high-profile positions around the house, choose some plants that will look good for a long period of time, such as those with evergreen or colourful foliage, or long-lasting flowers.

Variegated Hedera helix trained up a spiral frame

TIPS FOR SUCCESS

- *Select the largest container you can find. For vigorous climbers opt for one 50cm (20in) deep and wide, for herbaceous go for 45cm (18in) deep and wide and for annuals a pot at least 25cm (10in) deep and wide.*
- *Place 5cm (2in) of crocks in the bottom of containers without drainage holes.*
- *Use a soil-based John Innes No. 2 compost for stability.*
- *Match the support to the vigour of your climber and size of container.*

Clematis 'Niobe' with Fatshedera

Clematis, early summer

Shape and size

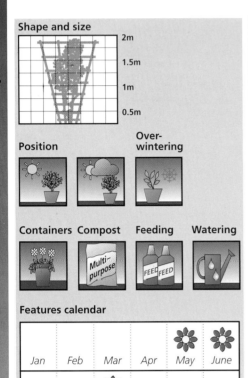

2m
1.5m
1m
0.5m

Position

Over-wintering

Containers Compost Feeding Watering

Features calendar

Jan	Feb	Mar	Apr	May	June
				✿	✿
July	Aug	Sept	Oct	Nov	Dec
		✿			

Buying tips *Spring and autumn are the best times to plant and there should be a wide selection of plants available. Select plants that are strong and well-branched. Clematis are grown in different-sized pots, and often there is little to choose between a well-grown plant in a smaller pot and a more expensive one in a larger pot. However, it is worth comparing specimens to be sure of getting the best plant.*

'Pink Champagne'

Growing guide

With masses of showy blooms in a range of jewel-like colours, large-flowered hybrid clematis are excellent for containers. However, they dislike exposed sites and hot roots. The optimum position is for their roots to be in the shade and their 'heads' in the sun. Place the clematis in an east- or west-facing site where it gets sun for only part of the day, avoiding the hottest temperatures. For clematis with pale and bicoloured flowers this is ideal as the colour can fade badly in full sun.

Pruning

After planting, prune back any weak or damaged stems to a strong pair of buds. Spread out the stems and tie them on to the support, spaced an even distance apart. Tie in the stems regularly as the plant grows or they can soon form a tangled mass of growth if left unattended. Annual pruning depends on when the plant flowers. Those that bloom early in the season do so on wood produced the previous year, and they are pruned by removing dead stems and cutting weak ones back to a strong pair of buds in late February or early March. If there is any vigorous growth that needs to be contained, cut it back in early summer after flowering. Plants that flower in early summer are also pruned in late February or early March in the same way as described above, though other shoots can also be shortened at the same time. With both types, hard prune a few of the older stems each year to encourage bushy growth to break from the base.

Propagation

Clematis can be propagated by cuttings or by layering. Take cuttings in late spring and early summer, selecting a healthy, non-flowering stem and cutting it into sections about 8cm (3in) long. Cut the stem just above a pair of leaf buds. Insert the cuttings into compost made up of a half-and-half mixture of potting compost and grit or horticultural vermiculite. Cover with polythene or a plastic cover and place the pot or tray in a warm place out of direct sunlight. In 4-6 weeks, when the cuttings have rooted, pot them up individually in 8-cm (3-in) pots.

Clematis are best layered in late spring to early summer. Select a strong, healthy shoot that can be bent down to the ground, and add a little sharp sand and potting compost to the soil underneath.

Troubleshooting
Clematis wilt

Large-flowered hybrids are most susceptible. Plants wilt but do not recover when watered. Cut back affected stems to ground level. Wilt-free shoots develop from buds below ground but may take up to six months or even more. Plant clematis 15cm (6in) deeper than in their container to improve chances of recovery if new plants are affected. It is worth remembering, however, that healthy plants are much more resistant to attack, so make sure the plant has a regular supply of water and fertiliser to keep it growing at a healthy rate.

Slugs and snails often attack the soft new shoots as they emerge from the ground. Put down slug bait, or surround the stems with a cut-down plastic bottle. Earwigs can chew holes in the foliage. Trap them each night in pots containing straw, or balls of screwed-up newspaper, and destroy them each morning.

Which variety?

Large-flowered hybrids that bloom in early to mid-summer are ideal for containers as they are reasonably compact in habit, while those hybrids that bloom later in the year tend to be more vigorous. The following hybrids are particularly compact yet free-flowering, blooming in early summer and often producing a second, smaller flush of flowers in early autumn. If you are growing a double-flowered variety, bear in mind that it is not unusual for single blooms to be produced during the first year and in the latter part of the season.

'Arctic Queen' Double, pure white flowers with golden stamens.
'Asao' Deep pink.
'Beauty of Worcester' Double, deep blue flowers.
'Carnaby' Deep pink flowers with a

'Dawn'

darker central bar, blooms in May and June with a second flush in September. Does best in light shade.
'Daniel Deronda' Semi-double blooms that open deep purple and gradually fade to blue-mauve. Flowers June to October. Does well in sun or shade.
'Dawn' Soft pearly-pink flowers.
'Fireworks' Vividly coloured flowers, purple-blue at the edges with a dark red stripe to each petal. Flowers May to June and again in September. Does well in sun or shade.
'Lasurstern' Rich, lavender-blue flowers in May and June with a second flush in September. Does well in sun or light shade.
'Miss Bateman' Creamy white blooms with contrasting chocolate-brown stamens; flowers in May and June with a second flush in September. Does best in sun or light shade.
'Pink Champagne' Cerise-pink flowers in May and June with a second flush in September. Flowers fade in sun so grow in light shade.
'Silver Moon' Unusual, pale mauve blooms.
'Sunset' Vivid red with a purple edge to the flowers.
'Vyvyan Pennell' Rosette-shaped double, violet-blue flowers appear in May and June with a second flush in September. Does well in sun or shade and will withstand exposed positions, but slightly more rampant than others listed.

The vivid flowers of 'Fireworks'

Clematis, species

Shape and size

2m
1.5m
1m
0.5m

Position

Over-wintering

Containers Compost Watering Feeding

John Innes

FEED FEED

Features calendar

Jan	Feb	Mar	Apr ✿	May ✿	June
July	Aug	Sept	Oct	Nov	Dec

Buying tips *In addition to the species and hybrids listed opposite, a wider range is available from specialist nurseries.*

Clematis macropetala in close-up and showing nodding habit of the blooms

Clematis alpina 'Pamela Jackman'

Growing guide

Species clematis bear flowers that are smaller and less flamboyant than those of the large-flowered hybrids, but they more than make up for it with their greater profusion and longevity. Attractive, feathery seed heads are produced after the flowers. These clematis are more tolerant of adverse conditions than the hybrids, making them better suited for container growing. There are also many attractive hybrids of the species. However, for permanent container plants choose between *Clematis alpina* and *C. macropetala*, which will grow in containers for many years. Other species, such as *C. montana* and *C. tangutica*, which are more vigorous, can be grown in a container for several years, but will eventually need to be planted out in a site in the border.

Propagation

Species clematis can be raised from seed, though it is necessary to propagate named hybrids by layering (see 'Clematis, early summer' page 140). Collect seed heads and separate the seeds from any debris. Prepare a tray of potting compost mixed half and half with sharp sand or horticultural vermiculite, water it first and allow the water to drain, then sow the seed thinly on the surface. Cover the seed with a thin layer of the same mixture. A cold period is needed in order for the seed to

Clematis alpina 'Willy'

Clematis macropetala blooms from April

germinate, so the tray can go in a cold frame or in a sheltered spot outside for the winter. In spring, pot the seedlings up individually into small pots.

Troubleshooting
Generally trouble-free.

Which variety?

C. alpina and *C. macropetala* are usually the first clematis to bloom in spring, flowering during April and May. Their fresh green leaves appear early in the season too, and look almost too delicate to withstand the

harsh weather. This foliage makes an excellent background to the small, nodding, pale blue flowers. In addition to the species, there are a number of different varieties. They are all quite tough plants, growing 1.8-2.4m (6-8ft) tall. Avoid pink forms in a sunny spot as the flowers will fade badly. Those marked * are the varieties you are most likely to find at garden centres.

C. ALPINA VARIETIES

'Frances Rivis'* Mid-blue flowers with contrasting white stamens. Flowers slightly larger than the

species.
'Pamela Jackman' Slightly darker blue flowers than the species.
'Ruby'* Red flowers with white stamens.
'White Columbine' Pure white flowers.
'Willy'* Pale-pink blooms.

C. MACROPETALA VARIETIES

'Blue Bird' Mauve-blue flowers, similar to those of the species but larger.
'Maidwell Hall' Deep blue.
'Markham's Pink'* Mid-pink.
'White Moth' Pure white.

Eccremocarpus scaber

Shape and size

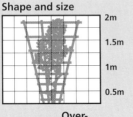

2m
1.5m
1m
0.5m

Position

Over-wintering

Treat as Annual

Containers

Compost

Multi-purpose

Watering

Feeding

FEED

Features calendar

Jan	Feb	Mar	Apr	May	June
✿	✿	✿			
July	Aug	Sept	Oct	Nov	Dec

Buying tips *It is more economical to raise from seed than buy mature plants.*

Eccremocarpus scaber flowers from mid-summer onwards

Plants can be trained on sticks

Growing guide

This fast-growing plant is easy and quick to raise from seed and it can be treated as an annual if desired, flowering well in its first year. It scrambles up by means of tendrils, rapidly covering its support with mid-green, finely lobed leaves, and it does best on a support of mesh or fine trellis. In warmer areas this plant can be evergreen, but it tends to die back to the ground and regrows in spring if hard frosts occur. From mid-summer, stems of exotic, tubular, brightly coloured flowers are borne in quantity (they are usually orange but red and yellow forms are available too). This plant needs full sun in order to flower well. Height 1.8m (6ft).

Propagation

Sow seed in February or early March at 13-16°C (55–60° F). Seed needs light to germinate. Pot seedlings individually in small pots and harden off before planting out in early summer.

Troubleshooting

Generally trouble-free.

Which variety?

There is only one species.

Hedera helix

Ivy

Shape and size

2m
1.5m
1m
0.5m

Position

Over-wintering

Containers

Compost   Watering   Feeding

Multi-purpose

FEED FEED

Features calendar

Jan	Feb	Mar	Apr	May	June
July	Aug	Sept	Oct	Nov	Dec

Buying tips *In spring, named varieties of ivies are sometimes sold in small pots, which is an economical way to buy them.*

Ivies scramble over wooden barrels

Variegated ivies can make attractive specimens

Growing guide

An excellent and useful garden plant which comes in many superb varieties with glossy, handsomely variegated or attractively shaped foliage. Ivies are evergreen and grow almost anywhere, in conditions varying from full sun to total shade, as well as being tolerant of poor soil. They are invaluable for year-round interest. Ivies are self-clinging by means of aerial roots, which is an advantage in most cases, though it is advisable to avoid planting next to old walls where the mortar may be starting to crumble, because the ivy will root into it and speed up the process of deterioration. Keep ivy trimmed away from window frames and any other painted wood, as the aerial roots are liable to cling to and damage the paintwork. Ivies are also excellent trailing and ground-cover plants as well as climbers. Prune if necessary in late winter or early spring, and again in late summer to contain any vigorous growth.

Propagation

Take cuttings from shoot tips in July and August. Ivy often layers itself where the shoots touch the soil, and well-rooted shoots can be detached and potted up individually.

Troubleshooting

Variegated or coloured varieties may revert and start to produce shoots with plain green leaves. These should be pruned out immediately as they will be more vigorous than the variegated shoots.

Which variety?

The best species for containers is the small-leaved *Hedera helix*, and there are numerous varieties. As a general rule of thumb, the more green a variety has in its leaves, the quicker it will grow. Those with leaves that are completely green are the fastest-growing. The following is a selection of those which are generally available.

'Adam' Small leaves which are neatly variegated with cream.

'Buttercup' Attractive, bright lime-yellow, but in shade it turns green, and in full sun in mid-summer the leaves can scorch . This variety is slow-growing.

'Glacier' Greyish-green leaves marked with white.

'Goldchild' Grey-green leaves margined with creamy-yellow.

'Goldheart' Leaves splashed with yellow.

'Green Ripple' Small, dark green, jagged-edged leaves.

'Ivalace' Light green with crinkled leaf edges.

'Kolibri' Dark green leaves which are boldly streaked and blotched with creamy-white.

'Little Diamond' Compact habit, green leaves that are mottled with grey and edged with creamy-white.

'Luzii' Yellow marbled with green.

'Marginata Major' Small, greyish-green, slightly lobed leaves which are edged with cream.

'Parsley Crested' (also known as **'Cristata'**) Green, rounded leaves that are crinkled at the edges.

'Sagittifolia' Neat habit, five-lobed dark green leaves.

Ipomoea

Shape and size

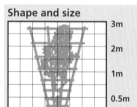

3m

2m

1m

0.5m

Position

Over-wintering

Treat as Annual

Compost

Multi-purpose

Containers

Watering

Feeding

FEEL FEED

Features calendar

Jan	Feb	Mar	Apr	May	June
July	Aug	Sept	Oct	Nov	Dec

Buying tips *It is best to raise your own plants from seed as ready-grown ones are rarely available. Some seed catalogues offer some lesser-known species in addition to those opposite.*

Ipomoea 'Heavenly Blue'

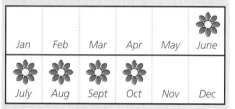

Ipomoea versicolor

Growing guide

Ipomoeas are supremely beautiful and exotic plants which are fairly easy to raise from seed. They are quick to grow once established and rapidly form a mass of green foliage that makes a good background for the brightly coloured flowers that are borne continuously from early to late summer. Ipomoeas need a sunny, sheltered spot in order to thrive, and they do particularly well in hot summers provided they are planted in rich, well-drained soil and have plenty of water and feed. Height 2.4–3m (8–10ft).

Propagation

Sow seed in March or April. Soak seeds for 24 hours in lukewarm water first, then sow at 18°C (65°F).

Troubleshooting

Whitened young foliage is caused by low night temperatures. Aphids and spider mite can be a problem, particularly on young plants. Treat aphids with a general insecticide and spider mite with a systemic one.

Which variety?

I. alba (moon flower) Produces large, fragrant, saucer-shaped flowers up to 10-15cm (4-6in) across. The flowers open in the evening and close up in the morning.

I. rubrocaerulea 'Heavenly Blue' (also known as **Convolvulus tricolor** 'Heavenly Blue') Huge, saucer-shaped blooms, up to 13cm (5in) across, that are a deep and exquisite sky-blue with a white centre. The individual flowers last for less than a day, opening early in the morning and closing by afternoon or evening, but they are borne in such profusion as to ensure a near-continuous supply. White and red-flowered forms are also available.

I. versicolor (also known as **Mina lobata**) Bears many small, tubular flowers on short stems. At first the flowers are crimson and then gradually age to shades of yellow, so at any time a stem of flowers can be an attractive mixture of colours.

I. quamoclit (also known as **Quamoclit lobata** or cypress vine) An annual with finely cut leaves and and narrow tubular red or orange flowers

WARNING

The seed of this plant is poisonous

Jasminum officinale

Shape and size

2m
1.5m
1m
0.5m

Position

Over-wintering

Containers
Compost
Watering
Feeding

Features calendar

Jan	Feb	Mar	Apr	May	June
❀	❀	❀	❀		
July	Aug	Sept	Oct	Nov	Dec

Buying tips *Jasmines are generally easy to obtain. Autumn or early spring are the best times to plant.*

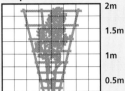

Close-up of flower

Jasminum officinale brightens up a shady corner

Growing guide

This vigorous, deciduous climber has deliciously fragrant flowers, the scent of which is often strongest in the evening. Long, twining stems are covered with dark green, pinnate leaves that make an excellent background for the clusters of white flowers which are borne from early summer through until autumn. This species is happy in sun or shade, though flowers tend to be more freely produced in a sunny site.

In addition to the green-leaved species there are several varieties with variegated or coloured foliage, and their leaves colour best if given a reasonable amount of sun. These varieties also produce flowers, though not as freely as the species. Prune in late winter by thinning out entire branches; do not shorten them as this encourages lots of thin, bushy shoots to be produced.

Propagation

Shoots often layer themselves where they touch the ground, and these layers can be detached and potted up individually. Semi-ripe cuttings can be taken in July and August.

Troubleshooting

Generally trouble-free.

Which variety?

Jasminum officinale Dark green leaves and white, strongly scented flowers.
J. officinale affine Its scented flowers are slightly larger than the species and tinged with pink.
'Argenteovariegatum' Green leaves that are attractively edged with white. White, strongly scented flowers.
'Aureum' Green leaves are blotched with yellow. White, strongly scented flowers.
'Fiona Sunrise' Attractive new variety with leaves that are completely suffused with gold.

Lathyrus odoratus

Shape and size

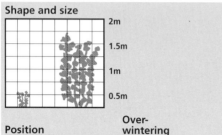

2m
1.5m
1m
0.5m

Position

Over-wintering

Treat as Annual

Containers

Compost

Multi-purpose

Watering

Feeding

FEED FEED FEED

Features calendar

Jan	Feb	Mar	Apr	May	June
July	Aug	Sept	Oct	Nov	Dec

Buying tips *If buying young plants, they should be short, bushy and with plenty of healthy green foliage. Avoid thin, straggly plants.*

'Knee High'

Old-fashioned sweet peas are highly scented

Growing guide

An old, much-loved garden favourite which is easy to grow and produces many stems of blooms in a wide range of colours. The flowers usually have a delicious fragrance, though some varieties are more scented than others. They make excellent cut flowers, and need regular deadheading to encourage continuous flowering through the summer. Sweet peas climb by means of tendrils, so they can be supported with mesh, netting or twiggy sticks. They love a cool, deep root run and prefer a large, deep container with plenty of good compost. Feed weekly with liquid fertiliser and do not allow plants to go short of water.

Propagation

Seed can be sown in September or March at 15°C (60°F). The seedlings are deep-rooting and benefit from being sown individually in long tubes. Autumn-sown seedlings produce plants that are particularly sturdy and which flower early. Pinch out the growing tips when plants are 10cm (4in) high to encourage bushy growth. Harden off before planting outside in April or early May. Autumn-sown plants benefit from cloche protection in cold areas.

Troubleshooting

Thrips can cause flecking and silvering of the leaves; control with a systemic insecticide as soon as symptoms are noticed. Aphids can be a problem on young shoots in particular; treat with an aphid-specific insecticide to avoid harming pollinating insects. Foot rot and root rot can cause plants to yellow, wither and collapse; dig up and destroy affected plants. Small, dark, pollen beetles often infest the flowers, and although they rarely cause damage they are a nuisance if cut flowers are taken into the house. Put cut stems in a shed or garage with a window for an hour or so, and the beetles will leave the flowers in search of light.

Which variety?

There is a huge range of varieties listed in seed catalogues. For showy flowers, look for the **'Spencer'** and **'Giant Waved'** varieties. Many of these are scented but not all. For the most fragrance, choose the smaller-flowered, old-fashioned varieties such as **'Antique Mixed'** or **'Painted Lady'**. Most sweet peas are climbers that grow to around 1.8m (6ft), though there are also several semi-dwarf and dwarf varieties that can be grown in containers. For example, **'Bijou Mixed'** is widely available and at only 45cm (18in) high is ideal for window-boxes and containers.

Rhodochiton atrosanguineus

Shape and size

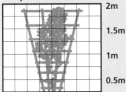

2m
1.5m
1m
0.5m

Position

Over-wintering

5°c

Treat as Annual

Containers

Compost

Multi-purpose

Watering

Feeding
FEED FEED

Features calendar

Jan	Feb	Mar	Apr	May	June
✿	✿	✿	✿		
July	Aug	Sept	Oct	Nov	Dec

Buying tips *Mature plants are sometimes available, particularly in early to mid-summer, though they can be expensive. Raising plants from seed can be a better proposition.*

Rhodochiton looks stunning when allowed to trail from a large pot

Close-up of the extraordinary flowers

Growing guide

This quick-growing plant has particularly unusual flowers that are borne in profusion throughout the summer. They are of such a dark shade of purple as to appear almost black, with a dark 'ruff' at the base and a long, tubular corolla. Heart-shaped green leaves make an attractive background to the flowers. The slender stems climb by means of their twining leaf stalks. This plant thrives in a sunny, sheltered spot, and it can be perennial if overwintered in a frost-free place. Height 1.8m (6ft).

Propagation
Sow seed in March at 16°C (60°F).

Troubleshooting
Generally trouble-free.

Which variety?

There is only one species.

Thunbergia alata

Shape and size

1.2m
1m
.75m
0.5m

Position

Over-wintering

 Treat as Annual

Containers

Compost   Watering   Feeding

Multi-purpose   FEED FEED

Features calendar

Jan	Feb	Mar	Apr	May	June
🌼	🌼	🌼	🌼		
July	Aug	Sept	Oct	Nov	Dec

Buying tips *Plants can be found on sale in early summer, though they quickly go past their best. Make sure plants are healthy and disease-free before buying.*

The distinctive blooms of Black-eyed Susan

Annual climber T. alata looks equally good trailing over a container

Growing guide

A compact climber with heart-shaped green leaves which bears many brightly coloured flowers through summer. It prefers a sheltered site in sun, though a little light shade can be beneficial in the height of summer. This plant can be grown either as a climber, where it grows to around 1.2m (4ft), or as a trailing plant in a hanging basket.

Propagation

Sow seed in February or March at 20°C (68°F).

Troubleshooting

This plant is susceptible to spider mite. Inspect the leaves regularly and treat with a systemic insecticide or, if growing under cover, use a biological control.

Which variety?

There is only one species, though seed is often sold as a mixture that gives flower colours varying from deep orange-yellow to white, either pure colours or with a distinctive black eye.

Tropaeolum

Shape and size

3m
2m
1m
0.5m

Position **Over-wintering** **Containers**

Treat as Annual

Compost **Watering** **Feeding**

John Innes

FEED

Features calendar

Jan	Feb	Mar	Apr	May	June
					✲
✲	✲	✲	✲		
July	Aug	Sept	Oct	Nov	Dec

Buying tips *Tropaeolum species and varieties are readily available as seed.*

Tropaeolum major 'Climbing Mixed'

Tropaeolum peregrinum (canary creeper)

Growing guide

There are two main climbing species of Tropaeolum, both of which are quick and easy to grow. The popular nasturtium (*T. majus*) is the easiest annual of all to grow. Within just a few weeks of pushing the seeds into the soil, they produce long, rambling stems and masses of bright flowers in glowing shades of red, orange and yellow. An added bonus is that both leaves and flowers are edible; add the leaves to a salad to give a peppery, spicy flavour and scatter the flowers on top for a colourful decoration. The young seeds can be used as substitutes for capers. The other species, less well known but still popular, is *T. peregrinum* (canary creeper). They both climb by means of winding their leaf stalks around their support, and are excellent for quickly concealing ugly objects such as chain-link fencing or an oil tank. Both these plants will often self-seed readily. They thrive in full sun.

Propagation

Sow seed directly into the container in April. If early-flowering plants are desired, sow seed under cover in March, pot on as necessary and harden off before planting out in April-May.

Troubleshooting

Black fly and caterpillars can be a problem but they are easily controlled with a ready-to-use spray containing pyrethrum.

Which variety?

T. majus (nasturtium) has mid-green, rounded leaves that are wavy at the edges and give off a pungent smell when crushed. The brightly coloured flowers are borne from early summer until the first frosts. Seed is available as a mixture with flower colours including scarlet, orange, yellow and cream. **'Jewel of Africa'** has leaves that are streaked and marbled with cream. Nasturtiums flower best on a fairly poor soil as a fertile one will encourage leaf growth at the expense of flowers. Height up to 2.4m (8ft).

T. peregrinum (canary creeper) quickly develops long, scrambling stems clothed with five-lobed, fresh green leaves, and from mid-summer to autumn it bears many small, bright yellow flowers that are prettily fringed at the edges. It prefers a site in full sun, though it will tolerate shade, and a reasonably fertile soil. Height 3m (10ft).

Roses round the patio

Modern developments in rose breeding have resulted in a considerable selection of roses that are suitable for containers. Whereas once the choice was confined to a few miniature bush roses, we can now choose from a substantial range of miniatures, dwarf floribunda and ground-cover roses for containers, window-boxes and even hanging baskets. There are also miniature standard roses for tubs, and several dwarf climbing roses that will thrive in containers.

Because of their thorny stems, roses need to be sited with care on the patio. The spreading, ground-cover types in particular can easily snag the legs of unwary passers-by, so it is best to place any with trailing stems well out of the way. All roses need full sun, and a reasonable amount of shelter will help ensure the blooms stay in good condition. As with all flowering plants, roses benefit from regular deadheading, both to keep the bush looking tidy and to encourage the production of more blooms. They do best in a soil-based compost and should be top-dressed every spring with fresh potting compost and controlled-release fertiliser (see page 16-17).

'Gentle Touch' – a pale pink dwarf floribunda

The miniature 'Little Buckaroo'

Propagation

Roses can be propagated by cuttings, 23–30cm (9–12in) long, taken in August or September. Remove all the leaves apart from the top few, and place the cuttings in a slit-trench 15–20cm (6–8in) deep in a sheltered spot outside. The base of the trench can be lined with about 2.5cm (1in) of sharp sand to improve drainage and rooting. Water well and leave in place until the following autumn, when the cuttings should be well rooted and ready to pot up. Miniature varieties can be raised from 5–10cm (2–4in) heel cuttings taken from mid-summer to autumn, and rooted in a cold frame.

Troubleshooting

It is important to feed and water roses grown in containers regularly as plants under stress through lack of water are more susceptible to attack by several different pests and diseases.

Blackspot develops as conspicuous black blotches on the leaves, often causing yellowing and early leaf fall. Once an attack is established it is hard to eradicate. The disease overwinters on infected plant

'Top Marks' – a miniature standard

'Pink Sunblaze' – a miniature rose

'Flower Carpet' – a ground-cover variety

'Suffolk' – a ground-cover rose

material, so clear up and bin all fallen leaves. The following spring, begin preventative spraying with fungicide.

Powdery mildew appears on the leaves as white blotches that spread rapidly, often to stems and buds as well. Leaves become crinkled and yellowed and can fall early. Clear up and burn infected leaves, prune out infected stems and buds, and spray with a fungicide to limit further spread of the disease.

Rust appears as raised orange spots on the stems and leaves, starting on the underside. Control and prevention similar to blackspot.

Aphids tend to infest young stems, buds and leaves. They can be controlled with an insecticide; those containing pirimicarb are designed to kill only aphids.

Leaf-rolling sawfly lays its eggs in the leaves during late spring and early summer, causing them to roll up until they resemble small green cigars. Small amounts of infected leaves can be picked off by hand, preferably as soon as possible. Larger infestations can be treated with a systemic insecticide.

Miniature and dwarf floribunda

Shape and size

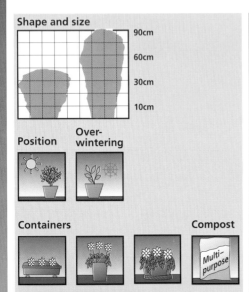

90cm
60cm
30cm
10cm

Position

Over-wintering

Containers

Compost

Multi-purpose

Watering

Feeding

FEED FEED FEED

Features calendar

Jan	Feb	Mar	Apr	May	June
					✿
✿	✿	✿	✿		
July	Aug	Sept	Oct	Nov	Dec

The multicolour blooms of 'Baby Masquerade'

The vivid blooms of 'Orange Sunblaze'

MINIATURE AND DWARF FLORIBUNDA

Although these two groups of roses are distinctly different in appearance, they are often grouped together and sold under the single banner of 'patio' roses. Both groups are ideal for containers, being rounded and neat in habit.

Pruning is best done in late winter or early spring by cutting out any dead or damaged wood, cutting weak stems hard back and shortening other stems by about one-third.

Miniatures

Smallest of all the bush roses, miniature varieties grow to around 45cm (18in) high and bear many tiny flowers that are about 2.5cm (1in) across. Several varieties are available, and the following is just a selection of the most popular ones:

'Baby Masquerade' Mixture of red, yellow and orange.
'Bobalink' Rose red.
'Colibri' Golden apricot flushed with reddish-pink.
'Easter Morning' Ivory white.
'Little Buckaroo' Red flowers with a white centre.
'Orange Sunblaze' Orange and scarlet flowers.
'Pink Sunblaze' Salmon pink.
'Pour Toi' White with creamy tints.
'Yellow Doll' Bright yellow flowers.

Miniature standards

Shape and size

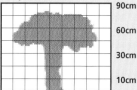

90cm
60cm
30cm
10cm

Position

Over-wintering

Containers

Compost

Multi-purpose

Watering

Feeding

Features calendar

Jan	Feb	Mar	Apr	May	June
					✸
July	Aug	Sept	Oct	Nov	Dec
✸	✸	✸	✸		

'Sweet Magic' – a dwarf floribunda often sold as a standard

'Sweet Dreams' – a miniature standard

Dwarf floribunda

These neat, compact bushes reach a height of 45–90cm (18–36in) and bear flowers that are 5–8cm (2–3in) across. As with miniatures, there is a wide range of varieties available and new ones are being introduced every year.

'Anna Ford' Clear, orange-red blooms.
'Cider Cup' Deep apricot.
'Crystal Palace' Creamy-peach flowers.
'Gentle Touch' Pale pink.
'Honey Bunch' Golden yellow.

MINIATURE STANDARDS

Miniature standards are varieties of the miniature and dwarf floribunda described above, which are budded on short stems about 75cm (30in) high. They have considerable potential for use in large containers such as wooden half-barrels, where the bushy head of the standard creates some instant height on the patio, and the rose can be under-planted with a selection of bushy and trailing plants to give a spectacular display. Prune as described above, and rub out any suckers produced on the main stem under the knobbly graft union as soon as they appear. The following varieties are all commonly grown as miniature standards.

'Festival' Large, crimson-scarlet blooms with petals that are silver on the reverse.
'Little Bo-Peep' Rose-pink flowers fading to pale pink.
'Perestroika' Bright yellow.
'Queen Mother' Soft pink.
'Robin Redbreast' Red blooms with a contrasting white eye.
'Sweet Dreams' Peachy-apricot flowers.
'Sweet Magic' Orange tinted with gold.
'Top Marks' Small, double, bright vermillion-red flowers.

Ground-cover roses

Shape and size

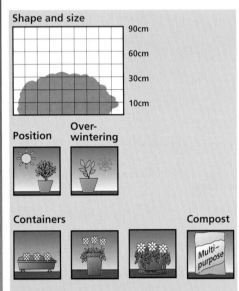

90cm
60cm
30cm
10cm

Position

Over-wintering

Containers

Compost
Multi-purpose

Watering

Feeding
FEED FEED FEED

Features calendar

Jan	Feb	Mar	Apr	May	June
					✿
✿	✿	✿	✿		
July	Aug	Sept	Oct	Nov	Dec

'Hampshire' – a useful and colourful ground-cover rose

'Nozomi' – a pink ground-cover grown here as a standard with red miniature 'Anne Ford' in the foreground

'The Fairy' – an old, sprawling ground-cover variety

GROUND-COVER ROSES

Most ground-cover roses were introduced comparatively recently, and the compact varieties do particularly well in containers, where they form a spreading bush around 30–60cm (12–24in) high and wide. Many have been bred to produce repeated flushes of flowers from June to October, as well as being selected for other attributes such as resistance to disease. Little pruning is required; in late winter or early spring, remove any dead or damaged shoots, and cut back branches if necessary to contain growth.

The **'County'** series of ground-cover roses are named after the counties of England:

'Avon' Double white flowers that are blush-pink in bud.

'Hampshire' Single scarlet blooms with contrasting golden stamens.

'Norfolk' Bright yellow, fragrant, double flowers.

'Suffolk' Bright crimson flowers with contrasting golden stamens.

'Warwickshire' Single, rose-red blooms with a prominent white eye.

'The Fairy' Small, double, pale pink blooms in large clusters.

'Flower Carpet' Dusters of double, bright pink flowers. Excellent disease resistance.

'Nozomi' Single, pale, pearly pink flowers for a period of about two months in early summer.

'Snow Carpet' Double, pure white flowers against fern-like foliage.

Miniature climbing roses

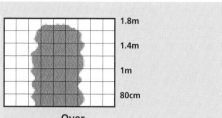

Position

Over-wintering

Containers

Compost
Multi-purpose

Watering

Feeding

Features calendar

Jan	Feb	Mar	Apr	May	June
					✿
✿	✿	✿	✿		
July	Aug	Sept	Oct	Nov	Dec

'Laura Ford' blooms through June and July

Tie climbing roses firmly to their support

MINIATURE CLIMBING ROSES

Until recently there were no climbing roses that could sensibly be grown in containers, because they have deep root systems that are too large to be accommodated in a container for any length of time. However, a few years ago the first varieties of a new breed of miniature climbing roses were introduced. These new climbers grow to around 1.8m (6ft) in height and bear many clusters of flowers which, although smaller than those of traditional climbing roses, still give a very effective and colourful display.

Prune in late winter or early spring by removing dead and damaged shoots and trim side shoots back to 5–8cm (2–3in). Tie shoots firmly to their support to avoid wind damage.

'Laura Ford' Amber-yellow flowers.
'Little Rambler' Blush pink.
'Nice Day' Pale salmon-pink.
'Rosalie Coral' Orange-yellow blooms.
'Warm Welcome' Bright orange.

Shrubs for permanent containers

Shrubs are invaluable for providing a permanent framework of foliage on the patio. A number of fully hardy shrubs with evergreen foliage can lend interest through the winter months when there is little else to look at. A good proportion of the evergreens detailed in this section have been chosen for their attractively shaped, coloured or variegated foliage, so they not only provide extra colour during winter, but in summer they make a foil for the many seasonal plants with bright flowers.

Tender shrubs are ideal for a ready-made summer display. Although they need winter protection in a greenhouse or conservatory, they can be moved outside in late spring to create an instant display. Some of these tender shrubs such as lantana and mimulus are often to be found on sale alongside tender perennials, under the overall banner of 'patio plants'.

Only a little care is needed to keep shrubs in good condition from one year to the next. If the plant has become potbound, it will benefit from being potted on in spring. When this becomes impractical, give the plants a top-dressing of fresh potting compost and controlled-release fertiliser (see page 16-17). Some sup-

Pinus mugo 'Pumilio' is a tough, drought-resistant dwarf pine

plementary feeding later in summer is beneficial in the case of tender plants and those that will be overwintered under cover. Shrubs that will remain outside through winter should not be given nitrogen-rich fertiliser after mid-summer as it encourages soft growth that can be damaged by frost.

Watering

Regular watering is vital for container shrubs. Most will require watering daily in warm weather during spring and summer. Soak the whole rootball thoroughly each time, until water runs out through the drainage holes. Use tap water or rainwater for most shrubs, but try to collect rainwater for use on lime-hating shrubs.

Alternatively, put a teabag in a watering can filled with water and allow it to stand for 24 hours before sprinkling over the plants.

In winter, reduce watering to once a fortnight – it is important not to stop altogether, especially with evergreens.

Phormium 'Yellow Wave' creates a focal point

Success with shrubs in containers

- Buy container-grown plants as they will have already developed the, fibrous root systems needed for life in a container.

- Check the root system by tipping the rootball out of its pot. Avoid plants which have just been potted up or are likely to be potbound, and those with masses of roots.

- Before planting, tease out the roots a little from the base. Cut off roots that curl around the bottom of the rootball.

- Where several shrubs are combined, plant the one with the largest rootball first and add a little compost before positioning the next largest rootball. Repeat until the whole container is planted up.

- After all the shrubs are planted, level the compost, leaving a gap of 2.5-5cm (1-2in) below the rim to allow for easy watering.

- Mulch with a layer of gravel or chipped bark to set off the foliage and help retain moisture.

- Turn the container regularly (at least once a fortnight) to keep growth balanced, unless the display is designed to be viewed from one side only.

Viburnum tinus 'Eve Price' provides winter and spring blooms

Abutilon

Shape and size

- 1.8m
- 1.2m
- 60cm
- 20cm

Position

Over-wintering
 7°c

Containers

Compost

John Innes

Watering

Feeding

FEED FEED

Features calendar

Jan	Feb	Mar	Apr	May	June
					✿
July	Aug	Sept	Oct	Nov	Dec
✿	✿	✿	✿		

Buying tips *Although garden centres should stock a limited range of species and hybrids, it is usually necessary to go to a specialist supplier for a comprehensive selection. The best time to find abutilons in garden centres is early to mid-summer.*

'Souvenir de Bonn'

Growing guide

These tall, slender plants make ideal centrepieces for large containers, and they are also excellent for a cool conservatory. They have large, attractive leaves which in some cases are brightly variegated or edged with yellow or white, and bear many vividly coloured flowers throughout summer. The blooms are either bell-shaped or, in the case of a few species and hybrids, they are longer and more slender, forming a lantern-shape. Abutilons prefer a sunny, sheltered spot, though they can still flower freely in light shade providing the site is sheltered. They produce their blooms over a long period from early to late summer. Plants are generally sturdy and self-supporting, though later in the summer they may need a little additional support from bamboo canes. In autumn, move outdoor plants under cover, preferably to a frost-free environment. In mild areas, abutilons can survive outdoors all year. Overwintered mature plants can be pruned in March by cutting back main stems by half and lateral shoots to 10-15cm (4-6in). Pot on at the same time if necessary.

Propagation

Take half-ripe cuttings from early to late summer. Plants can also be raised from seed, though named hybrids do not come true from seed.

Troubleshooting

Scale insects and mealy bugs can be a problem. Treat with a systemic insecticide, or control small infestations by hand-cleaning with cotton wool buds dipped in methylated spirits.

Which variety?

There are a number of hybrids and species available. They can grow up to 1.8m (6ft) high, but in the restricted environment of a container they generally grow to 0.9-1.2m (3-4ft).

Abutilon megapotamicum

'Boule de Neige' Pure white flowers show up well against dark green foliage and greeny-black stems.

'Canary Bird' Clear yellow flowers and fresh green foliage.

'Cannington Carol' Small red flowers contrast well with its yellow-variegated leaves.

'Cannington Peter' Crimson flowers and yellow-variegated foliage.

'Hinton Seedling' Clear orange flowers among soft green foliage.

'Kentish Belle' Long, bell-shaped flowers with apricot petals and a red base. The petals can be faintly veined with red.

A. megapotamicum Lantern-shaped flowers with crinkled petals that are red with a yellow base.

***A. megapotamicum* 'Variegatum'** Green leaves heavily mottled with yellow.

***A. x milleri* 'Variegatum'** Apricot flowers that have a brown base, and yellow variegated leaves.

'Nabob' Flowers are an unusual shade of dark maroon, with stems that are almost black and dark-green foliage.

'Patrick Synge' Rusty orange, lantern-shaped flowers shaded with maroon.

'Souvenir de Bonn' Orange flowers and large green leaves broadly margined with white.

Acer palmatum

Shape and size

1.8m
1.2cm
60cm
20cm

Position

Over-wintering

Containers

Compost

Multi-purpose

Watering

Feeding

FEED FEED

Features calendar

Jan	Feb	Mar	Apr	May	June
July	Aug	Sept	Oct	Nov	Dec

Buying tips *Because there is so much individual variation in foliage shapes and colours, it is best to wait until plants are in leaf before buying.*

Acer palmatum 'Dissectum'

Growing guide

Japanese maples are grown for their attractive, lobed leaves, which come in an enormous range of shapes and colours. They can be divided into two groups; the *Acer palmatum* 'Dissectum' varieties that form a low, mushroom-shaped mound, and other *A. palmatum* varieties that have an upright habit.

Japanese maples are deciduous, and their leaves usually develop many different colourful tints before they fall in autumn. Even afterwards, the bare skeleton of the plant has an attractive shape through the winter. These slow-growing plants are ideal for providing long-lasting impact for a site in partial shade, though they do need a sheltered location which is protected from cold winds, and also one which does not get the early morning sun in spring as this, coupled with a late frost, may damage the newly emerging, delicate leaves. No pruning is required.

Propagation

Plants can be raised from seed sown in autumn in a cold frame, though named hybrids do not come true from seed.

Troubleshooting

Generally trouble-free, provided care is taken to site the plant correctly. Watch out for aphids on new leaves. Treat with an insecticide if seen. Check for coral spot, which appears as pink or orange pustules, and prune out back to healthy wood. Foliage can easily become brown and scorched if exposed to strong wind or full sun, or if the plant goes short of water.

Which variety?

There are numerous named varieties, and the following is a small selection of the most popular:
**Acer palmatum* varieties:
'Atropurpureum' Leaves are bronze-red through spring and summer, turning to brilliant red in autumn. Leaf colour can vary.

A. palmatum 'Dissectum Atropurpureum'

'Bloodgood' An excellent, coloured form with deep reddish-purple foliage that turns bright red in autumn.
'Butterfly' Small, deeply cut leaves that are pale-green edged with cream and tinged with pink when young.
'Linearilobum' Leaves are deeply cut, giving a light and elegant effect.
'Osakazuki' Superb for autumn colour, its lobed green leaves change to fiery scarlet before falling.
'Sango-kaku' (also known as 'Senkaki') The coral bark maple, so called because its young shoots are a bright coral-red which provide excellent winter colour.
'Seiryû' Finely dissected leaves are green tinged with red when young, changing to orange-yellow and crimson in autumn.
***Acer palmatum* 'Dissectum'** varieties:
***A. palmatum* 'Dissectum'** (sometimes called 'Viridis') Light, fresh green leaves.
'Atropurpureum' Deep purple leaves.
'Garnet' Reddish-green leaves.
'Nigrum' Bronze leaves that turn red in autumn.

Agave americana

Shape and size

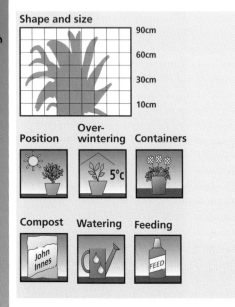

90cm

60cm

30cm

10cm

Position	Over-wintering	Containers

Compost	Watering	Feeding

Buying tips *Agaves are expensive, but they are slow-growing so buy the largest plants you can afford.*

Variegated agaves make stunning specimens once mature

Growing guide

Agaves are succulent-leaved plants grown for their foliage. They have bold, slightly undulating, sword-shaped leaves arranged in rosettes. The species has grey-green leaves, though those forms with variegated leaves look most eye-catching. The leaves are viciously spiny, so do not place this plant too near seats or paths, or where there are young children. In containers the plant generally grows to around 60-90cm (24-36in) across, though to reach this size takes a number of years.

Agaves like full sun and a well-drained, loam-based compost. They should be moved under cover in autumn before the first frosts to overwinter in a frost-free place. Repot plants every April, but only move up one pot size each year.

Propagation

Mature plants often produce small offshoots around the central rosette of foliage. These can be carefully removed and left to dry for a couple of days before being potted up in a loam-based compost.

Troubleshooting

Generally trouble-free.

Which variety?

Forms of **Agave americana** with variegated leaves look most ornamental. You may find these labelled either 'Marginata' or 'Variegata'.

Aloysia triphylla

Shape and size

1.2m
1m
60cm
30cm

Position	Over-wintering	Containers

Compost	Watering	Feeding

Features calendar

Jan	Feb	Mar	Apr	May	June
❀	❀				
July	Aug	Sept	Oct	• Nov	Dec

Buying tips *Occasionally lemon verbena is sold along with herbs as a small plant in a 8-cm (3-in) pot. This is much cheaper than buying larger plants and the small ones will soon reach a good size.*

Aloysia Lamontagne

Growing guide

Formerly known as *Lippia citriodora*, lemon verbena is one of the best plants for fragrant foliage. Its long, slender, mid-green leaves give off a strong lemon scent when crushed. The leaves can be used in a number of ways; they are a popular ingredient of pot-pourri and for making a refreshing herbal tea. Tiny, mauve flowers are borne in panicles in mid-summer, though the foliage is this plant's main attraction. In cold areas, lemon verbena can remain outside all year, provided it is planted in a well-drained soil and given a sheltered site in full sun, preferably against a south-facing wall. In such a location it can reach a height and spread of 1.5m (5ft). However, in a tub it stays much more compact. In autumn, container-grown plants should be moved under cover; the plants can survive in an unheated greenhouse provided the rootball is kept on the dry side. Repot annually in March and prune by half in April.

Propagation
Take cuttings of side shoots in July and August.

Troubleshooting
Generally trouble-free.

Which variety?

There is only one species.

163

Azalea

(evergreen or Japanese varieties)

Shape and size

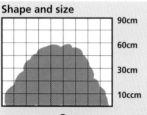

90cm
60cm
30cm
10ccm

Position	Over-wintering	Containers

Compost	Watering	Feeding

Features calendar

Jan	Feb	Mar	Apr	May	June
				✿	✿
July	Aug	Sept	Oct	Nov	Dec

Buying tips *Buy plants in flower to be sure of getting the colour you want.*

White varieties such as 'Persil' provide a stunning contrast to pinks and reds

Growing guide

Evergreen azaleas have a neat, compact shape and make long-lasting plants for containers. In late spring they are covered with many small flowers, usually in vivid shades of red, pink and orange, though pale pink and white forms are also available. They thrive in a woodland-type habitat, so on the patio this can be replicated by placing them in the partial shade of an east- or west-facing site or by siting them underneath a larger plant. This is particularly important in warmer parts of the country, though in the cooler North they do better in a more open position in years when there is not much sun.

Azaleas are lime-hating, so it is best to use a lime-free (peat-based) potting compost, and to use rainwater for watering in hard-water areas. No regular pruning is required, though straggly stems can be cut back hard in early spring.

Propagation

Cuttings can be taken in mid-summer, though it takes several years to produce flowering plants.

'Hino-mayo'

'Addy Wery'

Troubleshooting

Leaf hoppers may bore holes in flowers to lay their eggs. This can allow the bud blast fungus to enter, which causes buds to remain hard and brown. Remove and destroy damaged buds. Azalea gall causes waxy swellings on the leaves, and these should be picked off by hand as soon as possible.

Which variety?

A considerable range of varieties is available. The following is a selection of the most popular:
'Addy Wery' Deep crimson-red.
'Blaauw's Pink' Salmon-pink blooms.
'Blue Danube' Violet-blue.
'Hino-crimson' Crimson-scarlet.
'Hino-mayo' Clear pink flowers.
'Kirin' Deep rose-pink.
'Mother's Day' Rose-red.
'Palestrina' White with a tinge of green.
'Persil' White with yellow blotch.
'Salmon's Leap' A new variety with leaves that are boldly variegated with white and green, and deep pink flowers.
'Vuyk's Rosyred' Deep rose-red.
'Vuyk's Scarlet' Bright red.

Bamboo

Shape and size

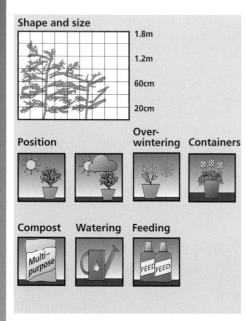

1.8m
1.2m
60cm
20cm

Position

Over-wintering

Containers

Compost

Watering

Feeding

Buying tips *Spring and summer are the best times to buy and plant bamboos. They grow quickly so smaller plants are good value.*

Fargesia nitida

Pleioblastus auricomus

Growing guide

Bamboos have slender, elegant leaves in a range of colours, and create some lush foliage interest. Sizes range from dwarf species that grow from around 45cm (18in) high to larger specimens that can reach 1.8m (6ft) or more. They are particularly suited to sites in full or partial shade. Bamboos combine well with a water feature and are ideal for an Oriental-type setting. The slender leaves and stems rustle in the slightest breeze to give a soothing background noise. Bamboos adapt to containers and, as a number of species have invasive roots, this is often the most trouble-free way in which to grow them. They are best in a sheltered site, as windy conditions can cause the edges of the leaves to become brown and scorched.

Propagation

Established clumps can be divided in spring. Small, rooted offshoots can be separated from the parent plant at the same time, potted up individually and grown on in a cold frame or greenhouse.

Troubleshooting

Generally trouble-free.

Which variety?

A number of bamboos have been reclassified in recent years, which can cause confusion as plants are sold under both new and old names. With the plants listed below, the new name is given first, followed by the old name(s).

Fargesia murieliae (Arundinaria murieliae) A tall variety bearing masses of slender green leaves on stems that arch slightly outwards. Height: 1.8m (6ft).

Fargesia nitida (Arundinaria nitida) This variety has narrow leaves on purplish stems. Height: 1.8m (6ft).

Phyllostachys nigra (black bamboo) A tall, elegant plant with stems that are upright yet slightly arching. The stems are dark green when young and become almost black with age. Height: 1.8m (6ft).

Pleioblastus auricomus (Arundinaria auricoma or A. viridistriata) A compact form with green leaves that are brightly striped with yellow. Height: 90cm (3ft).

Pleioblastus humilis 'Pumilis' (Arundinaria pumila) A dwarf bamboo with attractive, fresh green leaves. Height: 60cm (24in).

P. pygmaeus is similar.

Brugmansia

Shape and size

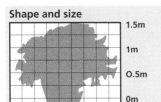

1.5m
1m
0.5m
0m

Position

Over-wintering

7°C

Containers

Compost

Multi-purpose

Watering

Feeding

FEED FEED

Features calendar

Jan	Feb	Mar	Apr	May	June

July	Aug	Sept	Oct	Nov	Dec

Buying tips *Brugmansias are often sold in the houseplant section of garden centres.*

The enormous fragrant blooms of Brugmansia

Brugmansia make ideal specimens for a sunny patio

Growing guide

These tall, handsome shrubs make excellent specimens for the greenhouse or conservatory, and they can also be moved out on to the patio for the summer. They bear enormous, drooping, trumpet-shaped flowers from June to August, and they usually give off a rich, heady fragrance. Brugmansias do well when grown in large pots on their own and repotted annually in March. Plants are best moved under cover in autumn and over-wintered at a minimum temperature of 7°C (45°F). Prune in February or early March. The large, long, dark green leaves are evergreen, though plants may be deciduous if overwintered in cool conditions.

Propagation

In May take heel cuttings of side shoots 10-15cm (4-6in) long.

Troubleshooting

Spider mites can be a problem under glass. Control with systemic insecticide or the biological control Phytoseiulus.

Which variety?

Named varieties and species are available, though plants are generally sold by flower colour alone. They are red, pink, white and yellow.

WARNING

All parts of this shrub are poisonous.

Buxus sempervirens

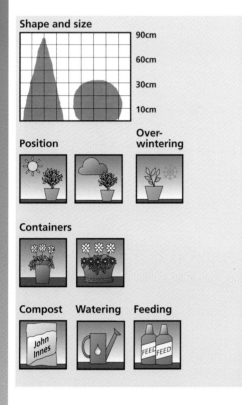

Shape and size

90cm
60cm
30cm
10cm

Position

Over-wintering

Containers

Compost   **Watering**   **Feeding**

John Innes

FEED FEED

Buying tips *Avoid buying pot-bound plants or ones with yellowing foliage. Simple shapes are easy to form and you can save a lot of money by training your own.*

Ball-shaped box stands sentinel in Versailles tub

Clipped box with ivies and pansies

Growing guide

Box is a useful shrub for year-round foliage interest on the patio. It is compact and slow-growing with tiny, rounded, evergreen leaves borne on a dense bush. Box is very tolerant of being trimmed, and it is therefore ideal in containers to create topiary shapes such as balls, spirals and pyramids. A pair of trimmed box flanking a flight of steps or a path, for example, can look stunning, particularly during winter when there is little else of visual interest in the garden or on the patio. Ready-grown topiary specimens are expensive to buy so it is worth training your own from young plants, although it will take a number of years. Trim plants annually in July or August.

Propagation

Take semi-ripe cuttings in August and September.

Troubleshooting

Box suckers can cause distortion of the foliage. Control with a systemic insecticide in early May and again in June.

Which variety?

As well as **Buxus sempervirens** which has dark green leaves, there are a number of varieties with attractively coloured or variegated foliage. Generally, they are slower-growing than the species.
'Argenteovariegata' Grey-green leaves that are edged with creamy-white.
'Aureovariegata' Green leaves that are striped or mottled with creamy-yellow
'Elegantissima' Green leaves with a creamy-white margin.
'Notata' (also known as **'Gold Tip'**) Shoots are tipped with yellow.

Calluna vulgaris

Shape and size

90cm
60cm
30cm
10cm

Position

Over-wintering

Containers

Compost

Multi-purpose

Watering

Feeding

FEED

Features calendar

Jan	Feb	Mar	Apr	May	June
🌿	🌿	🌿	🌿		
July	Aug	Sept	Oct	Nov	Dec
❀	❀	❀	🌿	🌿	

Buying tips *Look for compact, bushy plants and check for root damage before buying.*

Calluna vulgaris 'Winter Chocolate'

Calluna vulgaris 'Gold Haze'

Growing guide

The callunas or summer-flowering heathers are often overlooked for use in containers as there are so many other plants that bloom at the same time. The main flowering period is July to September, though a few varieties bloom in October/November. However, their period of interest can extend throughout the year as their foliage is evergreen, and those with coloured foliage are particularly valuable for adding interest from autumn to spring. The shoot tips of some varieties become brightly coloured in spring, producing a lovely effect. Callunas need an acid soil, so it is important to use an ericaceous or multipurpose potting compost, and to ensure good drainage as they dislike waterlogging. They tolerate some shade but flower best in a sunny position. The flower stems can be pruned out after flowering has finished, though pruning of varieties with attractive foliage is best done in March.

Propagation

Cuttings can be taken from early to mid-summer. Callunas can also be propagated by layering.

Troubleshooting

Generally trouble-free given the right growing conditions.

Which variety?

There is a huge range of varieties, and the following is a selection of the most popular ones which have attractively coloured foliage or shoot tips. Heights range from 30-45cm (12-18in).

'Aurea' Gold-tinted leaves turn bronze-red in winter. The flowers are purple.

'Beoley Gold' Bright yellow leaves and white flowers.

'Blazeaway' Green leaves turn to rich red in winter. The flowers are mauve.

'Cuprea' Young shoots are gold in summer and bronze in winter. The flowers are pale mauve.

'Gold Haze' Bright yellow foliage and white flowers.

'Golden Carpet' Orange-yellow leaves and purple-pink flowers.

'Multicolor' Green foliage tipped with gold and pink in summer, and red in winter. The flowers are purple.

'Robert Chapman' Leaves are gold in spring, changing to orange and then red. The flowers are purple.

'Spring Cream' Dark-green leaves are strikingly tipped with cream in spring. The blooms are white.

'Spring Glow' Green leaves tipped with pink and red, with lilac flowers.

'Spring Torch' Green leaves tipped with orange-red. The flowers are mauve.

'Winter Chocolate' Foliage is yellow-green and orange, turning dark chocolate-brown tipped with red in winter. The flowers are purple-pink.

Camellia

Shape and size

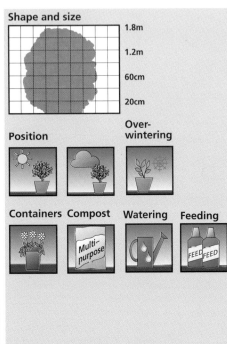

1.8m
1.2m
60cm
20cm

Position

Over-wintering

Containers Compost Watering Feeding

Multi-purpose

FEED FEED

Features calendar

Jan	Feb	Mar	Apr	May	June
		✱	✱	✱	
July	Aug	Sept	Oct	Nov	Dec

Buying tips *Late winter and early spring are the best times to find a good selection of camellias on sale. As there is so much subtle variation in flower shape and colour it is advisable to buy plants in flower. Prices and plant quality can vary enormously so shop around.*

'Donation' drops its petals as flowers fade

Growing guide

These evergreen shrubs give a beautiful display of showy and exotic flowers in spring, and the dark green, glossy leaves look attractive all year. The plants themselves are hardy, although they have an undeserved reputation for being tender and difficult to grow. However, the flowers are vulnerable to damage from frost and wind, as they are borne mostly in March and April when weather conditions can be extremely variable. For best results, camellias should be grown in light shade in warmer parts of the country, while in the cooler north they do well in a sunny site. Avoid sites exposed to wind, and if possible avoid placing camellias where they will receive the early morning sun as the sudden warmth on frozen buds and flowers can cause damage. Camellias are lime-hating, so use a lime-free (peat-based) potting compost and, in hard-water areas, water with rainwater if possible. Do not let plants dry out, particularly during mid-summer to early autumn when next year's flower buds are just starting to form. No regular pruning is required, though straggly growths can be cut back in spring.

Propagation

Shoots can be layered in early spring.

Troubleshooting

Bud drop is usually caused by insufficient watering the previous summer (see above). Aphids and scale insects can be a problem, as they secrete a sticky substance called honeydew on which a sooty mould then develops.

Which variety?

There are hundreds of camellia varieties available, virtually all of which are forms of **Camellia japonica** and **C. x williamsii**.

'Lady Clare'- like all C. japonica varieties, faded blooms remain on the plant

Peony-like 'Debbie'

Flower types are single, semi-double, double, anemone (flat outer petals with a raised centre) and peony (rounded blooms containing a mass of petals). A selection of the most popular varieties is listed below.

Camellia japonica varieties
'**Adolphe Audusson**' Bright red, semi-double flowers.
'**Alba Plena**' Pure white, double blooms.
'**Debutante**' Light pink, peony-type flowers.
'**Elegans**' Peach-pink, anemone-type blooms.
'**Lady Clare**' (also known as '**Akashigata**') Large, deep peach-pink, semi-double flowers.
'**Lady Vansittart**' Semi-double blooms that are white striped with rose-pink.

C. x williamsii varieties
'**Anticipation**' Crimson, peony-type flowers.
'**Brigadoon**' Rose-pink, semi-double flowers.
'**Debbie**' Deep rose-pink, peony blooms.
'**Donation**' An extremely popular and reliable variety with light pink, semi-double blooms.
'**J.C. Williams**' Rose-pink, single flowers.
'**Jury's Yellow**' White with wavy petals that are creamy-yellow in the centre.

In addition to the spring-flowering camellias above, **C. sasanqua** is a delightful species that blooms in winter and early spring. This species is best grown in a conservatory during the winter months, though it can go outside during summer. Two reliable varieties are '**Crimson King**' with bright red, single flowers, and '**Narumigata**' which has large, fragrant, creamy-white flowers that are tinged with pink at the edges.

Conifers

Shape and size

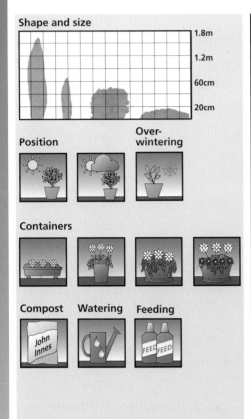

1.8m
1.2m
60cm
20cm

Position

Over-wintering

Containers

Compost **Watering** **Feeding**

John Innes

FEED FEED

A colourful winter display of conifers, heathers and ivies

Taxus baccata 'Repens Aurea'

Growing guide

With a wealth of foliage colours and plant shapes, conifers are tough and hardy plants that are excellent for lending year-round interest in containers. During the winter they take centre stage, and in the summer they make an attractive foil for seasonal flowering plants.

A huge selection of species and varieties are available, ranging in size from tiny dwarfs that are suitable for alpine troughs (see page 194-197) to larger specimens that do well in large tubs.

When buying conifers, it is important to check their eventual size, as many varieties look deceptively compact when young but can soon develop into substantial shrubs. It is very useful to look out for mature conifers when visiting gardens, and make a

172

Use bulbs and bedding plants to add seasonal colour to conifers in pots

note of their size and shape.

Most conifers prefer a site in light shade. They can be grown in full sun, provided their roots are shaded with stones and other pots to prevent overheating. Junipers are the exception as they will tolerate full sun. Conifers do best in a John Innes compost and they should be sited away from exposed positions where wind can cause rapid drying in summer and frost scorch in winter. During severely cold spells, it is worth giving the rootballs some protection to prevent frost-damage. Ensuring that containers have good drainage will also help avoid the compost freezing. Throughout the growing season the roots should be kept evenly moist, and do not overlook the need for occasional watering in winter if the weather is dry.

The smallest and slowest-growing conifers grow to around 15-30cm (6-12in) high and wide, and they are perfect for planting with alpines and dwarf bulbs to create a miniature landscape. The best upright variety is *Juniperus communis* **'Compressa'.** For a rounded shape the choice includes *Juniperus squamata* 'Blue Star', *Chamaecyparis lawsoniana* 'Green Globe', *C. lawsoniana* 'Gnome', *C. pisifera* 'Nana Albovariegata' and *C. pisifera* 'Plumosa Compressa'.

Petunias add a touch of summer interest to this conifer

Chamaecyparis

(cypress)

Growing guide

This is the most popular group of conifers and comes in an enormous range of shapes and sizes. Their attractive foliage covers a range of colours from gold through every shade of green to steely blue. However, cypresses do not like an exposed position and must not be allowed to dry out.

Propagation

Take basal cuttings in March.

Troubleshooting

Generally trouble-free. However, they can be attacked by aphids which secrete sticky honeydew that may become colonised by sooty mould.

Varieties

Chamaecyparis lawsoniana **'Gnome'** Holds its green foliage attractively in flattened sprays. Height: 25cm (10in) after 5 years.
C. lawsoniana **'Green Globe'** Soft green foliage on a bun-shaped plant
C. pisifera **'Nana Albovariegata'** Forms a low mound of green leaves variegated with yellow.
C. pisifera **'Plumosa Compressa'** Makes a tight bun of yellow foliage.

Juniperus

(juniper)

Growing guide

Junipers are particularly well suited to containers because they are far more tolerant of drought than most other conifers. They will also be happy in the alkaline conditions that often build up if containers are regularly watered using hard tap water.

With the exception of the vigorous prostrate varieties, virtually any juniper would make a good specimen for a large tub. However, if you are looking for one for a small container, your choice is much more limited. Perhaps the best is *J. communis* 'Compressa' which grows only a few centimetres a year – making it an ideal choice for a window-box or alpine trough.

Propagation

Take basal cuttings in April or semi-ripe cuttings in September or October.

Troubleshooting

Generally trouble-free. But if foliage turns yellow look for conifer spinning mite; if it turns brown suspect juniper webber moth.

Varieties

Juniperus communis **'Depressa Aurea'** Bushy yellow foliage conifer that turns bronze in winter. Height: 30cm (12in) in five years.
J. communis **'Hibernica'** Neat grey-green column tinged with bronze in winter. Height: 90cm (36in) in five years.
J. horizontalis Spreading habit,

keeping very low. Both green and greyish varieties available. Height: 15-20cm (6-8in) in five years. Shade-tolerant.

J. x media **'Old Gold'** Compact, semi-prostrate. Foliage stays golden-yellow all year. Height: 60cm (24in) in five years.

J. scopulorum **'Skyrocket'** Very slim and pointed pencil shape with grey-green foliage. Height: 1.4m (5ft) in five years.

J. squamata **'Blue Carpet'** More spreading than 'Blue Star' with silvery foliage. Height: 20cm (8in) in five years.

J. squamata **'Blue Star'** A compact, bushy, spiky plant with steel-blue foliage. Height: 20cm (8in) in five years.

J. squamata **'Meyeri'** Bushy blue conifer. Height: 30cm (12in) in five years.

Pinus

(Pine)

Growing guide

Most pines form large trees and are unsuitable for growing in containers, but there are some slow-growing, dwarf forms that make excellent container plants. These dwarf forms have a more open habit than many other conifers, so can be underplanted with bulbs and ground-cover plants. However, pines are less tolerant of shade and pollution than some other conifers.

Propagation

Selected forms of dwarf pines, such as *P. sylvestris* **'Beuvronensis'**, can only be propagated by grafting. However, the species can be raised from seed in autumn.

Troubleshooting

Generally trouble-free. They can be attacked by woolly aphids which secrete sticky honeydew that may become colonised by sooty mould.

Varieties

Pinus mugo Forms a compact mound of dark green foliage. Height: 45cm (18in) in five years.

P. sylvestris **'Beuvronensis'** Dwarf form of Scot's pine. Tolerates exposed position. Height: 60cm (24in) in five years.

Taxus baccata

(common yew)

Growing guide

Yews are tolerant of drought, pollution and shade which makes them ideal for growing in containers. They are also slow-growing, particularly in the first few years after planting so make good centrepieces for a permanent container display.

Propagation

Take semi-ripe cuttings in September or October.

Troubleshooting

Generally trouble-free.

Varieties

'Repens Aurea' Semi-prostrate golden yew. Height: 30cm (12in) in five years.

'Semperaurea' Golden, irregularly shaped bush. Height: 60cm (24in) in five years.

'Standishii' Very slow-growing golden form of yew. Height: 50cm (20in) in five years.

'Summergold' Semi-prostrate golden yew. Height: 30cm (12in) in five years.

Juniperus squamata 'Blue Carpet'

Cordyline australis

Shape and size

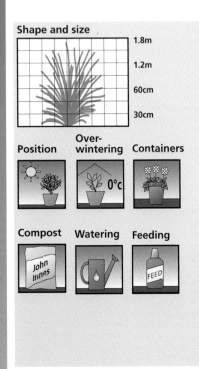

1.8m
1.2m
60cm
30cm

Position   **Over-wintering**   **Containers**

0°c

Compost   **Watering**   **Feeding**

John Innes

FEED

'Torbay Sunset'- one of the slower-growing, coloured leaved varieties

Cordyline australis with red polyanthus for winter interest

Growing guide

A spiky-leaved plant that gives excellent foliage contrast to other plants on the patio. The green-leaved species is cheapest and most widely available, though there are several forms with striped or coloured foliage that look exceptionally handsome. Cordylines need full sun and a sheltered site in order to thrive. Although hardy outdoors in mild areas, it is safest to move cordylines under cover to a porch or greenhouse during the winter. An unheated structure usually provides adequate protection, particularly if the rootball is kept on the dry side. If it is not possible to move the plant under cover, tie up the foliage and wrap the whole stem in bubble polythene or hessian during spells of severely cold weather. In time, the plant will start to develop a small trunk, which initially gives space for underplanting it with seasonal plants or flowers. However, after a number of years a cordyline will eventually become too large for a container and it will need to be planted out in the border. In mild areas, *C. australis* can develop into a small tree.

Propagation

Offshoots may be produced around the stem of the parent plant and these can be detached and potted up individually.

Troubleshooting

Generally trouble-free.

Which variety?

C. australis has plain green leaves and is the fastest-growing form. The following varieties have coloured foliage and are slower-growing.

'Albertii' Leaves attractively striped with red, pink, cream and green.
'Black Tower' Dark, purple-red leaves.
'Torbay Dazzler' Dark red leaves.
'Torbay Sunset' Green leaves with a red central vein.
'Torbay Surprise' Leaves which are variegated with dark green and yellow-green.

Erica carnea

Shape and size

90cm
60cm
30cm
10cm

Position

Over-wintering

Containers

Compost

Multi-purpose

Watering

Feeding

FEED

Features calendar

Jan	Feb	Mar	Apr	May	June
🌸	🌸	🌸	🍃	🍃	

July	Aug	Sept	Oct	Nov	Dec
				🌸	🌸

Buying tips *Avoid plants which are straggly or have bare stems, Choose bushy, compact ones.*

Euonymus, heathers and polyanthus

Winter colour from pansies, heather and ivies

Growing guide

These tough, hardy plants are invaluable for winter flower colour in containers. They bloom from November to April, although the main flowering season is from January to March. Many tiny, bell-shaped flowers are produced along slender, wiry stems, and some varieties have colourful foliage to provide even more ornamental interest. Winter-flowering heathers can be combined with other plants such as winter-flowering pansies, ivies, and early-flowering spring bulbs like crocuses to create an attractive and colourful display. Unlike callunas (summer-flowering heathers), *Erica carnea* varieties are tolerant of lime so there is no need to use a special potting compost. They flower best in a sunny spot. After flowering, trim the whole plant with shears to remove dead flowers and to encourage bushy growth.

Propagation

Cuttings of shoot tips can be taken in mid-summer. Plants can also be propagated by layering.

Troubleshooting

Generally trouble-free.

Which variety?

The following is a selection of the wide range of *Erica carnea* varieties available:

'Aurea' Bright golden foliage in spring and summer. Flowers are deep pink fading almost to white.
'December Red' Dark green leaves and rose-red flowers.
'Foxhollow' Greenish-yellow foliage that in winter turns dark yellow tinged with red. The flowers are pale pink.
'Kramer's Rubin' Reddish-pink flowers.
'March Seedling' Dark green leaves and rose-purple flowers.
'Myretoun Ruby' Deep green leaves and rose-pink flowers.
'Pink Spangles' Lots of bright pink flowers.
'Springwood White' Masses of white flowers.
'Westwood Yellow' Golden foliage and deep-pink flowers.
'Whitehall' White, with a more compact habit than 'Springwood White'.

Euonymus

(evergreen varieties)

Shape and size

90cm
60cm
30cm
10ccm

Position

Over-wintering

Containers

Compost

Watering

Feeding

Features calendar

Jan	Feb	Mar	Apr	May	June

July	Aug	Sept	Oct	Nov	Dec

Buying tips *Young plants in 8-cm (3-in) pots are often available in garden centres; these are good value as euonymus are fast-growing.*

Euonymus fortunei 'Emerald 'n' Gold'

Euonymus fortunei 'Golden Prince'

Growing guide

These useful shrubs have glossy leaves that are mostly variegated in bright colours. They are tough plants that thrive in sun or shade, so they are ideal for providing winter colour on the patio. Evergreen euonymus for containers broadly divide into two groups: *E. fortunei* varieties that have a low, spreading habit, and *E. japonicus* varieties which are narrow and upright. Young plants are useful for providing some winter foliage interest in window-boxes, containers and hanging baskets. After they have been used for one season, they can either be potted on into a larger container or planted out in the garden borders. No regular pruning is required, though old, straggly stems can be cut hard back in early spring. Variegated forms can sometimes revert and produce plain green shoots and these should be pruned out as soon as they appear.

Propagation

Take semi-ripe cuttings from early to mid-summer.

Troubleshooting

Generally trouble-free.

Which variety?

Euonymus fortunei varieties:
All grow to around 30cm (12in) high with a spread of up to 60cm (24in).

'Blondy' Green leaves with a large, creamy yellow central blotch.
'Emerald Gaiety' Grey-green leaves edged with white, often become tinged with pink in winter.
'Emerald 'n' Gold' Green leaves brightly variegated with gold.
'Golden Prince' (also known as **'Gold Tip'**) Leaves are edged with golden-yellow. Its habit is more upright than other varieties.
'Harlequin' White and green foliage.
'Silver Queen' Spring foliage is creamy-yellow maturing to green with a creamy-white edge.
'Sunspot' Deep green leaves with a long, central, golden blotch. The stems are yellowish in colour.

Euonymus japonicus varieties:
All grow to around 90cm (36in) high in containers.
'Aureus' (also known as **'Aureopictus'**) Deep green leaves which have a bright golden blotch in the centre.
'Microphyllus Albovariegatus' A small-leaved, compact form with foliage that is variegated green and white.
'Ovatus Aureus' (also known as **'Aureovariegatus'** and **'Marieke'**) Leaves are edged and flushed with yellow. It colours best if given a reasonable amount of sun.

WARNING

All parts of euonymus can be harmful if eaten.

Gaultheria procumbens

Shape and size

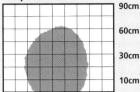

90cm
60cm
30cm
10cm

Position **Over-wintering**

Containers

Compost Watering Feeding

Features calendar

Jan	Feb	Mar	Apr	May	June
🫐	🫐	🫐	✿		

July	Aug	Sept	Oct	Nov	Dec
			🫐	🫐	🫐

The cherry-like berries of G. procumbens make a stunning contrast to the reddish foliage

Buying tips *Autumn is the best time to find small, reasonably priced plants on sale.*

Growing guide

This creeping, evergreen shrub looks at its best in autumn and winter, when it bears many small, bright-red berries. The oval, glossy, mid-green leaves also develop attractive reddish tints in winter. A large specimen looks eye-catching in a container on its own, while small plants can be used as part of a mixed display in window-boxes, hanging baskets and the edges of containers. Small, urn-shaped, white flowers are borne in spring. Gaultheria needs a lime-free (peat-based) potting compost. It does best if given a site that is partially shaded in summer.

Propagation

Rooted suckers are often produced, which can be separated from the parent plant and potted up individually.

Troubleshooting

Generally trouble-free.

Which variety?

Gaultheria procumbens is the only species suitable for containers.

Mimulus

Shape and size

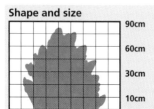

90cm
60cm
30cm
10cm

Position

Over-wintering

0°c

Containers

Compost   Watering   Feeding

Multi-purpose

FEE FEED ED

Features calendar

Jan	Feb	Mar	Apr	May	June
					✿
July	Aug	Sept	Oct	Nov	Dec
✿	✿	✿	✿		

The glorious apricot blooms of Mimulus aurantiacus

Buying tips *Late spring to early summer is the best time to find mimulus on sale. Look for compact, bushy plants.*

Growing guide

The shrubby mimulus are outstanding for summer flowers on the patio. Many trumpet-shaped flowers appear in profusion from late spring right through to autumn; these are produced along long, lax stems among slender, sticky, dark green leaves. The flowers of the most widely grown species, *M. aurantiacus*, are an unusual and attractive shade of peachy-orange, and other colours available include red and pale peach. This plant grows readily from cuttings and soon flowers. Plants are best overwintered in a frost-free place, though they can tolerate a little frost so long as the rootball is kept on the dry side. Overwintered plants can be pruned by half in late winter to encourage bushy growth.

Propagation

Take heel cuttings in spring or mid- to late summer.

Troubleshooting

Aphids can be a problem on young shoots. Treat with a general insecticide.

Which variety?

M. aurantiacus Rich, warm apricot flowers.
***M. aurantiacus* 'Puniceus'** Brick-red.
***M.* 'Popacatapetl'** Ivory white.

Myrtus communis

Shape and size

		90cm
		60cm
		30cm
		10cm

Position

Over-wintering

 0°c 7°c

Containers

Compost Watering Feeding

Features calendar

Jan	Feb	Mar	Apr	May	June
July	Aug	Sept	Oct	Nov	Dec

Buying tips *Early to mid-summer is the best time to find myrtle on sale.*

Myrtus communis 'Variegata'

The unusual flowers of Myrtus communis

Growing guide

An evergreen shrub with small, pointed, glossy leaves that are pleasantly aromatic when crushed. There is also a form with foliage that is attractively variegated. Small, fragrant white flowers up to 2.5cm (1in) across are borne through the middle of summer. They are notable for their prominent central mass of stamens. Myrtles can be left outside all year in mild areas, but in most parts of the country they benefit from winter protection. They prefer a sunny, sheltered site. No regular pruning is required, though straggly shoots can be cut hard back in spring.

Propagation

Take heel cuttings of semi-ripe shoots in mid-summer.

Troubleshooting

Generally trouble-free.

Which variety?

Myrtus communis Plain, dark green leaves, white flowers.
'Flore Pleno' Double flowers.
M. communis tarentina (also called **'Jenny Reitenbach'**, **'Microphylla'** and **'Nana'**) A compact variety with flowers and leaves that are smaller than those of the species. It is particularly suited to a container.
'Variegata' (also known as **'Tricolor'**) Leaves are variegated creamy-white.

Nandina domestica

Shape and size

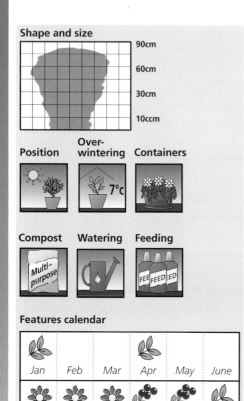

90cm
60cm
30cm
10ccm

Position	Over-wintering	Containers
	7°c	

Compost	Watering	Feeding
Multi-purpose		FEE FEED EED

Features calendar

Jan	Feb	Mar	Apr	May	June
July	Aug	Sept	Oct	Nov	Dec

Buying tips *Early summer is the best time to find well-shaped, bushy plants on sale.*

The berries of Nandina domestica

Growing guide

An attractive shrub for both flower and foliage interest, with the added bonus of autumn colour. The bold, pinnate leaves bear some resemblance to those of a bamboo. In spring the young leaves are green flushed with red, becoming completely green in summer and then developing fiery tints of red and purple in autumn. Large panicles of white flowers are borne in mid-summer and, in a hot summer, are sometimes followed by clusters of scarlet fruits that last for several months. Nandina prefers a sunny, sheltered position. Severe frosts can scorch the foliage, so it is worth giving the plant some protection during cold spells.

No regular pruning is necessary, though weak shoots can be thinned out after flowering.

Propagation

Cuttings of side shoots can be taken in late summer. Offshoots can be separated from the parent plant and potted up individually in spring.

Troubleshooting

Generally trouble-free.

Which variety?

N. domestica Green leaves in summer with red and purple autumn tints. It grows to around 90cm (36in) in a container.
'Firepower' More compact, growing to around 60cm (24in) and with brighter autumn colour.
'Richmond' A more reliable fruiting form, bearing large clusters of showy red berries.
'Wood's Dwarf' A compact, bushy habit and light greeny-gold foliage that is flushed with red in winter.

Phormium

Shape and size

90cm
60cm
30cm
10cm

Position

Over-wintering

Containers

Compost

Watering

Feeding

Buying tips *Buy phormiums from mid-summer onwards when the new season's stock has arrived in garden centres. Plants on sale in early spring may have suffered some frost damage.*

'Cream Delight'

Phormium tenax 'Purpureum'

Growing guide

The bold, sword-shaped leaves of phormiums make a striking contrast to other plants on the patio. Varieties with foliage colours ranging from greens and yellows to reds and purples are available. The coloured forms are particularly ornamental and give an exotic, tropical air to the patio. Although phormiums are hardy, when grown in containers there is a risk of the rootball freezing solid in winter. This would kill the plant, so in colder areas it is prudent to move them into a sheltered spot or into an unheated structure. Phormiums do best in a sunny, sheltered position. No pruning is required, though dead or damaged leaves can be cut out at the base in spring.

Propagation

Mature plants can be divided in spring.

Troubleshooting

Generally trouble-free.

Which variety?

There are two main species, ***Phormium cookianum*** and ***P. tenax***, plus a number of hybrids. Those with coloured or variegated leaves give much more ornamental value in containers than the green-leaved species. Most phormiums grow to around 90cm (36in) in containers.

'Apricot Queen' Pale yellow arching leaves flushed with apricot in the centre, and dark green and bronze leaf edges.

'Bronze Baby' Dark bronze leaves and grows to 60cm (24in).

'Duet' A dwarf form reaching 30cm (12in) high, with green and cream foliage.

'Maori Queen' Leaves are striped with rose-red on a bronzey-green background.

'Maori Sunrise' Leaves are light red, pink and bronze.

'Sundowner' Coppery leaves with pink and salmon bands.

'Tricolor' Green leaves striped with white and red.

'Yellow Wave' Arching, bright yellow foliage.

Rhododendron

(dwarf varieties)

Shape and size

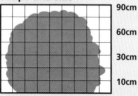

90cm
60cm
30cm
10cm

Position

Over-wintering

Containers

Compost

Multi-purpose

Watering

Feeding

FEED FEED

Features calendar

Jan	Feb	Mar	Apr	May	June
	✿	✿	✿	✿	
July	Aug	Sept	Oct	Nov	Dec

Buying tips *Look for healthy, bushy plants and avoid any that have yellowing foliage, damaged leaves or stunted growth.*

R. cilipense

'Molly Miller'

Growing guide

Dwarf rhododendrons are acid-loving (lime-hating) plants. They do well in containers, provided they are potted in ericaceous compost which is kept evenly moist, and given a sheltered site in light shade. Growing rhododendrons in containers is a useful option if your soil is limy and unsuitable for such ericaceous plants. There is an enormous range of varieties and flower colours, and it is often best to choose plants in flower to be sure of having your desired flower type and colour.

Alternatively, it is well worth visiting rhododendron gardens in spring and noting your preferred varieties. A few species flower as early as February, though the main flowering period is from March to May.

Propagation

Plants can be layered in spring or autumn. Layers take a year or more to root after which time they can be detached and potted up individually.

Troubleshooting

Leaves that are browning at the edges or curled are a sign of frost, drought or sun scorch. Correct siting will avert most problems. Leaf hoppers appear in the foliage from July to October and cause holes in the buds which can allow infection by rhododendron bud blast fungus, which turns the buds black. Pick off any infected buds.

'Dopey'

'Bashful'

Which variety?

There are hundreds of varieties to choose from.

Rhododendron yakushimanum hybrids:

They are particularly good in containers as they have large, attractive leaves, yet only grow to around 90cm (36in) high. Their flowers come in a range of splendid colours and flushes.

'Bambi' Red in bud, opening to soft pink tinged with yellow.

'Bashful' Rose-pink with a reddish-brown blotch.

'Chelsea Seventy' Salmon-pink shaded with carmine.

'Doc' Light pink ageing to white.

'Dopey' Rich red.

'Dusty Miller' A mixture of pale pink and cream.

'Grumpy' Primrose yellow fading to creamy-white flushed with shell pink.

'Molly Miller' Cream flushed with apricot.

'Percy Wiseman' Cream and pink ageing to creamy-white.

'Silver Sixpence' Creamy-white with yellow spots.

'Sleepy' Pale mauve with brown spots.

'Surrey Heath' Rose-pink.

Dwarf species and hybrids:

'Baden Baden' Scarlet-red blooms.

'Blue Diamond' Violet-blue flowers.

R. cilipense Deep pink.

'Elizabeth' Large, blood-red flowers.

R. impeditum Tiny blue flowers.

'Pink Drift' Pinky-mauve.

R. praecox Lilac-mauve blooms in February.

'Scarlet Wonder' Bright red flowers.

Sarcococca

Shape and size

90cm
60cm
30cm
10ccm

Position

Over-wintering

Containers

Compost Watering Feeding

Multi-purpose FEED

Features calendar

Jan	Feb	Mar	Apr	May	June
🌸	🌸	🌸			

July	Aug	Sept	Oct	Nov	Dec
					🌸

Buying tips *Plants tend to be on sale in winter, though spring or autumn are the best times to pot up plants for containers.*

The highly scented blooms of Sarcococca confusa

Growing guide

This evergreen comes into its own in winter for both flower and foliage interest. The flowers are small, creamy-white tassels borne along the stems from mid- to late winter, and though they are not particularly ornamental, the strong vanilla-like fragrance more than makes up for it.

The overall shape of the plant is neat and upright, with a dense thicket of stems clothed with pointed, glossy, dark-green leaves. Sarcococca thrives in sun or shade, and placed near a frequently used path, gate or doorway its penetrating scent can be fully appreciated. A plant in a container could even be moved into an unheated porch or conservatory to get the full benefit of the scent.

Propagation
Lift out of pot in early spring and divide with sharp knife.

Troubleshooting
Generally trouble-free.

Which variety?

There are several species available which are all similar. They are: **S. confusa, S. hookeriana 'Digyna', S. hookeriana 'Humilis'** and **S. ruscifolia**.

Skimmia japonica

Shape and size

90cm
60cm
30cm
10ccm

Position

Over-wintering

Containers

Compost Watering Feeding

Multi-purpose

FEED FEED

Features calendar

Jan	Feb	Mar	Apr	May	June
●	●	❀	✿	✿	
July	Aug	Sept	Oct	Nov	Dec
		●	●	●	●

Buying tips *Look for plants which are compact and bushy with healthy foliage; avoid any with leaves that are very pale green or showing signs of yellowing.*

Skimmia combines with dwarf daffodils, polyanthus and pansies to produce a colourful display

Early spring flowers from heather and skimmia

Growing guide

These shrubs offer several different periods of interest throughout the year. They are evergreen, forming neat, rounded domes of glossy leaves. A number of varieties have attractive flower buds that are formed in late summer and autumn, staying on the plant throughout winter and opening in early spring to give off a pleasant scent. There are both male and female forms; the males have larger and more fragrant flowers, while the females have brightly coloured berries in autumn and winter. There needs to be a male variety nearby in order for the females to be pollinated and produce berries. However, if space for more than one plant is a problem, there is a hermaphrodite variety that bears both male and female flowers on the same plant. Skimmias are hardy, though the roots can be damaged if severe frosts occur, so it is worth insulating the containers in spells of very cold weather. They like a lime-free soil, and in hard-water areas it is worth watering with rainwater to avoid any build-up of lime.

Propagation

Take cuttings in mid- to late summer.

Troubleshooting

Generally trouble-free.

Which variety?

'Fragrans' A male form with white, fragrant flowers.

'Nymans' A good fruiting variety bearing large red berries.

'Rubella' A male, one of the most ornamental varieties for containers. Its leaves are flushed with dark red and the flower buds, which are also dark red, are held in large panicles through winter, opening to reveal white flowers in spring.

'Veitchii' (also known as **'Foremanii'**) is a female form bearing large clusters of red berries.

'Reevesiana' Bears male and female flowers on the same plant, so there is no need to have other plants in order for berries to be produced. This is a compact form that grows to 30-45cm (12-18in) high and wide, and which bears many large, bright red berries.

Tweedia caerulea

Shape and size

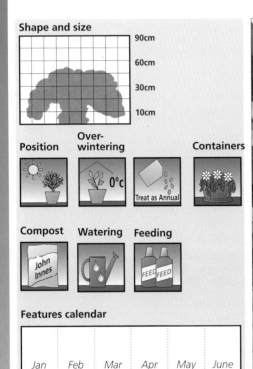

90cm
60cm
30cm
10cm

Position   **Over-wintering**   **Containers**

0°C

Treat as Annual

Compost   **Watering**   **Feeding**

John Innes

FEED FEED

Features calendar

Jan	Feb	Mar	Apr	May	June
❀	❀	❀	🌰		
July	Aug	Sept	Oct	Nov	Dec

Buying tips *Ready-grown plants tend to be fairly expensive, so it is well worth raising your own from seed.*

The striking blue flowers of Tweedia caerulea

Growing guide

This attractive little plant (also known as *Oxypetalum*) has a habit halfway between that of a shrub and a climber. Although the stems do sometimes twine up a support, the plant generally benefits from being tied on to canes, where it can reach a height of 60-90cm (24-36in). The flowers, which are borne in clusters in summer and early autumn, are an unusual and exquisite shade of powder-blue, and are followed by long, pointed, swollen seed pods. The hairy leaves are heart-shaped and grey-green. This plant can be overwintered in a frost-free place, but it can also be treated as an annual as it flowers within a reasonably short time of sowing.

Propagation

Sow seed in early spring at 16-18°C (60-65°F). Flowers are usually produced within five months of sowing.

Troubleshooting

Overwatering causes leaf drop. Keep the soil constantly moist but not waterlogged.

Which variety?

There is only one species.

Viburnum tinus

Shape and size

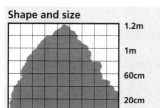

1.2m
1m
60cm
20cm

Position

Over-wintering

Containers

Compost

John Innes

Watering

Feeding

FEED FEED

Features calendar

Jan	Feb	Mar	Apr	May	June
🌼	🌼	🌼	🌼 🔵🔵		

July	Aug	Sept	Oct	Nov	Dec
				🌼	🌼

Buying tips *Look for plants which are compact and bushy with healthy foliage. Avoid plants that look pot-bound.*

Viburnum tinus 'Eve Price'

Viburnum tinus 'Variegatum'

Growing guide

Its shiny, dark green leaves and rounded habit make *Viburnum tinus* an ideal specimen plant in a large container. In the depths of winter, its beautiful fragrant blooms will cheer up a dull, dismal patio. It is worth moving the container close to a window in autumn where it can be viewed in comfort. From December to March the pink buds open to whitish pink flowers and are followed by clusters of dark blue berries. The species will reach 1.2x0.9m (4x3ft) in five years, so needs a large tub. However, the slow-growing compact form **'Eve Price'** is a useful plant in patio pots and other containers.

Prune in spring to maintain a tidy shape and to restrict the size of the plant.

Propagation

Take semi-ripe cuttings in September and root in a cold frame using peaty compost. Alternatively, take stem cuttings in June or July from young shoots. Root these in a pot of compost covered with a polythene bag.

Troubleshooting

Generally trouble-free.

Which variety?

Viburnum tinus Forms a dense evergreen shrub. Flowers are borne from October for about 16-20 weeks, and blue-black berries in spring. You may come across the following varieties:

'Eve Price' Dwarf form 90x90cm (36x36in) with smaller leaves than species. Deep pink flower buds opening to pink last from February for 8-10 weeks.

'Gwellian' Dwarf form 90x90cm (36x36in) with smaller leaves than species. Deep pink flower buds opening to whitish pink. Flowers from November for 16-20 weeks.

'Variegatum' Dwarf form 90x90cm (36x36in). White flowers from November lasting 16-20 weeks. Needs a sheltered spot.

Vinca minor

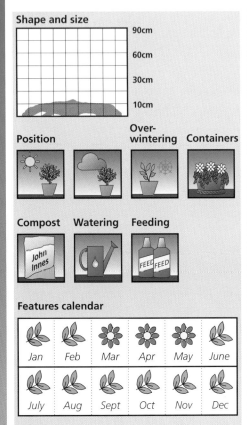

Shape and size

90cm
60cm
30cm
10cm

Position   **Over-wintering**   **Containers**

Compost   **Watering**   **Feeding**

John Innes

FEED FEED

Features calendar

Jan	Feb	Mar	Apr	May	June
July	Aug	Sept	Oct	Nov	Dec

Vinca minor in bloom

Buying tips *Periwinkles are often sold in small pots amongst selections of herbaceous perennials and ground-cover plants, which is an economical way to buy them.*

Periwinkles and ivies spill over the edge of the pot

Growing guide

This hardy, carpet-forming evergreen is widely used for ground-cover in garden borders, but less so in containers, although it makes a handsome display of flowers and foliage when allowed to trail over the edges of a container or a hanging basket. Being hardy, it is particularly useful in winter containers where it can be combined with plants such as dwarf bulbs and winter-flowering pansies. Those forms with variegated foliage are especially valuable for winter interest. No regular pruning is required, though plants can be cut hard back in spring to encourage vigorous new growth.

Propagation

Plants can be divided in spring. Cuttings can also be taken in late summer.

Troubleshooting

Generally trouble-free.

Which variety?

Vinca minor Dark, glossy, green leaves and blue flowers in spring.
'Alba' has white flowers.
'Argenteovariegata' Silver-edged leaves and blue flowers.
'Atropurpurea' Green leaves and purple flowers.
'Aureovariegata' Green leaves edged with gold and blue flowers.
'Azurea Flore Pleno' Double, blue flowers.
'Gertrude Jekyll' White flowers.
'La Grave' (also known as **'Bowles' Blue'** and **'Bowles' Variety'**) Large blue flowers and green leaves.

Yucca

Shape and size

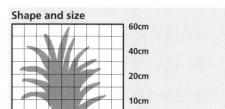

60cm
40cm
20cm
10cm

Position

Over-wintering

Containers

Compost

John Innes

Watering

Feeding

FEED

Features calendar

Jan	Feb	Mar	Apr	May	June

| July | Aug | Sept | Oct | Nov | Dec |

Buying tips *Early to mid-summer are the best times to find a selection of yuccas on sale.*

Yucca gloriosa 'Variegata'

Yucca flaccida 'Ivory'

Growing guide

Yuccas provide excellent foliage interest in containers with their large, bold rosettes of spiky leaves. They give an exotic, Mediterranean effect to the patio, and the leaves make a good contrast to rounded and prostrate plants. Although their foliage is the main ornamental attribute, particularly in the case of those with variegated leaves, flowers are occasionally produced on mature plants. Generally one bold spike of flowers is borne, consisting of many creamy-white, bell-shaped blooms. Plants can be left outside in mild areas, though in colder places it is worth moving them into an unheated structure for the winter. Varieties which have variegated foliage are more susceptible to frost damage than the green-leaved species.

Propagation

Offsets can be removed in spring using a sharp knife, and potted on individually.

Troubleshooting

Generally trouble-free.

Which variety?

Yucca filamentosa Plain, green leaves. The variety **'Bright Edge'** has yellow-edged leaves.
Y. flaccida **'Golden Sword'** striped with yellow. *Y. flaccida* **'Ivory'** has green leaves.
Y. x *floribunda* **'Garland's Gold'** has a broad, gold central band to each leaf.
Y. gloriosa Plain, green leaves. The variety **'Variegata'** has leaves edged with cream.

WARNING

The leaves of this plants have sharp tips and serrated edges, so avoid placing near pathways or where there are young children. Wear glasses to protect your eyes when working near yuccas.

Herbaceous perennials and alpines

Although annual and tender plants with brightly coloured flowers tend to be more popular for patios, there is considerable potential for using hardy perennial plants such as herbaceous plants, alpines, ornamental grasses and ferns. They provide a diverse range of foliage and flower colour. The great advantage that many of these plants have is that a good number of them thrive in full or partial shade, so they are perfect for cheering up any gloomy corners.

In general, they are more subtle in appearance than most annuals and tender perennials that have eye-catching flowers, but as permanent plantings they develop imposing shapes that have an enduring appeal from spring until autumn. Indeed, some of these plants are at their best in containers, particularly alpines which have a charm that can be fully appreciated at close quarters. These dainty miniatures can be planted in troughs and combined with other dwarf plants to create a delightful small-scale landscape.

Buying tips *Many of the plants you already have in the garden can be lifted and divided in autumn or spring. Small divisions can then be used to fill containers.*

The softening effect of a pot of scabious

Herbaceous perennials

When choosing perennials for containers, it is advisable to look for plants that fulfil one of two functions. Either choose plants with attractively shaped or coloured foliage that will look stunning from spring to autumn, or those varieties that give a relatively short burst of flowers and which are brought on to the patio just while they are at their best. In both cases, the size of the plant is important as its habit needs to be reasonably compact.

In the first category, hostas are excellent candidates for containers. They thrive in full or partial shade. Their large, bold leaves come in many colours and shapes; there are varieties that are handsomely variegated with cream or white and green, while others have gold-flushed or blue-green leaves.

Most herbaceous perennials flower in the summer, but you can extend the season of interest on the patio by choosing a few early- and late-flowering types for containers. For spring colour, consider one of the many euphorbias or pulmonarias. Agapanthus and *Sedum spectabile* will add stunning highlights in late summer.

When planting up herbaceous perennials in containers, it is usually best to grow them as single specimens as mixed plantings usually become dominated by one particular plant. The type of compost is not critical but for a permanent container, where the compost will be outside for several years, a John Innes No2 is recommended.

Brighter foliage colour can be provided by *Houttuynia cordata* 'Chameleon', which has heart-shaped leaves flushed with red, green and white.

Achillea 'Moonshine' brightens up a winter garden

The delicate flowers of Anthemis cupaniana

Lamium maculatum

Variegated hostas make striking specimens

Container choice

Acanthus spinosus (bear's breeches) Huge, arching leaves, deeply cut and spiny. Tall spires of purple and white flowers in July. Needs full sun. Height: 1.2m (4ft).

Achillea 'Moonshine' Graceful, feathery, greyish foliage, which often survives well into winter. Pale yellow flowers in June and July. All achilleas do well in containers. Stake in an exposed position. Needs full sun. Height: 60cm (24in).

Agapanthus (African lily) Ideal as single subject or specimen in a container. Fresh green, strap-shaped leaves, large heads of rich-blue flowers in late summer. **'Headbourne Hybrids'** have a range of shades. Wrap up or take under cover during winter in very cold areas. Needs full sun. Height: 75cm (30in).

Anthemis cupaniana Silvery-grey, ferny foliage. White, daisy-like flowers in spring with occasional blooms later. Shelter from hard frosts (or overwinter as cuttings). Needs full sun. Height: 20cm (8in).

Aquilegia vulgaris (columbine) Delicate, slightly bluish foliage. Pretty purple, cottage garden flowers in May or June. **'McKana Hybrids'** have larger flowers in many colours. Generally short-lived, however. Sun or light shade. Height: 60cm (24in).

Astrantia major (masterwort) Attractive, deeply divided foliage. **'Sunningdale Variegated'** is splashed with yellow. Tiny pale pink flowers surrounded by greenish papery bracts in June and July. *A. maxima* has deep pink flowers and bracts. Light or full shade. Height: 60-90cm (24-36in).

Doronicum plantagineum (leopard's bane) Large, yellow, daisy-like flowers appear above the light green, heart-shaped leaves in

Sedum spectabile varieties are a magnet for butterflies

April. Cut back after flowering to encourage fresh leaves. Needs full sun. Height: 60cm (24in).
Euphorbia myrsinites Bluish evergreen foliage in whorls on trailing stems. Greenish-yellow flowers in April. Needs full sun. Height: 15cm (6in). Other euphorbias such as the imposing *E. characias wulfenii* at 90cm (36in) are also suitable.

All Euphorbias are poisonous and have irritant sap.

Helleborus orientalis (Lenten rose) an evergreen perennial with green leaves and stunning winter flowers in a range of colours depending on the variety. Sun or partial shade. Height: 30cm (12in). **Poisonous.**
Hosta Hostas do well in containers provided you do not let the compost dry out. ***H. fortunei* 'Albopicta'** (yellow with green margins); ***H.* 'Frances Williams'**,

(irregular, broad, pale yellow margins); ***H. lancifolia*** (narrow green and glossy); and ***H. undulata*** (wavy green with splash of white) are all worth trying. Light shade or shade is best. Height: 60-75cm (24-30in).
Houttuynia cordata Pointed, heart-shaped bluish-green leaves on red stems. The variety **'Chameleon'**, is similar but the leaves are flushed with red, green and white. This plant can be invasive in the border, so planting it in a container can be the perfect solution. Light shade or shade is best. Height: 30-45cm (12-18in).
Incarvillea delavayi Dark, fleshy leaves appear with the large, exotic, deep pink flowers in May. Flowering often continues until July. Shelter, or take under cover in cold areas in winter. Needs full sun. Height: 60cm (24in).
Lamium maculatum Silver-splashed leaves, pink or white

'deadnettle' flowers according to variety. Sun or light shade. Height: 25cm (10in)
Pulmonaria saccharata Low-growing plant with attractively marbled leaves, and pink or blue flowers in March and April. The leaves on the variety **'Argentea'** are almost completely silvered. Best in partial shade. Height: 30cm (12in).
Scabiosa There are many varieties in shades of pink to blue. All make useful cut flowers. The heavily promoted **'Butterfly Blue'** is more compact. Needs full sun. Height: 45-90cm (18-36in).
Sedum spectabile Succulent, pale green leaves topped with flat heads of pink flowers in late summer, turning deeper mauve in autumn and remaining eye-catching even when dead. Attractive to butterflies. Needs full sun. Height: 45-60cm (18-24in).

Long-flowering and scented, Dianthus 'Pike's Pink'

Alpines

There is a huge range of alpines that provide both flower and foliage interest for containers. These dwarf plants are shallow-rooting and therefore ideal for troughs and sinks where a combination of plants can create a contrasting mix of flower and leaf colours. Popular and easy-to-grow plants to look out for include campanula (bellflower), alpine dianthus (pinks) and *Phlox douglasii*, all of which have attractive flowers. The many varieties of saxifrage include plants offering both flower and foliage interest, while sedum and sempervivum have fleshy leaves in a myriad of shapes and colours. A collection of alpines could also include one or two of the tiniest conifers such as *Juniperus communis* 'Compressa'

(see Conifers, pages 174-175), or a dwarf shrub like one of the smallest hebes. A few dwarf bulbs could be added for spring interest, such as *Scilla sibirica* with its deep blue flowers or *Chionodoxa lucillae*, which has pale blue blooms.

Good drainage is vital for alpines. Ensure that containers have adequate drainage holes and cover the base with a 5-cm (2-in) layer of drainage material, such as broken clay pots, followed by a layer of coarse leaf-mould or plastic mesh to prevent the drainage layer becoming clogged up with compost. Mix about one-fifth of coarse grit into the compost to ensure an open growing medium. After planting, finish off with a layer of fine gravel chippings, which makes an attractive finish to a container and prevents the tiny plants becoming dirtied by rain-splashed soil.

Making an alpine trough

Stone troughs are difficult to find and expensive to buy. Old glazed butler sinks coated with hypertufa are often recommended, but frost tends to lift the coating after a few years. It is better to make your own hypertufa troughs. To do this you need a mould – two very strong corrugated cardboard boxes one slightly smaller than the other, so that when the smaller one is placed inside the larger there is a 5-cm (2-in) gap all round.

The hypertufa mixture is made with one-part sand, one-part cement and two-parts sphagnum peat (all by bulk). Add water until the mixture is workable. Then fill the bottom of the larger box with a 2.5-cm (1-in) layer of hypertufa. Place a sheet of galvanised chicken wire for reinforcement and add another 2.5-cm (1-in) layer of hypertufa, so that the chicken wire is sandwiched between the two layers. Make sure there are drainage holes before placing the smaller box in the centre of the larger one. Then fill the gap between the sides of the boxes with hypertufa, again sandwiching a sheet of galvanised chicken wire for reinforcement.

The hypertufa will take several days to harden before you can take it out of the mould. The surface will still be soft enough to texture with a stiff brush or trowel. Leave for another week or so before planting.

Phlox douglasii 'Crackerjack' is both colourful and accommodating

Buying tips *Avoid leggy plants as well as those with brown, dead or withered leaves.*

Aubrieta 'Rose Queen'

Container choice

Anacyclus depressus White flowers borne in May. Prefers a sunny position and an alkaline compost. Handsome foliage. Petals red underneath. Dislikes winter wet. Height x spread: 8x15cm (3x6in)

***Arabis ferdinandi-coburgii* 'Variegata'** Cushion-forming plant which is good for troughs. Grown for its variegated leaves. White flowers are borne from April to May. Grow in full sun. Prefers an alkaline compost. Height x spread: 8x15cm (3x6in).

Aubrieta A very popular and reliable alpine, with many shades available. Grows well in walls. Can be invasive. Flowers are pink, mauve or purple and borne from March to June. Site in a sunny position. Prefers an alkaline compost. Height x spread: 10-15cmx20-30cm (4-6inx8-12in)

Campanula garganica Long, star-shaped blue flowers from June to July. Prefers sun or partial shade and an alkaline compost. Also ideal for walls and crevices. Height x spread: 10x20-30cm (4x8-12in).

Cotyledon simplicifolia Yellow flowers from June to July. Graceful, droopy habit. Long-lived and ideal for large containers. Fleshy leaves. Likes moisture. Not fussy about site, but prefers an alkaline compost. Height x spread: 15x20cm (6x8in).

***Dianthus* 'Pike's Pink'** Scented variety, with pink flowers from May to August. Likes a sunny site and an alkaline compost. Height x spread: 15x15cm (6x6in).

Erinus alpinus Short-lived but self-seeding. Lilac, pink or mauve flowers are borne from May to June. Also good for crevices. Height x spread: 10x10cm (4x4in).

Gentiana septemfida The easiest gentian to grow. Blue flowers from

June to August. Buy in flower as colour can be variable. Prefers a sunny site. Height x spread: 20x20cm (8x8in).

***Helianthemum* 'Henfield Brilliant'** Red flowers in June. Prefers a sunny site. Height x spread: 20x30cm (8x12in).

Hypericum olympicum Yellow flowers from June to August. Good for wall tops and crevices. Glaucous foliage. Prefers a sunny site Height x spread: 30x30cm (12x12in).

***Lithospermum diffusum* 'Heavenly Blue'** Blue flowers from May to August. Dark green, hairy foliage. Site in a sunny spot. Also attractive on walls. Height x spread: 10x30cm (4x12in).

Mazus reptans Mauve flowers from June to July. Flowers blotched white and yellow. Useful for paving and cover for bulbs. Prefers a shady site. Height x spread: 5x30cm (2x12in).

Oxalis adenophylla Pink flowers from April to June. Grey-green foliage. Site in a sunny position. Height x spread: 10x10cm (4x4in).

***Phlox douglasii* 'Crackerjack'** The best red phlox. Flowers from April to May. Grows to form a tight cushion. Not fussy about soil type, but prefers a sunny spot. Height x spread: 5x20cm (2x8in).

Pulsatilla vulgaris (Pasque flower) Purple flowers are borne from April to May. Plant also has attractive seed heads and ferny foliage. Buy in flower. Hates being moved. Prefers a sunny site. Height x spread: 20-30x15-20cm (8-12x6-8in).

Raoulia australis Yellow flowers in June. Good for troughs. Fast-spreading, silver carpeter. Prefers a sunny site. Height x spread: 2x20cm (1x8in).

***Saxifraga* 'Four Winds'** Red flowers in May – useful for late spring colour. Scorches easily in full sun if dry at roots. Best replaced every 2-3 years. Prefers a shady site and an alkaline compost. Height x spread: 10x15cm (4x6in).

***Sedum spathulifolium* 'Capa Blanca'** Useful for ground cover, crevices and sinks. Yellow flowers from June to July. Leaves covered in white bloom. Site in a sunny position. Height x spread: 5x12cm (2x5in).

***Sempervivum arachnoideum* 'Laggeri'** Pink flowers in June. Thrives in sinks. Grow in a sunny position. Height x spread: 8x10cm (3x4in).

***Thymus* 'Doone Valley'** Mauve flowers from June to July. Foliage deep green speckled with gold. Prefers a sunny spot. Height x spread: 12x20cm (5x8in).

Pulsatilla vulgaris

Sempervivums are ideal for sinks and bowls

Ornamental grasses

These handsome foliage plants are rarely seen as part of a patio display, although they have considerable potential for use in containers. In recent years many attractive grasses have been introduced, with a wide selection of leaf colours and plant shapes, and a good proportion of these are suitable for growing in pots. With their slender, delicately shaped leaves and a graceful habit, these plants excel either as specimens on their own or grown in individual pots and placed as part of a group of containers.

Ornamental grasses which form small neat clumps are ideal for mixed containers. *Festuca glauca* combined with a garden pink such as Dianthus 'Doris' will create a soft, hazy blue and pink group. They also combine well with small spring bulbs as the grasses cover the bulbs as they fade. Grasses are useful for edging large containers, too. For example, *Carex stricta* 'Bowles' Golden' and *Hakonechloa macra* 'Albo-Aurea' produce arching stems that will tumble over

Buying tips *Look out for good leaf colour and plenty of new unblemished growth. In particular, check the centre of the clump for signs of die-back or rot. Young plants are generally a good buy as they tend to establish in containers better than larger specimens.*

A collection of potted grasses creates a striking architectural effect

the edge of a container. Grasses with tall, delicate flowering stems, such as *Stipa gigantea* or *Milium effusum* 'Aureum' also look best in a container where their fine shape can be appreciated.

Some grasses are worth including for their flowers as well as their foliage. *Pennisetum orientale* has beautiful pinkish-grey plumes from July to September.

A few ornamental grasses are invasive, so growing them in containers is one way of keeping them in check. Taller varieties can be grown in troughs to form a mobile, living screen, but they can look a little tatty by the end of the season. Although many do better in full sun, some grow just as well in shade (see list overleaf).

Winter-interest grasses

Many ornamental grasses remain attractive throughout the year. Evergreens, such as **Festuca glauca** and *Carex hachijoensis* 'Evergold' are obvious choices for a winter container, but some of the deciduous grasses also have much to offer. For instance, the leaves of **Helictotrichon sempervirens** and *Molinia caerula* 'Variegata' fade to a pale parchment colour and remain on the plant all winter.

All-grass containers

Choose the appropriate grasses and you can create an eye-catching and very unusual container display. Take care to select grasses of different sizes and forms so that they contrast and complement one another. For example, try **Miscanthus sacchariflorus** with **Stipa gigantea** and *Miscanthus sinensis* 'Variegatus'.

The evergreen Carex hachijoensis 'Evergold'

Container choice
GRASSES THAT NEED FULL SUN:

Festuca glauca Clump-forming plant with fine, grey-blue evergreen foliage. Flowers are also grey-blue in colour, borne in summer. Divide every other year. Height x spread: 15x23cm (6x9in).

***Molinia caerulea* 'Variegata'** Dense, deciduous grass with cream-striped foliage which turns beige during winter. Purplish-coloured flowers appear in autumn. Height x spread: 60x60cm (24x24in).

Pennisetum orientale (also known as ***P. setaceum***) Clump-forming, deciduous grass with hairy foliage and mauve-grey flowers in summer. Treat as an annual in the coldest regions. Height x spread: 45x45cm (18x18in).

***Phalaris arundinacea* 'Picta'** (gardener's garters) Deciduous grass with white-striped foliage and creamy flowers in summer. Invasive in garden so best grown in containers. Height x spread: 90x60cm (36x24in).

Stipa gigantea Clump-forming, semi-evergreen grass with arching, grey-green blades. Silver-purple flowers appear in summer, turning to yellow. Height x spread: 45x90cm (18x36in).

GRASSES THAT TOLERATE LIGHT SHADE:

***Carex hachijoensis* 'Evergold'** Clump-forming plant with yellow-striped evergreen foliage. Brown flowers borne during summer. Height x spread: 25x45cm (10x18in).

***Carex riparia* 'Variegata'** Invasive deciduous plant with white-striped foliage, bearing brown flowers in

The elegant and eye-catching Hakonechloa macro 'Albo-Aurea'

Carex stricta 'Bowles' Golden' in autumn. The new growth is bright yellow.

summer. Height x spread: 60x60cm (24x24in).

Carex stricta 'Bowles' Golden'
Deciduous, clump-forming plant with arching, green and gold foliage. Turns buff-coloured in winter. Fluffy brown flowers are borne in summer. Height x spread: 60x45cm (24x18in).

Hakonechloa macra 'Albo-Aurea'
Deciduous plant with dense, spreading habit. Arched foliage is striped brilliant yellow, and green flowers appear in autumn. Height x spread: 60x45cm (24x18in).

Helictotrichon sempervirens (also known as **Avena candida**) Clump-forming plant with blue-grey evergreen foliage. Flowers are also blue-grey, turning light brown during summer. Height x spread:

1.2x0.6m (4x2ft).

Luzula maxima 'Marginata Variegata' Very invasive, carpet-forming plant with cream-edged evergreen foliage. Brown flowers appear during summer. Height x spread: 30x60cm (12-24in).

Milium effusum 'Aureum' (Bowles' golden grass) Clump-forming, deciduous grass with greenish-yellow blades and bright greenish-yellow flowers in spring. Self-seeds. Height x spread: 25x30cm (10x12in).

Miscanthus sinensis 'Variegatus' Clump-forming, deciduous grass with white-striped blades. Brown flowers are borne in autumn. Height x spread: 1.8x0.6m (6x2ft).

M. sinensis 'Zebrinus' Clump-forming, deciduous grass. Blades

Control the vigour of Phalaris by planting in a container

Fluffy heads of pennisetum orientale

are horizontally striped with yellow. Brown flowers are borne in autumn. Height x spread: 1.8x0.6m (6x2ft).

Stipa pennata Clump-forming deciduous grass with arching blades. Silvery-buff flowers, with drooping stems, borne in summer. Height x spread: 60x45cm (24x18in).

Tips for success

- Divide grasses every two years, in late spring, to keep them vigorous and healthy.

- Don't overfeed grasses in containers. Use a slow-release feed in spring rather than liquid feeding.

- Remove dead foliage in spring. Leaving the dead foliage over winter helps to provide some frost protection.

- Make sure pots don't get waterlogged during the winter. Grass roots are particularly prone to rotting. Stand containers on bricks or 'pot feet'.

- Start annual grasses off in small pots in March or April and plant them up into their main containers during early summer.

Ferns for foliage effect

Hardy ferns are all too often overlooked for use in containers, despite the fact that they thrive in complete shade. On the patio, they are ideal plants to bring foliage interest to any dark, north-facing corners, and a considerable range of varieties offer a wide selection of attractive leaf shapes. Although virtually all ferns have green leaves, a surprising number of shades can be combined to make appealing and subtle contrasts.

A few ferns are evergreen and thus afford foliage interest all year on the patio. They combine well with other shade-loving perennials such as hostas. Hardy ferns thrive in both multipurpose and John Innes composts as long as they are not allowed to dry out, and in a part- or fully-shaded spot sheltered from wind.

Of the evergreen ferns, one of the easiest to grow is *Asplenium scolopendrium* (hart's tongue fern). It has wide, strap-shaped, rich green leaves. A less common variety, *A. scolopendrium* 'Crispum', has stunning wavy margins to its leaves. *Polystichum setiferum* (soft shield fern) has soft green fronds, and there are several extremely ornamental forms including *P. setiferum* 'Divisilobum' that has finely divided leaves. *Dryopteris erythrosora* has bold leaves that are an attractive shade of reddish-brown when young, ageing to rich green.

Ferns that die back to the ground in winter include: *Athyrium filix-femina* (lady fern) which has lacy, fresh green fronds; *Adiantum pedatum* which has feathery leaves; and *Adiantum venustum,* similar but smaller and even more dainty in shape. One of the most attractive varieties of all is *Athyrium nipponicum* 'Pictum' (painted fern) which has deeply cut, silvery leaves and purplish stems, the purple spreading out to colour the base of the fronds.

Left to right: Adiantum pedatum, Asplenium scolopendrium 'Undulatum' and Asplenium trichomanes

Asplenium scolopendrium 'Crispum'

Watering and feeding
Once established, ferns need very little attention. They must not be allowed to dry out, however, so regular watering is essential while they are actively growing. Also a dilute general-purpose liquid feed can be applied fortnightly during the summer. Avoid fertilisers which contain a lot of nitrogen because this encourages soft growth which is susceptible to disease.

Which fern?
Adiantum pedatum (maidenhair) Deciduous blue-green fern with clump-forming habit and small, tapered fronds. Height: 80cm (32in).

Adiantum pedatum 'Subpumilum' Short, clump-forming, deciduous fern with small, tapering fronds. Blue-green colour. Height: 15cm (6in).

Adiantum venustum Pale green deciduous fern with spreading habit. Height: 30cm (12in).

Asplenium scolopendrium (hart's tongue fern) Pale green evergreen fern with a clump-forming habit. Non-feathery, strap-shaped fronds. Height: 45cm (18in).

Asplenium scolopendrium 'Crispum' Evergreen fern with pale green foliage and a clump-forming habit. Single-leaved fronds with wavy edge. Height: 40cm (16in).

Asplenium trichomanes 'Cristatum' Dark green fern with tuft-forming habit and evergreen foliage. Long, thin fronds with tiny leaves. Height: 10cm (4in).

Athyrium filix-femina (lady fern) Clump-forming, deciduous fern. Its pale green stems sometimes turn to red. Fine-leaved fronds are feather-shaped. Height: 90cm (36in).

Athyrium filix-femina 'Frizelliae' Mid-green-coloured deciduous fern with clump-forming habit and slim, tapered fronds. Height: 20cm (8in).

Athyrium nipponicum 'Pictum' (painted fern) Clump-forming deciduous fern. Mid-green foliage, flushed with silver and purple, wide, tapering feathery fronds. May need protecting with straw or bracken in winter in cold areas. Height: 25cm (10in).

Athyrium filix-femina with ivies and violas

Blechnum tabulare Dark green, glossy evergreen fern with spreading habit. Feathery, elliptical fronds. Height: 90cm (36in).

Dryopteris affinis (golden male fern) Also known as **D. pseudo-mas, D. borreri**. Golden when young, turning dark green with age. Should stay green until mid-winter. Grows to form a shuttlecock shape. Feathery, tapered fronds. Height: 90cm (36in).

Dryopteris affinis 'Cristata' (also known as **'The King'**) is slightly smaller. Height: 80cm (32in).

Dryopteris erythrosora Shuttlecock-shaped fern with feathery fronds. Red when young, turning yellow, then green. Should stay green until mid-winter. Height: 60cm (24in).

Dryopteris filix-mas (male fern) Deciduous fern which grows into shuttlecock shape. Mid-green in colour with feather-shaped fronds. Height: 90cm (36in).

Dryopteris filix-mas 'Grandiceps Wills' Deciduous fern with clump-forming habit, mid-green in colour. Feather-shaped fronds. Height: 80cm (32in).

Dryopteris wallichiana Feather-shaped fronds form a shuttlecock shape. Yellow and green with black mid ribs; should retain colour until mid-winter. Height: 60cm (24in).

Dryopteris affinis

Dryopteris felix

Polypodium vulgare elegantissimum

Polypodium vulgare 'Bifido-cristatum' Pale green evergreen fern with long thin fronds, edged with tiny leaves. Height: 30cm (12in).

Polypodium cambricum sometimes sold as **P. australe** Pale green evergreen fern with clump-forming habit. Feather-shaped fronds. Height: 25cm (10in).

Polypodium vulgare 'Cornubiense' Pale green evergreen fern with clump-forming habit and feather-shaped fronds. Height: 30cm (12in).

Polystichum setiferum

'Divisilobum' Evergreen fern which grows to form a shuttlecock shape. Pale green colour with feather-shaped fronds. Height: 80cm (32in).

Polystichum setiferum 'Iveryanum' Shuttlecock-shaped evergreen fern. Pale green in colour with feather-shaped fronds. Height: 60cm (24in).

Polystichum setiferum 'Plumoso-divisilobum' Evergreen fern which grows to form a shuttlecock shape. Feather-shaped fronds. Height: 60cm (24in).

Buying tips *For the widest choice of species and varieties, visit a specialist nursery. Hardy ferns are available all year round.*

Herbs, vegetables and fruit

Herbs and strawberries have always been a popular choice for growing in containers, but other fruit and vegetables can now be grown on the patio too. Breeders are increasing the range of varieties suitable for this growing medium all the time. Not only are they a feasible size, but many varieties are chosen for their ornamental value so they make a display that is attractive, unusual and edible into the bargain.

Watering is the critical factor with all pot-grown vegetables and fruit. To get a decent crop they will need frequent watering during warm spells. This could easily mean twice a day on a sheltered patio when plants are growing vigorously. To make watering easier, leave at least a 1-cm ($\frac{1}{2}$-in) gap at the top of the pot which can be flooded with water. For fruit trees, consider covering the surface of the compost with a mulch or pebbles to cut down the water loss through evaporation.

Herbs for scent and flavour

Herbs are most useful when grown near the kitchen door. Pots, window-boxes, tubs and troughs are all suitable, provided they are at least 15cm (6in) deep. In larger containers, try growing herbs together: sage, thyme and parsley combine well and should not overwhelm each other.

Basil flowers are attractive but flowering ruins the flavour

Basil

Ocimum basilicum

Annual 30x30cm (12x12in).

Growing guide Prefers a sunny spot. Pinch out shoots to promote leafy growth. It is tender and needs shelter from the wind. Protect from slugs. Resents root disturbance.

Uses Sweet, pungent flavour. Essential ingredient of Italian cooking. Particularly compatible with fresh tomatoes. Leaves are used with tomatoes, eggs, fish, pasta, pizza and in salads. Best preserved by freezing.

Buying Look for a bushy plant with no sign of flowering.

Bay

Laurus nobilis

Evergreen shrub. 1.5x0.8m (5x2½ft) (if clipped).

Growing guide Needs a sheltered position. In cold areas bring indoors for winter.

Uses Mature leaves can be used fresh and added to soups, sauces, casseroles and milk puddings. Rip the leaves before adding to food to release the flavour.

Buying Watch for scale insect on stems and undersides of leaves and canker (brown lesions on stems).

Borage

Borago officinalis

Hardy annual 80x30cm (30x12in).

Growing guide Easy to grow. Self-seeds readily but does not like being transplanted.

Uses Young leaves and flowers have a refreshing flavour and can be used in drinks and fruit salads. Preserve by crystallising with sugar.

Buying Best raised from seed.

Chervil

Anthriscus cerefolium

Hardy annual 60x60cm (24x24in).

Growing guide It prefers light shade and a moist soil. Sow in succession from early spring to mid-summer.

Uses The young leaves have a delicate aniseed flavour but this is quickly lost, so pick just before using. Good as a garnish and in soups, egg dishes or potato salads.

Buying Choose well-established plants that are compact and not starting to flower.

Trim back plants after flowering for fresh young leaves

Chives

Allium schoenoprasum

Perennial. 15x15cm (6x6in).

Growing guide Best in sun or partial shade and a moist soil. They need a short dormant period, so leave potted plants out in frost over winter. Easily grown from seed, or divide established clumps every two to three years.

Uses Use fresh as a garnish on salads or added to cucumber and yoghurt dips as a cool accompaniment to curries and other spicy dishes. Complements potato salad.

Buying Look for large clumps. Leaves should be deep rich green, not brown or scorched.

Both the blue flowers and the leaves of borage can be used in Pimms or chopped and added to salads

Dill

Anethum graveolens

Hardy annual 1.2x0.9m (4x3ft).

Growing guide Best in a sunny position in moist compost. Sow seed every fortnight where the plants are to grow (as they do not transplant well) and keep well watered.

Uses Cut leaves while small and use with fish and potatoes – add towards the end of cooking to preserve its flavour. Good as a garnish on hot or cold savoury dishes. Dry seeds and freeze leaves in ice cubes.

Buying Best raised from seed.

The flavour of lemon balm is not as strong as its scent

Lemon balm

Melissa officinalis

Perennial 80x50cm (32x20in).

Growing guide Anywhere, provided the compost is moist but not waterlogged. Raise from seed or divide plants in spring. Variegated lemon balm is less invasive.

Uses Use lemon-flavoured leaves in drinks, fruit salads, herbal tea, salads or in stuffing for chicken. Leaves may be frozen (whole) or dried, but are best when fresh. Traditionally known as a bee plant; many beekeepers plant it near their hives.

Buying Look for small, round, bushy plants with deep green leaves.

Mint is a very versatile herb

Mint

Mentha species

Perennial 60x90cm (24x36in).

Growing guide Many forms exist including spearmint, peppermint, applemint and ginger mint. All are invasive so are ideal for growing in containers.

Uses Applemint is generally credited as the best culinary variety. Mint complements vegetables, especially potatoes and peas, and meat (particularly lamb) and makes a refreshing addition to cold drinks. Best fresh, but can be dried or used in preserves such as mint sauce and jelly.

Buying Plants can be wrongly labelled so check before you buy. Avoid any with small orange blobs on lower stems and under leaves – a sign of rust.

Curly-leaved parsley is best as garnish

Parsley

Petroselinum crispum

Biennial 30x20cm (12x18in).

Growing guide Make a succession of sowings (at 10-15°C/50-60°F for best results) to ensure a good supply. Damp sites in partial shade are ideal. Protect from slugs.

Uses The curly type is ubiquitous as a garnish. For adding flavour to almost any savoury dish, use the flat-leaved form. Can be chopped and frozen.

Buying Look for compact plants (several to a pot). Leaves should be dark green.

Sage

Salvia officinalis

Perennial 90x90cm (36x36in).

Growing guide Cut hard back every spring to prevent it getting leggy. Golden varieties can look green if they have been kept in the shade.

Uses Has strong and distinct flavour, use sparingly in stuffings for poultry and with pork. Preserve by drying as it holds its flavour well.

Buying Look for a bushy plant that fills the pot. The coloured-leaved varieties are just as good for use in the kitchen as the species.

Thyme

Thymus species

Perennial 30x30cm (12x12in).

The common thyme (*T. vulgaris*) is the most useful for cooking, but lemon thyme (*T. citriodorus*) is also used. Variegated forms like 'Doone Valley' are not prolific enough for culinary use.

Growing guide Best in a warm, sunny place. Can get 'woody' so is best from cuttings replaced every two or three years.

Uses The warm, spicy flavour goes well with all meat, eggs, cheese and pasta. It retains its flavour well in long cooking.

Buying Look for small, strong, bushy plants that are slightly woody.

Container vegetables

Some vegetables are attractive in their own right or as part of a group of containers. Vegetables such as chard, carrots, lettuce or leeks, have striking foliage and can be used as a foil for flowers. Be careful, however, to check the fertiliser requirements of different vegetables before growing them in the same container.

Almost any type of container will do, although very shallow containers, less than 20cm (8in) deep, should be avoided. In general, the bigger the better. Any good multipurpose compost will be suitable, but the cheapest is probably the compost from a growing bag.

Vegetables can hold their own for ornamental value amongst pots of flowers

Leafy crops such as lettuce, cabbage and chard need a balanced liquid feed, such as growmore, every fortnight. Fruiting crops such as tomatoes, peppers and podded vegetables need more potash, so give them a tomato feed instead.

Aubergine

Varieties 'Black Prince', 'Long Purple'.

Growing guide Sow in late March or early April in small pots somewhere frost-free. Plant out or move container outside after all risk of frost has passed (late May or early June in most areas). Plant one plant per pot and place in a sunny, sheltered spot. Keep a close watch for signs of whitefly as aubergines are prone to attack by this pest.

Yield 4-6 fruits per plant

Bean, broad

Varieties 'The Sutton' (dwarf), 'Witkiem Major' (tall)

Growing guide Sow in March or April, directly in container. Plant four plants per 10-litre pot, and support with canes and string. Watch out for blackfly and either squash them or control with pirimicarb.

Yield 0.3kg for a 30-cm (12-in) pot or a 10-litre container.

Bean, French

Varieties 'Pros Gitana' (green pods), 'Kinghorn Wax' (yellow pods), 'Purple Teepee' (purple pods).

Growing guide Sow between late April and mid-May in small pots somewhere frost-free. Plant out or move container outside after all risk of frost has passed, late May or early June in most areas. Sow two or three seeds per 8-cm (3-in) pot for transplanting, and plant

four plants per 10-litre pot. Support plants with canes and string. Pick pods regularly.

Yield 0.5kg for a 30-cm (12-in) pot or a 10-litre container.

Bean, runner

Varieties 'Desiree' (white flowers), 'Polestar' (red flowers).

Growing guide Sow between late April and mid-May in small pots somewhere frost-free. Plant out or move container outside after all risk of frost has passed (late May or early June in most areas). Sow two seeds per 8-cm (3-in) pot for transplanting and plant two per 10-litre pot. Provide 1.8-2.1m (6-7ft) high support. Pick pods regularly.

Yield 1kg per plant.

Beetroot

Varieties 'Boltardy', 'Detroit'.

Growing guide Sow in March or April. Seed capsules will produce up to five seedlings. Sow thinly, aiming for seedlings 2.5cm (1in) apart each way, and thin out to 7.5-10cm (3-4in) apart. Pull roots when 2.5-5cm (1-2in) in diameter.

Yield 1kg in a 30-cm (12-in) pot or a 10-litre container.

Spring cabbage and wall-flowers

Cabbage

Varieties Summer/autumn: 'Minicole', 'Castello'. Winter: Any Savoy (e.g. 'Wivoy', 'Wirosa'), 'Ruby Ball' (red).

Growing guide Sow between March and April in 8-cm (3-in) pots for transplanting, one plant per 5-litre pot.

Yield 1.2kg per plant.

Carrot

Varieties Any early variety (e.g. 'Early Nantes').

Growing guide Sow thinly in March or April, aiming for seedlings 2.5cm (1in) apart each way. Thin out to 4cm (1½in) apart. Eat the thinnings and leave the rest to grow on. Start pulling when roots are 1cm (½in) in diameter.

Yield 1kg for a 30-cm (12-in) pot or a 10-litre container.

Chard

Varieties Swiss or silver chard or 'Lucullus' (white stems), 'Ruby' (red stems).

Growing guide Sow in April, and plant one per 4-litre pot. Pick regularly, treating leaves like spinach and fleshy stems as a separate vegetable.

Yield 0.5kg per plant.

Courgette

Varieties 'Ambassador', 'Early Gem' (green fruit), 'Gold Rush' (yellow fruit).

Growing guide Sow from late April to mid-May, in small pots somewhere frost-free. Plant out or move container outside after all risk of frost has passed (late May or early June in most areas). Plant one plant per 30-litre pot, as plants are very large. Pick fruits regularly when they reach 10-15cm (4-6in) long

Yield 25 fruits per plant.

Cucumber

Varieties 'Bush Crop' (bush), 'Burpless Tasty Green' (trailing).

Growing guide Sow from late April to mid-May in small pots somewhere frost-free. Plant out or move container outside after all risk of frost has passed (late May or early June in most areas). Plant one per 30-litre pot, as outdoor bush varieties for large plants. Provide support for trailing varieties.

Yield 15-20 fruits per plant.

Endive

Varieties
Any

Growing guide Sow from April to June, and plant out one per 4-litre pot. Blanch head when fully grown by covering with a pot for a few days to reduce the bitterness of the leaves.

Yield 1 head per plant.

Kale

Varieties 'Dwarf Green Curled', 'Fribor'.

Growing guide Sow in May or June in 8-cm (3-in) pots for transplanting. Space one plant per 5-litre pot. Will stand outside all winter.

Yield 0.3kg per plant.

Kohl rabi

Varieties 'Purple Vienna', 'Rowel'.

Growing guide

Sow thinly in May or June, aiming for seedlings 2.5cm (1in) apart each way. Thin plants to 8-10cm (3-4in) apart. Eat the thinnings and leave the rest to grow on. Pull when 5-8cm (2-3in) in diameter.

Yield 1kg in a 30-cm (12-in) pot or a 10-litre container.

A pot of mixed salad

Leek

Varieties 'King Richard'.

Growing guide

Sow thinly from March to July (in succession), aiming for seedlings 2.5cm (1in) apart each way. Thin out to 4cm (1½in) apart. Eat the thinnings and leave the rest to grow on. Treat like spring onions and pull when 1cm (½in) in diameter.

Yield 1kg per 30-cm (12-in) pot or 10-litre container.

Lettuce

Varieties 'Saladin' (large crisphead), 'Little Gem' (small Cos). 'Lollo Rosso', 'Salad Bowl', 'Red Salad Bowl' (all loose-leaf, non-hearting types).

Growing guide

Sow from March to July (in succession), and plant one per 4-litre pot for one head per plant, 2-3 per pot for two heads. Pick the whole head before it starts to elongate (bolt).

Yield one or two heads per pot, depending on spacing.

A reasonable crop of onions and parsley from a 15cm (6in) pot

Marrow

Varieties 'Early Gem' (bush), 'Table Dainty' (trailing).

Growing guide

Sow from late April to mid-May in small pots somewhere frost-free. Plant out or move container outside after all risk of frost has passed (late May or early June in most areas). Plant one per 30-litre pot. Support the fruits of bush marrows. Train trailing varieties up a support.

Yield 3-5 fruits per plant.

Melon

Varieties 'Romeo', 'Sweetheart'.

Growing guide

Sow from mid- to late April in small pots somewhere frost-free. Plant out one plant per 30-litre pot and move container outside after all risk of frost has passed (late May or early June in most areas). Choose a warm, sheltered spot and train up a trellis support.

Yield 3-5 fruits per plant.

Butterhead lettuce and 'Lollo Rosso'

Onion

Varieties 'Hygro', 'Rijnsburger-Balstora' from seed or any variety from sets.

Growing guide Sow thinly in March or April, aiming for seedlings 2.5cm (1in) apart each way. Thin out plants to 8-10cm (3-4in) apart. Eat the thinnings and leave the rest to grow on. Growing from sets is easier than growing from seed.

Yield 1kg per 30-cm (12-in) pot or a 10-litre container.

Pea

Varieties Garden: 'Hurst Beagle', 'Kelvedon Wonder'; Mange tout: 'Sugar Snap' (tall), 'Sugar Rae' (dwarf), 'Honeypod' (dwarf).

Growing guide Sow from March to June in succession, and thin to eight plants per 10-litre pot. Push a few twiggy branches into the pot to support the plants.

Yield 0.5kg of pea pods per 10-litre pot.

Pepper

Varieties 'Redskin' (dwarf).

Growing guide Sow from late March to early April. Plant out one per 10-litre pot. Site container in a sunny, sheltered spot.

Yield Up to 12 fruit per plant.

Potato

Varieties Any early variety, e.g. 'Concorde', 'Maris Bard' or 'Pentland Javelin'.

Growing guide Plant tubers from February to March, or from June to July. Start early crops off in 10-cm (4-in) pots in a frost-free place. Later crops can be planted into final container or an old dustbin.

Use a large pot. As a guide, plant two tubers to a 80-cm (24in) pot or six to a dustbin. Fill container about one-third and gradually add more compost as the plants grow until it is full. Protect with a double layer of horticultural fleece while there is a risk of frost.

Yield 1kg per plant.

Radish

Varieties Any variety or a mixture.

Growing guide Sow thinly from March to June (in succession) aiming for seedlings 2.5cm (1in) apart each way. Thin out to 2.5cm (1in) apart each way. Eat the thinnings and leave the rest to grow on. Try leaving a few to flower – the green pods are edible and taste like capers.

Yield 10 bunches in a 30-cm (12-in) pot or a 10-litre container.

Spinach

Varieties Leaf beet (perpetual spinach).

Growing guide Sow from April to June, and thin to one plant per 4-litre pot. Pick young leaves as required.

Yield 0.3kg per plant.

Tomato

Varieties 'Pixie', 'Totem', 'Tumbler' (trailing variety suitable for a large hanging basket).

Growing guide Sow in late March or early April in small pots somewhere frost-free. Plant out one per 15-litre pot and move container outside after all risk of frost has passed (late May or early June in most areas). Use above varieties (which need no training) or 'Gardener's Delight' trained up a cane.

Yield 4kg per plant.

Potatoes in a dustbin carefully concealed by a pot of impatiens

Pots of fruit

As wood makes a good insulator, wooden tubs are recommended for growing fruit in containers. Terracotta pots are attractive, but make sure they are frost-proof and line them with polythene to help prevent the compost from drying out too quickly. Use a John Innes compost for stability. All pot-grown fruit trees need to be securely staked. Feed all fruit with a high-potash fertiliser such as tomato feed, every fortnight from when buds break out.

Most fruit crops require a sunny position, although currants and acid cherries will crop against a north-facing wall. Figs, peaches and nectarines will need a south-facing patio to do well, while the other types of fruit mentioned here require sun for at least half the day.

Established pot-grown apple trees

Apples

Varieties The following varieties are all well worth growing (eating periods are given in brackets): 'George Cave' (July-Aug), 'Katja' (Sept-Oct), 'Sunset' (Oct-Dec) and 'Spartan' (Oct-Feb). 'Ballerina' varieties form upright, unbranched trees. They look good in a container but the fruit tends to be of poor quality.

Apples are not self-fertile, but bees travel a fair distance and there is likely to be a compatible variety in your neighbourhood if you live in the suburbs. If there is not, you will need to grow at least two varieties that flower at the same time to ensure adequate pollination and a good crop. In colder areas, choose later-flowering varieties like 'Katja', 'Sunset' and 'Spartan'.

Buying Buy trees grafted on to dwarfing rootstocks such as M9 and M26. Trees grafted on to the very dwarfing M27 rootstock would also be suitable, but they may need more attention.

Pot size 30-38cm (12-15in).

Yield 3.5-4.5kg (8-10lb).

'Spartan'

'Sunset'

Pears

Varieties The most reliable pear for gardens is 'Conference' but, if you have a sunny, sheltered patio, you could try some of the really choice varieties in pots – for example, 'Doyenné du Comice' and 'Louise Bonne of Jersey'. However, like apples, they will need a suitable pollinator. Try 'Onward' (Sept-Oct) with 'Doyenné du Comice' (Nov) or 'Beth' (Sept-Oct) with 'Louise Bonne of Jersey' (Oct-Nov).

Buying The two most common pear rootstocks are Quince A and Quince C. The latter is more dwarfing and therefore a better choice for pot culture. A pyramid shape is best in a pot.

Pot size 30-38cm (12-15in).

Yield 3.5-4.5kg (8-10lb).

'Doyenné du Comice' pears

Cherries

Varieties Unless you are prepared to grow more than one tree, stick to the self-fertile varieties – 'Stella' and 'Cherokee' (both sweet varieties) and 'Morello' (an acid variety for cooking).

Buying Buy a tree grafted on to 'Colt' or the new dwarfing rootstock 'Inmil'.

Pot size 40-45cm (16-18in).

Yield 3.5-4.5kg (8-10lb).

Plums

Varieties Unless you want more than one plum tree on your patio or there is one in your neighbour's garden, choose a self-fertile variety such as 'Denniston's Superb' (Aug). If you live in an area where late frosts are common, choose 'Marjorie's Seedling' (Sept-Oct) as it flowers late.

Buying Buy plum trees grafted on to the dwarfing or semi-dwarfing rootstocks 'Pixy' and 'St Julien A'.

Pot size 30cm (12in).

Yield 3-3.5kg (6-8lb).

Blueberries

These are unlikely to flourish anywhere other than a container because they need soil with a pH of 5.5 or less, which is very acidic.

Varieties Most varieties are only partly self-fertile, so aim to grow at least two to be sure of fruit. Try 'Earliblue' with 'Bluecrop' (both early) or 'Herbert' with 'Ivanhoe' (both mid-season).

If you live in a hard-water area, water with rainwater to maintain the pH of the compost.

Pot size Using a lime-free, peat-based compost, pot them up in 15-cm (6-in) pots to start with, and pot on successively to a 38-cm (15-in) pot.

Yield 2-4kg (4½-9lb) per bush

Figs

A fig tree is an ideal candidate for growing in a pot because root restriction is vital for good crops.

Varieties 'Brown Turkey' (red flesh) and 'White Marseilles' (white flesh). Both are self-fertile.

When fruiting starts, the successful crop is produced in late summer at the end of young shoots. These embryo fruitlets will then over-winter and ripen the following year.

Bring the plant into an unheated greenhouse before severe frost or, if it is in a sheltered position outside, lag the pot and protect the leaves and embryo fruits.

Pot size Over the first three years, pot on from a 15-cm (6-in) pot to a 23-cm (9-in) pot and finally to a 30-cm (12-in) pot.

Yield 3.5-4.5kg (8-10lb).

Bush fruit

These can be grown as bushes. In pots, however, they are more manageable as cordons. Gooseberries also make very attractive standards.

Varieties *Red currants*: 'Laxton's No2' (July), 'Red Lake' (Aug), 'Rondom' (Aug). *White currants*: 'White Grape' (July). *Gooseberries*: 'Invicta' (June-July), 'Leveller (June-July).

Pot size Cordons 23cm (9in), standards 30cm (12in).

Yield Currants 3-3.5kg (7-8lb), gooseberries 2.5kg (6lb).

Peaches, nectarines and apricots

If your patio is warm and sunny, the trees should crop well, providing the flowers are protected from frost.

Varieties *Peaches*: 'Bonanza', 'Garden Anny' and 'Garden Lady' are older, yellow-fleshed varieties.

'Terrace Amber' and 'Terrace Diamond' are newer, earlier-flowering types. 'Garden Silver' has white flesh.
Apricots: 'Aprigold' and 'Golden Glow' are dwarf, orange-fleshed varieties.
Nectarines: 'Necterella' was one of the first dwarf types, 'Golden Beauty' has pink, double blossom and 'Terrace Ruby' is a new, improved type. Dwarf varieties require minimal pruning and are easiest to grow.

Pot size Standards 30-45cm (12in).

Yield Up to 6 fruit per tree.

Enjoy really fresh strawberries

Strawberries

Varieties 'Eros' (mid-season) produces a heavy crop of glossy, conical fruit among large leaves on vigorous plants. 'Tamella' (mid-season) produces a good yield of oval fruit that hang over the edge of the pot, making them easy to harvest when grown in a container. 'Rhapsody' (late) produces a heavy yield of dark red, pointed fruit on long trusses. 'Calypso' produces small crops of bright red, round fruit all summer. The fruits hang down, making them easy to pick when grown in a container.

Pot size Forget strawberry towers and growing bags – it is too time-consuming to keep them watered in a long, hot summer. Opt instead for a 25-cm (10-in) pot filled with multi-purpose compost.

Yield Up to 1kg (2lb) per pot of three plants.

Plant selector

Myrtus for scent

Lilium regale for fragrance

Rose 'Flower Carpet'

Narcissus 'February Gold' for spring colour

SCENTED PLANTS

The following plants all have either scented flowers or aromatic foliage. Site scented flowers in the most sheltered part of the patio in a sunny position. They are ideal for pots near seats or next to a door. Plants with aromatic foliage release their fragrance when their leaves are rubbed or crushed. By placing them next to the main thoroughfares of your garden, their fragrance will be released when passers-by brush against them.

Aloysia
Brugmansia*
Cheiranthus
Cosmos
Heliotropium
Herbs
Hyacinthus
Pelargoniums
(scented-leaf varieties)
Jasminum
Lathyrus
Laurus
Lilium
Mirabilis
Myrtus
Narcissus
(some)
Nemesia
denticulata
Nicotiana
Sarcococca
Skimmia
Solenopsis

TRAILING PLANTS FOR HANGING BASKETS AND WINDOW-BOXES

Trailing plants are ideal for covering up less attractive containers as well as for baskets and window-boxes. Foliage plants such as *Glechoma hederacea* 'Variegata' provide a long season of interest with their variegated leaves, while flowering plants such as diascias provide a mass of colour right through the summer.

Acalphya
Alonsoa
Begonia
(pendulous varieties)
Bidens
Nierembergia
Brachyscome
Centradenia
Convolvulus
Diascia
Fuchsia
Glechoma
Helichrysum
Hedera
Lobelia
Lotus
Lysimachia
Parochetus
Pelargonium
Petunia
Plectranthus
Roses
(ground-cover varieties)
Scaevola
Sutera
Verbena

SPRING COLOUR

Use spring bedding such as double daisies (*Bellis perennis*) and wallflowers (Cheiranthus) together with spring bulbs to create containers specifically for spring interest. Alternatively, go for more permanent plantings, choosing specimens that have eye-catching spring foliage such as ferns and Japanese maples, or those that flower in spring such as camellias and periwinkles.

Acer palmatum 'Atropurpureum'
Asplenium scolopendrium
(hart's tongue fern)
Azalea
Bellis
Camellia
Cheiranthus
Clematis alpina
Clematis macropetala
Crocus
Dryopteris filix-mas *(male fern)*
Hosta *(variegated)*
Hyacinthus
Muscari
Myosotis
Narcissus
Pinus mugo 'Mops'
Rhododendron
Tulipa
Vinca minor 'Variegata'
(lesser periwinkle)
Viola

SUMMER COLOUR

Annuals and tender perennials provide the mainstay of summer interest and colour in containers. The following shrubs, hardy perennials, grasses and herbs are also worth considering.

Achillea
Buxus *(variegated)*
Canna
Incarvillea
Lilium
Mirabilis
Molinia
Myrtus communis
Pennisetum orientale
Salvia officinalis 'Purpurescens'
Scabiosa
Stipa

Acer palmatum for its glorious leaves

AUTUMN FOLIAGE

For the most colourful autumn tints or brightly coloured autumn and winter foliage, this selection is hard to beat.

Acer palmatum
Gaultheria
Ornamental brassicas
Nandina

WINTER INTEREST

A selection of the following hardy and decorative evergreens will ensure that there is always something to admire on your patio, even in the dull depths of winter.

Bamboos	Gaultheria
Buxus	Hedera
Calluna	Juniperus
Conifers	Sarcococca
Erica	Skimmia
Euonymus	Vinca

PLANTS TO GIVE AN EXOTIC, TROPICAL EFFECT

The following plants all make excellent specimens. For the most dramatic effect, site them on their own in terracotta containers. Rocks and gravel help to enhance the exotic feeling.

Agave
Arctotis
Canna
Cordyline
Eucomis
Melianthus
Phormium
Yucca

PLANTS FOR A HOT SITE IN FULL SUN

Many popular plants simply cannot tolerate the heat in a scorching summer and either frazzle or stop flowering prematurely. The following can be relied on to give a stunning display no matter how hot it gets.

Acanthus spinosus (*bear's breeches*)
Achillea 'Moonshine'
Agapanthus (African lily)
Anthemis cupaniana
Arctotis
Bidens
Canna
Convolvulus
Doronicum plantagineum
(*leopard's bane*)
Eccremocarpus
Euryops
Euphorbia myrsinites *
Felicia
Gazania
Incarvillea delavayi
Juniperus squamata 'Blue Star'
Juniperus x media 'Old Gold'
Lotus
Melissa officinalis
Mimulus
Nandina domestica
Osteospermum
Phormium tenax
Sedum spectabile
Sempervivum tectorum
Sphaeralcea
Taxus baccata 'Standishii' *

Agapanthus (left) – a touch of the tropics

Ornamental cabbages and pansies make a curious but stunning planting

PLANTS FOR FULL SHADE

No matter how shady the position, it is possible to create a colourful display of container plants. The plants listed below are an excellent starting point.

Aquilegia vulgaris (columbine)
Astrantia major (masterwort)
Clematis *(species & some large-flowered hybrids)*
Fuchsias
Ferns
Glechoma
Hedera
Hosta
Impatiens
Jasminum officinale
Lamium maculatum
Lobelia
Lysimachia nummularia
Phalaris arundinacea 'Picta'
Pinus sylvestris 'Beuvronensis'
Pulmonaria saccharata
Scilla sibirica
Soleirolia

PLANTS REQUIRING LIME-FREE COMPOST

The following plants all require acid conditions and should be grown in peat-based multipurpose compost. Specialist ericaceous composts are available but, in *Gardening Which?* trials, they have been shown to have no advantages over ordinary peat-based composts.

Azalea
Calluna
Camellia
Gaultheria
Rhododendron
Skimmia

*WARNING: THESE PLANTS ARE POISONOUS

Brugmansia	– all parts harmful if eaten.
Euonymus	– all parts potentially harmful if eaten.
Euphorbia	– irritant sap and can cause burning sensation and stomach complaints if eaten.
Lantana	– toxic if eaten.
Taxus	– all parts poisonous.

Aquilegia (columbine) is ideal for shady sites on the patio

Hostas thrive in shady corners

Rhododendron 'Pink Drift'

Plant Index

ACKNOWLEDGEMENTS

Front Cover (Inset): Gardening Which?; (Background): The Garden Picture Library (photographed by Lynne Brotchie)

The Garden Picture Library

Photographers:
John Glover; 26, 51, 52, 90, 96, 106, 113, 117, 118, 130, 135, 137, 179
Roger Hyam ; 26, 115
Sunniva Harte; 31, 52, 94, 109, 110, 116
Rex Butcher; 34, 133
Christopher Fairweather; 38
JS Sira; 38, 69, 71, 85, 93, 114, 125, 128
Chris Burrows; 45, 62, 85, 89, 103, 113, 124, 132
Brian Carter; 56, 63, 70, 72, 78, 80, 101, 105, 107, 126, 182
Howard Rice; 65, 69, 77, 78, 93, 97, 102, 104, 112, 114, 115
Neil Holmes; 66, 136, Jerry Pavia; 72, 95, 112, Mel Watson; 81, Linda Burgess; 83, Ron Evans; 84, David England; 94, Noel Kavanagh; 99, Philippe Bonduel; 105, Steven Wooster; 118, Lamontagne; 119, Claire Davies; 127, Densey Clyne; 131, Brigitte Thomas; 132, Michael Howes; 137, Jane Legate; 138, Zara Mccalmont; 139, 147, Gary Rogers; 150
Laslo Puskas; 157, 218, Mel Watson; 218, Ron Sutherland; 219; (unnamed) 163

Photos Horticultural

28, 29, 30, 32, 36, 39, 40, 44, 46, 47, 50, 55, 56, 58, 59, 60, 61, 62, 66, 70, 71, 73, 75, 76, 79, 82, 87, 88, 89, 91, 92, 93, 140, 141, 142, 143, 146, 151, 192, 201, 204

Oxford Scientific Films Deni Brown; 35

Bruce Coleman Eric Crichton; 125, 129, 131, Jules Cowan; 130

Peter McHoy 24, 46, 54, 106, 108, 111, 146, 155, 156

Pat Brindley 152, 153, 154, 155, 169, 180, 181, 188

Elizabeth Whiting Associates 122, 167

Clive Boursnell 5

All remaining photographs were provided by Gardening Which? Picture Library